Praise for *The Clean Money Revolution*

Nothing less than the antidote for modern finance.
—Don Shaffer, partner, Jubilee, former CEO, RSF Social Finance

Amplifies the urgent need for capitalism to redefine its purpose.
—Kat Taylor, co-founder and co-CEO, Beneficial State Bank

A profoundly sensible 21st century roadmap.
—Gary Hirshberg, chairman and former president
and CEO, Stonyfield Farm

It's aspirational, it's unsettling, it's demanding—
but revolutions are like that.
—Danielle LaPorte, author, *The Desire Map* and *White Hot Truth*

Answering the most salient and unanswered question
in our quest to transform as a civilization.
—Alfa Demmellash, CEO and co-founder, Rising Tide Capital

Decades of wisdom are distilled in the book...
prepare to be transformed.
—Ziya Tong, host, *Daily Planet*, Discovery Channel

A fresh vision, insightful, wise and profoundly hopeful.
—Wade Davis, UBC leadership chair in
Cultures and Ecosystems at Risk

A powerful message!
—Annie Leonard, executive director,
Greenpeace USA and founder, The Story of Stuff

Could literally cause billions of dollars to move toward
saving the planet for future generations.
—Kevin Jones, founder, SOCAP

This book is long overdue. I cannot recommend it enough
for anyone who cares to build a better future.
—Paul Born, author, *Deepening Community*

Crisp and insightful…this vision could remake our world.
—Randy Hayes, executive director, Foundation Earth and
founder, Rainforest Action Network

This book is a non-negotiable for these times!
—Nikki Silvestri, co-founder and CEO,
Silvestri Strategies, and co-founder, Live Real

Joel Solomon is the Pied Piper of the Clean Money Revolution.
—Deb Nelson, vice-president, client and community engagement,
RSF Social Finance, and former executive director, Social Venture Network

…A rare contributor to the re-conception of business as a
blending of the best of enterprise with true social commitment.
—Drummond Pike, founder, Tides Foundation

Solomon is a rare capital-savvy elder
who inspires Millennials to have hope and take action now,
for a fair and secure long term future.
—David Karr, co-founder and chief brand cebador, Guayaki

This book transcends ideology and platitudes and merges vision
with clear case studies to give us a pathway to a better world.
—Tzeporah Berman, environmental activist, author,
adjunct professor, York University

Joel and *The Clean Money Revolution* show us how money,
rather than being the "root of all evil,"
can become the driver for a more just and sustainable world.
—Robert Gass, EdD, co-founder, Rockwood Leadership Institute
and the Social Transformation Project

The Clean Money Revolution is the culmination of
decades of work.… This book and all it represents
are truly seminal and the hope for our collective future.
—Alissa Sears, VP growth and Strategy,
co-founder, adVenturesAcademy

Joel's work is a clarion call to a deeper form of capitalism,
one that truly maximizes the productivity of
our money and time on this planet.
—Alex Lau, vice president, Golden Properties Ltd.

…From politics to supporting ChangeMakers,
to facilitating deep interpersonal work,
thank you Joel Solomon for your modelling.
—Jessica Norwood, executive director, ChangeMakers Network

Forces us to consider what our money is doing, right now,
to our common world; and invites all of us but particularly
those with inherited wealth to join a new movement
of clean money and literally save our planet.
—Deepa Narayan, author, Voices for the Poor series and
Moving Out of Poverty series;
former senior advisor in the Vice President's Office
of the Poverty Reduction Group of the World Bank

Five stars!!
—Jed Emerson, Independent Strategic Advisor to Impact Investors

Good helpful stuff to do with your filthy lucre, if any.
—Margaret Atwood, author, *Handmaid's Tale*

Joel sees the future more clearly than Ray Kurzweil.
He has already made the world a better place than he found it.
I think his Indian name just may be "sees many trillions".
—Denise Williams, executive director,
First Nations Technology Council

I've had the pleasure of knowing Joel for a decade. In that time,
he has come to occupy a nearly mythical status in my mind:
compassionate, challenging, whip-smart, and so, so insightful.
—Matthew Weatherley-White, co-founder and managing director,
The Caprock Group, and selection board member, Impact Assets 50

Joel Solomon so eloquently lights the path society needs
to take in order to ensure future generations
can flourish on a sustainable planet earth.
—Reverend Yearwood, President of the Hip Hop Caucus

Joel Solomon is one of the smartest, most caring people I know.
And this book represents the best of both. Read it now!
—Carol Sanford, author and executive producer of
The Regenerative Business Summit

Joel has done so much to create and shape the landscape
of impact investing. He's a beloved local financial superhero,
and this book is a brilliant roadmap to purposeful investing.
—Catherine Ludgate, Manager of Community Investment, Vancity

Joel's book offers the history and sets the stage well,
for everyone who wants to align their investments
with their values—no need to sacrifice results.
—Janet M. Morgan, managing director, Cornerstone Capital Group

I'm a superfan of Joel Solomon.
You should be after reading his book!
—Joshua Fouts, executive director, Bioneers

The world needs this wisdom now more than ever.
—Karen Mahon, Canadian director, Stand.earth

Nodding my head, appreciating, note-making, and enjoying
the @joelsolomon book, *The Clean Money Revolution*.
#bionomy #ethical #neweconomy
—Raffi Cavoukian, singer, founder of Centre for Child Honoring

This book dramatically changed how I look at my investments,
and the financial industry in general. I have a long list of people
who will be receiving this book from me as a gift.
—Fiona Douglas-Crampton, president and CEO
of Dalai Lama Center for Peace and Education

There are so many who need to read this text, including my now former investment advisor. If he had taken up my challenge to read this book, he would likely still be working for me!
—Michael Keefer, lead visionary and president,
Keefer Ecological Services Ltd.

Joel's thought leadership in the clean money space will leave a legacy for generations to come.
—Rosy Atwal, co-founder, Maple Organics,
The Organic Pharmaceutical Company

Clean Money is a real treasure, a beacon of wisdom.
—Sana Kapadia, chief impact officer, Spring Activator

Joel's clever weaving of history throughout made this book hard to put down!
—Emily Applegate, vice president of
Impact Investments, Change Finance

Joel speaks to the wisdom of our ancestors and galvanizes us all to act. He inspires us to be a great ancestor.
—Dharini Thiruchittampalam, adjunct professor,
Sauder School of Business, UBC

A great read, and very important.
—Hunter Lovins, co-author, *A Finer Future* and *Natural Capitalism*

Crisp and insightful, for the long-term health of the whole planet.
—Randy Hayes, director, Foundation Earth

The simple thought—"do you know what your money is doing?"—really stuck with me.
—Roger Dickhout, president and CEO, Pineridge Group

Humble and powerful. A gem.
—Michèle Soregaroli, founder, CEO and coach,
Transformation Catalyst Corporation

This is your call to action.
—Shivani Singh, founding and managing partner, PathFinder

Joel Solomon has inspired thousands of others along the path
of a more ethical and fulfilling life. We are fortunate to have him
among us as a soulful friend and authentic guide.
—Yosef Wosk, rabbi, philanthropist, author, and director
of interdisciplinary programs of continuing studies,
Simon Fraser University

Wasn't at all what I expected. Authenticity and depth.
—Holly Vipond, financial security advisor,
Freedom 55 Financial

A rockstar in the "make good with money" space.
—Fiona Rayher, filmmaker, Fractured Land,
and co-founder and CEO, Hoovie

Encourages all investors to question
how their money is affecting people and the planet.
—Julien Gafarou, investment and portfolio
analysis consultant, Toniic

THE CLEAN MONEY REVOLUTION

THE
CLEAN
MONEY
REVOLUTION

REINVENTING
POWER, PURPOSE,
AND CAPITALISM

JOEL SOLOMON
WITH TYEE BRIDGE

new society
PUBLISHERS

Cover design by Diane McIntosh. Cover image © iStock.

Printed in Canada.
Hardcover Edition © 2017 by Joel Solomon and Tyee Bridge.

This book is intended to be educational and informative. It is not intended to serve as a guide. The author and publisher disclaim all responsibility for any liability, loss or risk that may be associated with the application of any of the contents of this book.

Inquiries regarding requests to reprint all or part of *The Clean Money Revolution* should be addressed to New Society Publishers at the address below. To order directly from the publishers, please call toll-free (North America) 1-800-567-6772, or order online at www.newsociety.com

Any other inquiries can be directed by mail to:

New Society Publishers
P.O. Box 189, Gabriola Island, BC V0R 1X0, Canada
(250) 247-9737

LIBRARY AND ARCHIVES CANADA CATALOGUING IN PUBLICATION

Solomon, Joel, 1954– , author
The clean money revolution : reinventing power, purpose,
and capitalism / Joel Solomon with Tyee Bridge.

Originally published: 2017.
Includes bibliographical references and index.
Issued in prints and electronic formats.
ISBN 978-0-86571-892-0 (softcover).—ISBN 978-1-55092-685-9 (PDF).—
ISBN 978-1-77142-281-9 (EPUB)

1. Investments—Environmental aspects.   2. Investments—Moral
and ethical aspects.   3. Green movement.   I. Bridge, Tyee, 1970– , author
II. Title.

HG4515.13.S65 2018   332.6'042   C2018-903309-6
                                                C2018-903310-X

Funded by the   Financé par le
Government   gouvernement
of Canada   du Canada

Canada

New Society Publishers' mission is to publish books that contribute in fundamental ways to building an ecologically sustainable and just society, and to do so with the least possible impact on the environment, in a manner that models this vision.

new society PUBLISHERS

Certified (B) Corporation

FSC
www.fsc.org

MIX
Paper from
responsible sources
FSC® C016245

Regarding Pigs: A Note on the Cover of this Edition

Pigs are misunderstood animals. Seen in their muck-filled pens we usually think of them as dirty, lazy, and stupid. But they're actually intelligent problem-solvers. Given the chance, they're cleaner than most other animals, including dogs. In natural, open environments they don't excrete waste anywhere near where they live or eat.

As a symbol of money pigs have two faces. One is the prudent "piggybank" of long-term thinking. This archetype is tied to our innocent, patient, childhood relationship to money. The other image is of the "capitalist pig" driven by insatiable greed. This not-so-little piggy goes to market and leaves a trail of destruction, devouring everything to fatten itself.

The two symbolic pigs occupy opposite poles. Innocence versus greed. Patience versus ravenous destruction. I love them as symbols for this book because they provoke core ideas about money's use and misuse.

We need to suspend our assumptions about money and business so we can imagine a new archetype. We need a new kind of capitalist piggy—one that is both innocent and wise, ambitious and clever. What would such a pig look like? It may have qualities we desperately need at this point in history.

As with pigs in a pen, things are not always as they seem. Capitalism need not be the enemy. Willful innocence can be a trap. Greed can be driven by fear. We can all do better with our money relationship. If piled up into pens managed like factory farms, it's true, money can start to stink. If it is allowed free range to roam and get reconnected to the Earth, it can do amazing and important things. The values, beliefs, and relationships within capitalist societies can form the nexus of a new formula for smarter leadership and reinvention.

Let's not throw out the piggies with the mud bath!

—J.S.

May this book reduce suffering,
honor the biosphere,
and support thriving resilience
for future generations.

Joel Solo

Contents

Select List of Profiled Organizations and Businesses

B Corporation	PlayBig
BALLE	Renewal Funds
Bioneers	Renewal Partners
Business for Social Responsibility	RSF Social Finance
Guayaki	Seventh Generation
Happy Planet	SOCAP
Hollyhock	Social Venture Network
Investors Circle	Stonyfield Yogurt
Lunapads	Threshold Foundation
Patagonia	Tides Canada

Foreword

by Jessy Tolkan

Born in 1981, I am the beginning of the Millennial generation, a proud member of the world's biggest, best-connected, and most diverse cohort in history. In my first three decades on this planet I've witnessed a crippling global economic crisis, horrific wars, and the warmest years ever recorded due to the devastation of climate change. I've grown up amidst the perpetual background noise of ugly, scary, and pervasive global problems. At the same time I've seen innovation, prosperity, and political "firsts" that even two decades ago would have been unimaginable.

What is one to do with this confluence of daunting challenges and overwhelming possibility?

From where I stand there is really only one way to absorb and respond to such awesome circumstances. We need to seize the moment for total transformation.

We can transform our anxiety into passion. Fear can become hope. The moment demands deep and unwavering commitment to transforming it all. The economy. The planet. The way we treat, see, and live with one another.

Generations before me were wooed by making millions on Wall Street or amassing material stuff as a symbol of success. Some in my generation are also attracted by this. But I couldn't be prouder to work and live amongst a massive group of global peers who are just crazy enough, just bold enough to imagine a completely different future. In our vision we do far more than just survive climate change. We shift our energy grid to 100 percent renewables, while turning on the lights for nearly two billion people without energy access.

We don't just fight poverty. We achieve a universal basic income around the globe.

We don't just innovate and succeed in the Global North and make token gestures in the South. Instead we eliminate the educational, financial, and cultural divide between them.

Are these only the miraculous visions of a naive Millennial? Some might say that. But a generation committing their lives to a regenerated world—powered by the biggest transfer of wealth in human history—could make these visions a reality.

In these dynamic days, how heartening, how inspiring, and what a relief it is to see this fresh perspective on money and possibility from my favorite baby boomer, Joel Solomon. Joel is the ultimate mentor and blueprint sketcher. He has spent his life bringing the puzzle pieces of business, politics, leadership, and culture together to form livable and thriving communities and cities. He has invested not in Wall Street millions but in deep and lasting change. His revolution is not limited to a single political administration or a small sect of socially conscious consumers. Rather it's a long-game, big-tent strategy that catalyzes a better way of life for all people and the planet.

In his Vancouver backyard you can see the evidence: all the entrepreneurs, businesses, and political and non-profit leaders that have been touched by Joel's mentorship. Across North America you can find thousands of leaders who have ventured to Hollyhock and returned inspired, connected, and transformed. Joel's impact shines brightly.

In these pages he tells the story of the clean money movement that is now gathering huge momentum. But not only that. He prompts us to consider how the current generational wealth transfer—a hundred trillion dollars in inherited capital—can be redeployed with love and intention. Driven by all of us, including my mighty Millennials, this wealth has the power to remake the world.

The revolution is about wholesale system change. At the intersection of business, politics, and culture are solutions. In the business sector we need innovation and beating hearts powered by values, not just profits. We need progressive political leadership and engaged citizens to put collective good above high-paid lobbyists. We need need art, music, and soul-enriching communities that remind us of our shared humanity and destiny.

We need this revolution. Let's commit to making miracles happen and building the world we need.

— Jessy Tolkan

Jessy is the executive director of Here Now, accelerating climate solutions globally. At Purpose, a social-good agency building new solutions to global problems, she is Head of Labs. Former co-executive director of both Citizen Engagement Laboratory and Energy Action Coalition, she cofounded PowerShift, an annual youth climate change summit now in more than twenty-five countries. *Rolling Stone* magazine named her one of "100 Agents of Change in America."

Preface to the 2018 Edition

by Joel Solomon

It's game time.

A profound call to action is underway. Dangerous financial disparities and ecological crisis are growing. National instabilities across the planet are making a mess of democracy.

The 2016 US presidential election was an alarming wake-up call. Late 2017 brought one of the most egregious tax heists in American history. That blatant abuse of self-interest gave a grand gift to the wealthy at the expense of those who can least afford it. Economic injustice grows.

Climate change is accelerating at a rate that five years ago was dismissed as fantasy. Meanwhile, environmental regulation rollbacks continue to compound damage to the commons.

We can change this game. Wise engagement in political arenas is vital. Help the campaigns of leaders who have integrity and future vision. Give them support and strategy. And vote!

Beyond thoughtful political work, clean money must play a big role.

Money is a powerful force for good. As we awaken to what our money actually does to people and places, our responsibility rises, as do our options, to do better. We can reinvent the economy to broaden opportunity, and level the playing field for everyone.

The demand to align money with values is rising. Financial advisors are responding. Trillions are already shifting. Regenerative futures remain promising and plausible.

Innovation and ingenuity give real hope. We can build a bright long-term future for all. Think what can be accomplished as we redirect earth's trillions of dollars now in circulation.

Will we remain passive? Or will we make this transition go faster and deeper?

Clean Money Is Happening

The clean money revolution is growing from a spiritual evolution, as our hearts and minds are touched by the potential we see.

Capitalism is adapting with increasing speed. The wealth management industry knows this marketplace disruption is real. New product growth is underway for pensions, endowments, mutual funds, banking, consumer goods, and savings. Momentum is growing at increasing speed.

Are you seeing all the optimism yet?

You will soon!

- There's been a 33 percent increase in screening for environmental, social and governance (ESG) factors since 2014. That's $9 trillion in the US alone.
- BlackRock, the world's largest asset manager with $6 trillion, said in a 2018 CEO letter: "To prosper over time, every company must not only deliver financial performance, but also show how it makes a positive contribution to society." That signals a historic shift from the Milton Friedman "profit-only" orthodoxy era.
- About $3 trillion in assets at 18 financial institutions in the Netherlands—along with big funds in Sweden, Australia and Canada—are rallying around Sustainable Development Goals (SDG) as an investment framework.
- The $443 million Nathan Cummings Foundation announced its goal to move the entire endowment into impact, as their response to climate change and global inequality. CEO Sharon Alpert: "We believe this is the future of philanthropy."
- The Ford Foundation committed $1 billion over ten years to mission-related investing, focusing on affordable housing and financial services accessibility.

Clean money is still a moon shot endeavor. Against big odds, it's happening! The momentum will build faster now.

Spiritual Evolution for a Clean Money Revolution

Changing the money game is invaluable to social movements like Black Lives Matter, #MeToo, First Nations activism, and so many more. All demonstrate the rich diversity of societal forces putting fairness and decency front and center.

After centuries of a male-dominated, maximum-financial-return-regardless-of-consequences exploitive capitalism, we are building a new regenerative business culture. Feminization of the economy is part of this, making our financial system relational, co-operative, and with more balanced representation.

It will be an inclusive economy that embraces full responsibility for the long-term well-being of the whole ecosystem.

That economy will be made stronger by empowering our cultural mosaic—the rising demographics that add richness, breadth, and depth to society. As we achieve it, we will alter how we employ, retain, and benefit from each other's diverse talents and preferences.

These shifts add up to an essential decolonization of the conquering, imperialist model that has brought us to the brink of severe global crisis.

We must move rapidly to invent a more unifying, peace-loving, shared responsibility for our miracle of a planet.

Love is the guiding principle.

Love of life, nature, and the future, can guide us.

Global religions have "golden rules" that teach reciprocity and doing unto others fairly. These ethics are basic to many emergent forms of spirituality. New spirituality will find powerful new stories for these new times.

We are learning the meaning and purpose of our lives, and our responsibility as citizens. That's the root for the impending spiritual evolution about money. It will ground and empower us as lifelong change agents.

With real honesty, spiritual awakening, and a smarter, more sacred perspective of money, we will forge a movement to change the world. From a deeper understanding of what money *means*, and a practical understanding of what it *does*, we can change this whole crazy system we are now caught in.

That spiritual evolution will unleash a clean money revolution.

Trillions of dollars will move into new hands through death in the next few decades. The tools are available.

We can make plenty of money by doing the right things. The privilege of wealth and power requires a new ethical bottom line. We know in our hearts what that is.

Our sacred role as ancestors of the future requires us to go deeper. We must shift money from destructive to more positive uses. Love is an excellent moral guide.

Let's be billionaires of good deeds. Billionaires of love.

It's game time. Let's be *all in*.

—J.S.

Preface

by Joel Solomon

From my desk in downtown Vancouver I can turn and look outside to a giant neon sign a block away. It spells out four words: "Let's Heal the Divide."

The Flack Block, the restored 1899 heritage building where I work, sits on the corner of Cambie and Hastings streets. This is the border between the financial district and the Downtown Eastside—infamous as one of the poorest postal codes in Canada. The sign's yellow neon, installed on the brick wall of Vancouver Community College, is a reminder by artist Toni Latour. It prods passersby, and people like me who see it every day, to be aware of what's around us. To remember injustice and to work to heal it.

Vancouver is my home. Like all cities it's a microcosm of the larger world that surrounds it. Vancouver has its contradictions and its struggles to achieve inclusivity and fairness. It's a beautiful and amazing city as well as a complicated one. And it's a perfect place to open this book, because like few other cities in North America it has embraced the challenges of the clean money revolution.

Two decades ago Vancouver was mainly a resource town for selling off BC's lumber and minerals. Now it has emerged as one of the most thriving and resilient urban economies in North America, with a bold "Greenest City in the World" action plan seeking zero waste, zero carbon, and healthy ecosystems. Mayor Gregor Robertson is a social entrepreneur and friend of mine, and under his leadership of three terms, the city is making significant progress with renewable energy, bike lanes, electric car charging stations, and "Skytrain" rapid transit infrastructure. It is incentivizing the built environment toward green buildings that are optimized to be long-lasting and energy-efficient. It's working to protect clean water and clean air. It's encouraging the growth of local, organic food systems. Challenging problems around homelessness and housing affordability remain, along with multiple efforts to respond to them.

In all these ways Vancouver joins the list of cities worldwide that are responding to climate change and trying to clean up their act. If you want a vision of the hoped-for future that the clean money revolution will bring, this is a great place to look.

What is Clean Money?

Clean money is money aligned with a purpose beyond self-interest. Money for the commons. Money that makes the world better. Money regenerating ecosystems and engendering a healthy balance between people and planet. Money that builds true security: long-term, safe, fair resilience.

Clean money is a revolution and an evolution. It expands our view of finance from a bank balance, net worth calculation or the name of a company in which you own stock. It goes beyond the surface. It opens the hood of the car, reads the ingredient label, pops open the laptop to see what's inside. Clean money thinks through where materials came from, who assembled them, and whether that process was just or unjust, regenerative or destructive.

Capitalism is a pervasive and ever-more-confusing global reality. Its simple foundation is exchanging goods and services. Buy or produce for one price, then sell for higher. "Make a profit." Human ingenuity takes the idea to complex and sophisticated levels. Industries and corporations influence culture and exert concentrated power over government and legislation. Exploitation of people, places, rules, and public coffers generates more spoils. The world of finance and speculation adds another profit-making layer, where people bet on—and manipulate perceptions of—corporate performance.

If capitalism hasn't yet captured every nation, culture, and personal assumption, it is close. Money is its ephemeral representation. It's in our pockets. It's in rectangles of plastic in our purses and wallets. It's a key that opens doors to nearly every imaginable desire, for those who have enough of it. Our entire society is built around it. It is seductive. It is perhaps the dominant religion in the world today.

But money has no values of its own. Money doesn't account for fairness, justice, beauty, consciousness, or love. That's *our* role, and it's ever more crucial that we assume it. We need to start to talk about money in ways that dethrone it and make it subject to human ethics and standards of love and decency.

Where does it come from? What is it doing? To whom? Where? Do we want to know? Do we care? Does it matter?

I believe it does. This book is a small attempt, part of an emerging movement, to start making vital distinctions about how wealth is made and used in the world.

For over thirty years I've been helping businesses and investors shift their money and awareness from a strictly utilitarian or default approach focused only on "highest return rate" toward a mission-based, regenerative approach. I've seen and continue to see the early signals transforming the world of finance and investment. Already there is big money to be made from countless "clean" or cleaner opportunities. Divesting from fossil fuels into renewable energy can be a huge financial win. Dollars into organic foods, cleaner manufacturing, transformation, the built environment, consumer goods, preventive health, waste reduction, and energy efficiency are all arguably wise investment strategies.

These changes, however, are being driven by factors beyond self-interest or winning the default game of earning the biggest returns possible. The spread of clean money is about love. It's arising from our collective caring for each other and this planet. From a desire to regenerate rather than destroy.

A Coca-Cola Insight

I'm not from Vancouver originally: I was born in Chattanooga, Tennessee. Chattanooga was a Coca-Cola town. The famous Coke formula was invented in Atlanta, Georgia—where it was marketed as an "Intellectual Beverage and Temperance Drink" that cured hysteria, melancholy, and headaches—but the first bottling plant was built in my hometown in 1899. The bottling operation had a ripple effect on its growth, spurring the development of lumber, glass, and vending machine companies.

By the time I was in elementary school in the early '60s, I knew kids at school whose families were founded on Coca-Cola. I would hear "My daddy owns the Houston bottling plant," or the plant in this or that city. If you were from Tennessee or Georgia, one thing you did not do was sell off your Coke stock. It was like God and gold in a glass bottle. Coke made many millionaires in those days. There are no doubt many billionaire families today whose fortunes began with Coca-Cola.

A fringe concoction sold as a health tonic becomes the most iconic soft drink in the world. Now, a half-century after my Chattanooga childhood, Coke is still a major corporation but sales of its flagship products are steadily dropping, along with the fortunes of other soda-pop manufacturers. Consumers, and even government regulators, are concerned about the health effects of carbonated soft drinks and declining sales reflect a steady market switch. Meanwhile, sales of healthier beverages and products that were on the fringe a few years ago are surging. Think of Guayakí and Mamma Chia, two companies I love and that appear later in this book.

The point of this Coca-Cola story, and a theme of this book, is this: watch the fringes to know where the mainstream is headed. That fortunes rise and fall as tastes and technologies change is well known. Incumbents that stay stuck in their ways fade as anachronisms. Look back at the dominant corporations of each generation and you'll see the road littered with slow adaptors.

With that in mind, it's worth noting the megatrend currently transforming the global economy. You can call it conscious consumption, "green," or Lifestyles of Health and Sustainability (LOHAS), but the meaning is the same. The humble cup of coffee becomes fresh-ground. Then it becomes shade-grown. Then organic. Then fair trade. Soon, locally roasted and ground. Ethical innovators chip away at and transform (or topple) the dominant conglomerates that have controlled this $19-billion global commodity—a bean that grows on a bush.

Like growing numbers of people, you want to know the sources and ingredients behind what you buy, how those goods will affect your own health, and how their production may be damaging people and planet. You want to make good choices for yourself and your family, at the least. More and more of us are thinking beyond ourselves. We want to help sustain life on Earth.

The effects of this conscious push will continue to be felt everywhere, from soft-drink bottling plants in Tennessee to offshore oil rigs in Norway. And the biggest sector of them all, the financial sector, is now feeling the early rumbles.

On one hand, clean money is like clean food or clean energy. If you hold up the finance sector alongside food or energy, you can see it as just one part of this massive shift that is remaking our world. But money is more fundamental than that. Money is an energy, the essence extracted from the value of services and resources, held in reserves the way power is held in a battery. It can be shaped to the vision and intentions of those who control its movements and its uses. Used for investment, it drives the evolution of all other sectors. Without clean money, no other sectors will change.

For that reason, it's hard to overemphasize the critical role that finance and investment leaders can play right now. Those who provide fuel to entrepreneurs, invest our money, and choose winners have a crucial part to play in regenerating the world and building a better future for us all.

Disclaimer: A Few Caveats

I've written this book through the lens of an older, rich, white male heterosexual—living in one of the safest, most prosperous places on the planet. I believe I am one of the luckiest people in the world. Though my hardships in life have been real for me, I know they are a walk in the park compared to the real suffering many endure.

Writing about clean money begs for critique. It will come from the dominant financial system, powerful interests, and those who have accumulated big money. It will come justifiably from those with little: the working poor, refugees and immigrants fighting for a foothold, activists working for too little pay, and many others who have not enjoyed the privileges that allowed me to write this book.

I apologize in advance for my narrow context and perspective. I tell my personal story and the story of the clean money revolution, as I have experienced it, to stimulate thinking and action. As you read through what may annoy or anger you, my hope is that you consider the deeper call for action in these pages—and take from them what you need to play the role you want to play.

Please debate, improve, exceed, and be smarter about these issues than I have been. Money is an agitating and often taboo topic. It has many dimensions, emotional, practical, aspirational, and philosophical. We all need to talk more about money and what it does in the world.

This book includes the story of the $98-million Renewal Fund of which I am a founding partner, and also how and why I've dedicated my life to the clean money revolution. I gratefully draw from the stories of the innovative businesses I've been lucky enough to work with, my life experiences, and key mentors, organizations, and others I've learned from along the way. There are so many groups and networks I have failed to mention that have been invaluable and generative parts of this work. Your contribution is essential and I am deeply appreciative of your influences past, present, and future. Any omissions or discourtesy are from my own limitations.

This book is dedicated to you, the change agents using your own resources to create the new economy and a better world. You are our hope.

—J.S.

Preface

by Tyee Bridge

Revolution is a tricky word. It brings to mind violent uprisings and bloody struggles, the kind that usually end up replacing an old dictator with a new one. That's not the kind of revolution we're talking about in this book. Nor do we mean the sense of an Industrial Revolution or a Digital Revolution, where technology drives massive cultural shifts.

We have more in mind the "revolutionary" work of grassroots leaders who consciously spark change. African American and indigenous civil rights activists laboring over generations for equality and justice, for instance, or other global movements: labor, feminism, gay rights, environmentalism. You can even include the organic food sector, a world in which Joel has spent many years. As the edible subset of the environmental movement, organics are a revolution of ethics as much as they are of agriculture.

In all of these movements (and I hasten to add that they are all ongoing) a lot of people spent a lot of time over a long period trying to get mainstream culture to evolve. With no apologies to Adam Smith, it's not because they were acting strictly out of self-interest. Rather they gave energy to these causes because they felt it was, simply, the right thing to do. Many of them achieved their social goals through personal sacrifice.

In his 2013 book *Sharing the Prize*, historian Gavin Wright calls the civil rights movement a "true revolution" because it was "a fundamental break with past trends that cannot be explained away as the inevitable consequence of market forces or modernization."[1] I'm not sure if James Watt, the inventor of the steam engine, had any compassionate ideas about liberating people from hard labor. He may have. Either way, the changes wrought by his invention were not part of a movement to make the world a better place. The Industrial Revolution was fueled by profit, not principle.

Easier access to media and faster transportation may have helped some or all of the movements for social justice and ecological integrity in the past fifty years, but they were nevertheless led by people, not technology. People who loved something—other people, a river, a field, a species, their children—and felt that it deserved better. They wanted more justice, more stewardship, more caring.

The distinction is important. It's about acting intentionally rather than being swept along by larger forces.

The clean money revolution is the same. It is a new, transformative trajectory *chosen* and accelerated by people who care.

The Lead Pipe

I'll conclude on a personal note. One of the most fascinating things about this collaboration with Joel was researching the infamous strategy called the Powell Memo. Learning about it was like reading a whodunit about my own life. I am a bit younger than Joel, and I grew up—from age 10 to 22, roughly—under the successive Republican presidencies of Ronald Reagan and George H. W. Bush. Adolescents and teenagers are not always politically astute, but they have a sixth sense for when they're being lied to or manipulated. You could tell there was something not quite right about these men. They, and the world they presided over, seemed off-kilter, artificial, and dangerous. Unfortunately there appear to be more hucksters of their sort in North America these days rather than less. We can partly thank the mass social and economic engineering kicked off by Lewis Powell for that.

Jane Mayer, author of the 2016 book *Dark Money*, has said that the Powell Memo is a Rosetta Stone for understanding the world we live in. Yes. For me it was the lead pipe in the library, still bearing Colonel Mustard's dusty fingerprints. It's worth learning more about. While the memo doesn't explain everything, it made me better understand the world in which I'd grown up, from Reagan's welfare queen speeches to Jerry Falwell's Moral Majority to the polluting trees of that other James Watt.

Such revelations don't fix anything, of course. Solving a whodunit doesn't undo the crime. So rather than feeling relieved by our research, I have become newly outraged at the astronomical amount of money—I hesitate to call it unclean money, but it is tempting—that since the 1970s has been funnelled into remaking America and the world into a B movie to suit the ideologies of badly scripted, powerful people.

Like Joel, I hope this book will inspire the opposite approach: unleashing the power of money toward protecting and regenerating the Earth and its many dependents, and bringing back some of what has been lost.

I'd like to thank my parents, Robert and Barbara, and my wife, Michele, for their enduring support and love. I dedicate my part in this book to my son Jonah, with a prayer that the world he grows up in is one far saner and more reverent than the one I knew as a child—one being made more beautiful every day by people who care, whatever resources they may have.

—T.B.

Introduction: The $100 Trillion Question

WE ARE ON THE CUSP of an economic revolution.

This upheaval will remake all the systems we depend upon. In the coming decades it will transform energy, food production, buildings, transportation, infrastructure, and finance. Among other things, it may be the biggest opportunity to make money in human history.

Imagine our world three generations from now: the world of your great-grandchildren. The seeds planted in cities like Vancouver have taken root and proliferated. Industrial activity works to decarbonize the atmosphere and stabilize the climate. The oceans have been cleaned of the horrific plastic gyres now poisoning them. Farming mimics, restores, and enhances natural ecosystems. Renewable energy, smart transit, and "living buildings" are the norm. Population has stabilized at a sustainable level.

These would be the hallmarks of an economy that serves both people and planet, with everyone's basic needs being met and abundant opportunities for meaningful work. Goods produced in a closed-loop production cycle and the concept of waste no longer exists. Nature heals itself as we take off the pressure. A world of true security, no longer deeply divided between haves and have-nots.

This is the potential of the clean money revolution that is starting to rumble through our economy.

If this imagined future sounds utopian or impossible, consider how much can happen in fifty years. What was life like for your grandparents? Could they even imagine the world as it exists today? Our descendants will inhabit a world vastly different than ours. The only question is whether it will be better or worse.

My bet is that it will be better. Two massive global forces are fueling that evolution. The first is the "green" conscious consumer trend I discussed in my preface. The second is the massive wealth transfer currently underway as affluent Boomers pass their wealth to Generation X and the Millennials. Occurring over the next thirty years, it's the largest such turnover in history.

As this wave of inherited capital meets the green megatrend, the possibilities for building a regenerative economy are, yes, challenging and daunting, but they are also dazzling and inspiring.

Waking Up

Our spectacular human ingenuity gave us fire, agriculture, language, self-awareness, art, intellect, spiritual awe, nations, science, books, fossil fuels, extended lives, technology, and money. Likewise, our economic system has performed miracles for many. But our ingenuity and our economic successes have led us to a dead end.

We know we have deep and complex challenges to address. The list is long, depressing, and, to many of us, well known. Our most fundamental problem is that humanity has overreached the carrying capacity of nature. The results of that overreach are all around us. Global warming, ocean acidification, widespread species extinction. Epic self-inflicted environmental damage like the BP *Deepwater Horizon* oil spill and the Fukushima Daiichi nuclear disaster. Dangerous externalities are too often legal, or even subsidized as part of "business as usual." High-priced lobbying keeps tax revenues subsidizing damaging industries instead of incentivizing newer, cleaner technologies. Rather than rewarding "goods" like labor, we tax them, while allowing "bads" like pollution to happen free of charge and with impunity.

It's a grotesque caricature of the ideal of capitalism, which is supposed to reward effort and innovation. One 2010 study by the London consultancy Trucost found that the top 3,000 corporations caused $2.2 trillion USD in environmental and social damage in 2008 alone—all externalized onto the commons and untaxed.

This is madness.

We must begin to intelligently "degrowth" to reset the balance. Infinite growth is a fantasy. The Earth can no longer support our species in blindly expanding, dominating, and accumulating.

There are other profound challenges. Violence against women, human trafficking, and slavery remain rampant. Estimates say approximately 45 million people live as slaves worldwide as of 2016.[2] Racism is resurgent in North America and Europe. These phenomena have been worsened by the sharp increase in poverty and inequity in recent decades.

From 2002 to 2010, the wealth of the world's billionaires increased at the same rate as that of the poorest 50 percent of the population.[3] In only five years between 2009 and 2014, the wealth of the bottom half of the global population declined—while that of the world's billionaires *doubled*.[4] Just 42 billionaires control the same wealth as 3.7 billion people, nearly half the planet's population. The wealthiest 1 percent have more money than the other 99 percent combined.[5]

For a North American perspective on inequity, the magazine *Mother Jones* summarized a recent Institute for Policy Studies report this way: "In 2014, Wall Street's bonus pool was roughly double the combined earnings of all Americans working full-time jobs at minimum wage."[6]

Such gross inequity fuels distrust, resentment, and anger among citizens who have been left behind. They have reason to be upset. Manipulation by the powerful has steadily pushed the burden of taxation from the rich to the poor. Catastrophic market failures have further cost taxpayers trillions of dollars, and the playing field remains severely tilted in favor of the wealthiest individuals and the largest corporations. Demagogic politicians like Donald Trump use twisted rhetoric to rise on the building tide of anger. Mainstream leaders, meanwhile, fail to challenge the entrenched powers that write the rules for our financial and monetary systems.

This is a recipe for disaster, one we are currently watching unfold in politics and society. Much of our current mess can be traced to the world of finance. In three decades as an investor, entrepreneur, and change agent, I've more often seen money and business as the cause of problems rather than the solution. We can change that formula.

To date, money and finance have been managed under a mass-cultural state of dissociation. A gentle term would be sleepwalking; a more accurate one would be a mental disconnect, a kind of insanity. The mainstream mindset that money and investments are somehow value-neutral is the root of the problem. We give our money to managers, banks, retirement funds, insurance carriers, and others to invest in products and practices we would be horrified to claim as our own work. Our major institutions are complicit in this hypnosis of human spirit that is stealing the future.

Waking up from this state and reforming our economic system would be intelligent, functional, and offer a soft landing. Money can be a powerful driver of long-term resilience and a more just world. It's our choice. If we do nothing, change will be forced upon us. It will be radical, painful, and lead to unknown, dangerous consequences.

Bleak? Hopeless? Thankfully, no.

The $100 Trillion Question

In the two countries considered in this book, Canada and the United States, the affluent amount to about about 70 million people.* These families are going to hand over between $30 and $50 trillion

* Here I define the "affluent" as the top 20 percent of the global population in terms of wealth. As of 2014, the 20 percent controlled 94.5 percent of the money on the planet. That leaves 5.5 percent for the other four-fifths of the population.[7] Those in the 20 percent have more than enough to support their basic security, such as food, shelter, mobility, education, health care, retirement support. They can afford top universities, private schools, extended vacations, multiple vehicles, and many other things—and they almost universally have significant sums of money invested in private and public securities.

to the next generation. Worldwide, the total transfer is closer to $100 trillion.

Will these riches be used to further exploit the poor and fund greater destruction of the planet? Or will they be used to create a clean money future and a resilient civilization?

We are smart enough to choose and successfully travel the second path. Our dominant system of capitalist democracy has reached its limits. Now it must be reformed. We can turn our ingenuity to living intelligently and beautifully within Earth's limits. To coexisting with each other and with wild creatures and ecosystems. We can find joy and meaning beyond unlimited consumption. The wealth that has perpetuated injustice can transform the world.

Over the next three decades, I propose we shift that $100 trillion from destructive and misdirected uses to regenerative ones. It is essential that we do so to ensure a soft landing by 2050. (In Chapter 10 I lay out some symbolic sector-by-sector numbers, to stimulate the conversation.) As we choose the better course, we will unlock tremendous economic opportunities. These will accelerate the momentum that is now well begun.

Statistics from the US Social Investment Forum (US SIF) show that by 2016 over $8.7 trillion was invested according to socially responsible investment (SRI) strategies. That is one in five dollars under professional management in the United States.[8] These are incredible figures relative to twenty years ago. They are a signal of the tremendous scale of what is coming in the next decades.

Bloomberg New Energy Finance (BNEF) forecasts at least $7.8 trillion in clean-energy investments over the next 25 years.[9] Danny Kennedy, cofounder of Sungevity, the largest privately held solar company in the United States, notes that in terms of current investment in renewables—between $250 to $300 billion per year as of 2016—we have already reached the point where hydrocarbons are the "alternative" energy source. Danny suggests in these pages that to adequately respond to climate change we can and should quadruple our clean energy investment—to $1 trillion a year.

These numbers seem astronomical, but they are well within the range of the possible. This kind of catalyzing investment is possible in nearly every sector, and has already begun. The green genie has escaped from the bottle. It's a vital counter-trend that should give us hope.

Every day new companies offer better, less harmful products that displace those offered by established incumbents. Like the "force that through the green fuse drives the flower," this energy will push its way through all the branches of our economy, shrinking negative externalities like pollution. Every industry will instead produce positive by-products, as organic farms now do.

The world of money, finance, and investment is ripe for major reform and reinvention. We're seeing more and more clean food, clean energy, and clean buildings. Now clean money is also on the rise. It's still near the fringes but rapidly becoming mainstream. The logic is compelling. The practicality is proving itself.

We are our money. It has our name on it. All of us in the money business must take responsibility for where our capital is, right this moment; what it is doing; and who it is helping or harming. Those of us who have more money than we need must choose better where to put it. Looking the other way and offloading responsibility for how mutual funds, wealth managers, and financial institutions invest our dollars—without considering how they affect the world—must end.

We don't dump our garbage on the sidewalk or poison other people's children. But do you know what your money is doing in other families' backyards? We can no longer pretend that we're morally detached from the stocks and bonds we invest in, if the companies in which we own shares are doing damage. It is our responsibility to know, and to act accordingly.

Bold leadership will be required at the highest level. The 2015 Paris climate agreement hints at what's possible through peaceful cooperation. The revolution begins as a citizen movement. For it to succeed, we all need to change our patterns of consumption, raise our standards for political leaders, and insist upon new standards for how our bank accounts, mutual funds, pensions, and personal wealth are managed.

The new generation of investors will demand nothing less. At 85 million, Millennials, born between 1980 and 2000, already outnumber Boomers in North America. For them, Milton Friedman's worn libertarian maxim—that "the social responsibility of business is to increase its profits"—is already dead.

In a 2006 poll, 78 percent of the famously values-aligned Millennials said that businesses have a responsibility to build a better world.[10] That hasn't changed much as they've entered the workforce. Sixty-one percent Millennials in senior positions say they have "chosen not to undertake a task at work because it went against their personal values or ethics," according to a 2016 Deloitte poll.[11] Millennials are already insisting that their portfolios, self-generated or inherited, be in values-consistent, ethical, sustainable, and just investments.

These are global imperatives. Embracing them is an awakening driven by love. Money, finance, and wealth-management have ignored love for too long. Love is our antidote for fear and despair. Love is a shorthand way of saying that we must show we care by *acting* on our values, ethics, and morals—for ourselves, our families, all life on the planet, and the future.

The conscious consumer movement is about love. Love will drive us to know where our money is and what it is doing to the world (or for the world) at this moment. It the most important responsibility of our lives, and will lead us into the great adventure of creating the future.

The clean money revolution is on!

A Mighty Time

THE SOUTHEAST STORM is raging at gusts of 60 knots. The Salish Sea is frothy and churning in the December storm, tossing floating logs and downed trees like toothpicks. Tree branches are flying like spears in the gale-force winds.

Our small group has gathered on BC's remote Cortes Island in the northern Salish Sea. We are in a beach house, huddled around a cast-iron wood stove pumping out heat. Though we have to speak up to be heard over the howl outside, we are calling forth the biggest visions we can conjure. It's 1993, soon after the quincentenary of the "discovery" of the Americas by Christopher Columbus. I've proposed that we attempt a 50-year strategy that will undo some of the cultural and ecological destruction that has been ravaging the continent since 1492—and help build a regenerative economy that will benefit the next 500 years.

As audacious and far-fetched as that may sound, it's no academic exercise. We have a real task at hand: one of our group has inherited a fortune. She wants the majority of it deployed to reducing humanity's ecological footprint and ensuring that the biosphere supports future life on the planet—clean water, clean air, and clean food.

Idealistic? Of course. Silly? Not really. Impossible? Maybe. But we hope not.

At 39 years old, I'm about to embark on an amazing adventure: helping turn a friend's personal fortune into a tool for changing history.

Early Roots

With my younger sister Linda, I grew up Jewish in Tennessee in the 1950s and '60s. It was a momentous time in American history: the civil rights movement, Vietnam protests, the rise of feminism, and the clash of a burgeoning, multicultural liberalism with the dominant conservative values of white men. Until the Civil Rights Act of 1964, Tennessee was one of 17 states that enforced legal segregation, or so-called "Jim Crow" laws. Black and white citizens had been kept apart at schools, diners, baseball stadiums, movie theaters, even drinking fountains. (My family had owned several such "colored" theatres before our father went into the suburban mall-building business that made his fortune.)

As late as 1957 Chattanooga had a softball team openly sponsored by the KKK. A 1958 poll in the university town of Knoxville—considered then more liberal than Chattanooga and only two hours up the road—showed that 90 percent of white citizens were against desegregation.

I remember a party my parents threw about ten years after that particular poll. I was in my early teens and my job was to mix drinks and grill the steaks. What made it memorable wasn't only the adult duties I'd been given, but that it was an "integrated" party with both black and white guests. I was told it was one of the first Chattanooga society had seen. For my parents it was edgy, possibly even risky. It was around the time that Martin Luther King Jr. was assassinated in Memphis, sparking riots and inflaming racial tensions across the country—including, of course, Tennessee.

As Jews in the South our family already bore our share of prejudice and scrutiny. My grandfather had moved to Chattanooga from Atlanta after the KKK there began marching around his neighborhood. But Chattanooga, the proverbial buckle of the Bible Belt, was not a perfect haven. My father, Joel "Jay" Solomon, had gone into the mall-building business in part because he felt shut out by the downtown business community. My sister Linda remembers picking up the phone one night as a young girl, saying "Hello," and hearing a man's voice on the other end of the receiver say: "Fucking Jews." This was around the time our father and his cousins owned local movie theatres, and were showing one of the first movies to star an African American, *Guess Who's Coming to Dinner* with Sidney Poitier.

"Prejudice was always under the surface," Linda remembers. "Kids would come up to me at Easter and say, 'Linda, why'd the Jews kill Jesus?'"

One of the most disappointing moments of my youth happened the first time I asked a girl out. I'd called to ask her to school dance. She left me hanging on the telephone for a long time. When she returned she was quietly sobbing and said, "I can't go with you." Three days later my father heard from a business associate that her father was telling people "that Jew boy" tried to ask out his daughter. My dating life took some years to recover. These personal encounters with racism and bigotry were minor, of course, compared to the experience of black citizens of the South, who were having firehoses and police dogs set on them amid lynchings and the brutal assassinations of civil rights leaders. It was all part of an entrenched culture of de jure and de facto prejudice accepted by the "decent people" of dominant white society.

There were no incidents because of our integrated party. It all seemed normal to me, and I'm not sure if I even understood the significance for my family. But I appreciate the example my parents, particularly my mother, set for me in that party and in their lives generally. Do the right thing even when the results may be frowned upon.

Linda, who now is editor-in-chief of the progressive online newspaper the *National Observer*, remembers our early life in much the same way. "They taught us that it was our duty to always be involved in politics and in what was happening in the outside world. This came, I think, in large part from the fact that they'd grown up during World War II, and witnessed Hitler's rise, thankfully from the safety of the United States. They gave us a sense that there are always forces pushing against one another, you could call it 'good' and 'evil,' and that it's a basic part of being in a democratic society that you become part of the push toward good."

As the '60s era of challenging convention reached its crescendo, courageous people faced down power structures that had long been tainted and perverted by narrow minds. The societal backlash against civil rights, "women's liberation," and Vietnam War protests made it easy to feel powerless and confused. But throughout that tumultuous time I saw leaders of all kinds choose vision and action over silence and complacency. Single mothers, students, artists, businesspeople, politicians, and even Supreme Court justices challenged the status quo. They began dismantling cultural assumptions and laws that perpetuated injustice.

It's true that our world remains flawed and unjust. But the progressives and social innovators of that era made huge strides and won great victories. They were models whose bravery and optimism made the world better.

We can learn much from the challenges of those times, and from the people who rose up to meet them.

Amid all of the of chaos of the 21st century, we understandably want to bury our heads in the sand—or throw down a beach towel on it, grab a margarita, and just watch it happen, debating what others should do to solve it. Neither of these responses is helpful. One is denial; the other is self-disempowerment. Most of us have much to offer. As Donella Meadows, author of the 1972 book *The Limits to Growth*, put it: "I've grown impatient with the kind of debate we used to have about whether the optimists or the pessimists are right. Neither are right. There is too much bad news to justify complacency. There is too much good news to justify despair."[12]

To pull a lyric from an old John Lee Hooker song, this is a mighty time. The stakes are high. There is reason to take heart, to be inspired, to remember what we are capable of. In North America and across the globe we have faced overwhelming challenges at various points in history, and risen to the occasion. We will do so again.

I've felt fortunate to be part of a growing movement that has already shifted hundreds of billions of dollars toward regenerative enterprises and meaningful change. I know it can be done. We can reinvent capitalism. We can join the revolution. All of us, and in particular those involved in the world of investment and finance, have something to offer. Each of us must soul-search the deep questions about our purpose, our direction, and our dreams—and most vitally, our sense of responsibility to our children and future generations. Together we have the resources to achieve what may be the greatest ethical and economic shift in human history.

One benefit of being over sixty—and being able to look back at your past and ahead to the future—is having a clear sense of your life purpose. Mine is to be the very best ancestor I can be. I do that by moving capital to invest in change. It took time, and many teachers, to figure that out.

My journey began when I started helping another Southerner, Jimmy Carter, get to the White House.

The Dirty Campaign against Al Gore Sr.

From grade seven to eleven I attended a military school in Chattanooga called Baylor. The public schools in our town were considered weak, and a "good education" was thought to be available only at private schools. At that time, the choice of private schools in my hometown was either military or religious. My father had graduated from Baylor and wanted the same for me, though my mother, the photographer Rosalind Fox Solomon, had a strong resistance to a military academy for her son. She only agreed to send me there on the condition that I could leave if I wanted to.

My family life was liberal, egalitarian, and lively. Baylor, on the other hand, was cut whole cloth from the dominant Southern culture of white male supremacy. Racism and misogyny were the norm. My parents were active in Democratic politics, and the dissonance between my days at Baylor and my home life were part of my awakening to the social and political rifts of the time. In 1970 I was sixteen and Nixon was in the White House. There he presided over the secret "Operation Menu" carpet-bombing of Cambodia and the Kent State murder of four students by the National Guard. This only heightened the tensions over racial desegregation, Vietnam, hippie culture, the sexual revolution, and what kind of blue jeans or haircut you wore.

At Baylor I was one of about ten Jewish boys in a school of five hundred. The discrimination against us was mainly of the subtle, exclusionary type, rather than overt intimidation, but I felt it and never truly settled in. I was a child of privilege like many of my peers, but unlike most of them, on Christmas and spring breaks my parents took Linda and me to New York City museums and Broadway shows instead of going en masse to party in Florida.

The highlight of my Baylor years—besides several close, lifelong friends—was attaining a degree of touch football stardom as a long-throw quarterback. By grade 11 I had transferred to the local public school, Chattanooga High. I was relieved that one third of the student body was black and, even more compelling, one half were girls. My long hair ended up frizzy and stacked on my head like a turban, but I wasn't much of a hippie. I was on whatever side of the spectrum you're on when you're a white kid in the South whose first two concerts were James Brown and Wilson Pickett, not Tammy Wynette and Merle Haggard.

In 1970 I had my first experience of the realities of power and politics while working on the campaign to re-elect Democratic Senator Al Gore Sr., a nationally significant, liberal, pro-civil rights Southerner. I went out many nights putting up signs, knocking on doors, licking envelopes, and helping as much as I could with ground-level political grunt work. Mostly I was a teenager using politics to get out of the house and avoid the mainstream teenage culture of sports and alcohol. I was able to have nighttime adventures with my pals learning new parts of town and leafleting football game parking lots, when otherwise we would have been home watching television or sitting in those football bleachers. It was fun, and without knowing it, I was finding early empowerment. Exposing young people to politics is valuable learning.

It can also reveal ugly realities of human nature. Senator Gore was a stately Southern politician of a kind you don't see much anymore, and I respected his stand for peace and civil rights. The campaign fought against him by the Republican Bill Brock was notoriously bitter and vicious. Brock was a Chattanooga native whose family owned one of the largest candy companies in the country. His race-baiting attack ads triumphed with the state's large contingent of white, conservative, anti-integrationist voters. His victory in that election was the first time I'd felt crushing defeat by forces that had abandoned ethics and truth in favor of power. It wouldn't be the last. Tennessee today sadly remains one of the most politically backward and conservative states in the country, even as its cities leap forward with a progressive, creative, and diverse urban culture.

I remember my spine tingling at Senator Gore's speech after the election results were announced. "The causes for which we fought are not dead," he thundered with the cadence of a gospel preacher. "The truth shall rise again!"

It's a fundamental truth in business and politics: failure is never final. You get up, dust yourself off, and start again.

To the White House Door with Jimmy Carter

While Brock's victory depressed me, the campaign hooked me on the necessity and importance of politics. I wanted to experience Washington, D.C. After my first year at Columbia University in 1973, my father helped me get a summer internship with the Democratic National Committee's campaign arm. It was chaired by a new and relatively unknown Georgia governor named Jimmy Carter.

One of my favorite stories from that period is that I told my political science professor at Vassar that Carter was going to win the presidency because I had read the strategy document that outlined how it would happen. They were impressed enough with my earnestness to agree to bundle my classes on Tuesdays and Thursday afternoons. This allowed me to travel around New England on various duties during the rest of the week. I organized groups of Young Democrats on college campuses and drove Carter family members to small-town campaign stops. One memorable assignment was to help raise the $5,000 needed in 20 different states to qualify for federal election campaign matching funds. The Allman Brothers—one of my then-favorite rock bands—agreed to hold a concert in

Providence, Rhode Island, where young concert-goers had to fill out election donation forms at the door. They booed when Carter came on stage to talk. They had no idea who he was and wanted the band they had paid to see. But we raised the money we needed.

I spent most of the campaign attempting to garner support for Carter in mostly obscure locations: the South Bronx; Vicksburg, Mississippi; and Lawton, Oklahoma. This was unpromising terrain, given to me as a kind of exile after being on the wrong side of an internal power struggle with the campaign manager and future White House chief of staff, Hamilton Jordan. I spent the final weekend of the 1976 election driving to rural Louisiana radio stations, dropping off cassette-tape ads in which former Alabama governor (and infamous segregationist) George Wallace gave Carter his endorsement. Talk about strange bedfellows! I lost a good deal of naive innocence in my encounter with political realities.

But I didn't lose my idealism. Carter's victories in Mississippi and Louisiana won him a razor-thin victory. The peanut farmer from Plains, Georgia—who had been a virtual unknown in federal politics at zero percent in the polls two years before the election— had risen to the most powerful political office in the world. This experience dramatically expanded my sense of the possible.

What inspired me most from the campaign was the original strategy document that chief strategist Jordan had drawn up at age 28, a strategy that mapped out Carter's victory in the Democratic nomination in 1976. That a virtual unknown on the national stage could ascend so quickly to the presidency, on the strength of well-considered strategy, timing, and tactical rollout, made a lasting impression. You can be as out of the box as a Georgia peanut farmer and pull off almost anything if you're determined and creative.

Dark Money: Lewis Powell's Legacy

Ignoring the realities of power and politics is a big mistake for anyone who wants to use business to create deep change. Public policy is inseparable from commerce. Small strokes of the pen can shift entire industries. With this in mind, it's enlightening to look back at the 1970s, because in many ways the degraded world we now live in, and are working hard to regenerate, is the result of ideas and policies that coalesced in that decade.

Well-organized forces forged a system intended to capture hearts and minds and shift America and its allies to the right—unleashing an era of rapid profiteering for the few at the expense of the many.

The right wing, like Hamilton Jordan, knew that strategy papers and focused work can change the world. The Powell Memo of 1971 is a little-remembered document that used long-term social engineering to remake American culture. It makes Jordan's strategy look like a dandelion puff in a hurricane. This well-articulated and powerful map was written by corporate lawyer Lewis F. Powell, Jr., who sat on the boards of several large corporations, including Philip Morris, and would later be nominated to the Supreme Court by Richard Nixon.[13]

As the 1970s began, Powell and his conservative peers were worried by what they saw happening in America. Naive trust in political and corporate leaders had shifted to suspicion and even hostility. New values were taking root in young people, part of a consciousness that was increasingly ecological, feminist, anti-war, and egalitarian. Powell's mindset, by contrast, had been shaped by the World War II glory years of American military and economic domination. He remained a staunch believer in American exceptionalism—and in the idea of business, and political power, concentrated in few hands. Most board members and executives of the Fortune 500 brands (almost entirely white men) shared his views.

The emerging Boomer generation didn't. Their dissent and outright protests were seen across the country. Meanwhile, a long list of factors—among them oil-price shocks and new legislation for civil rights, employee safety, and environmental protection—was chipping away at their oligarchical model and the profits it made for them.

Powell's response was an attempt to solidify a right-wing ruling class that would control the levers of power in perpetuity. "No thoughtful person can question that the American economic system is under broad attack," he wrote, before setting out his call to action: "The overriding first need is for businessmen to recognize that the ultimate issue may be survival—survival of what we call the free enterprise system, and all that this means for the strength and prosperity of America and the freedom of our people."

In the memo Powell singled out consumer-rights advocate Ralph Nader as a special threat. Nader was an early crusader against the disastrous impact of unregulated corporate activities.

"Perhaps the single most effective antagonist of American business is Ralph Nader, who—thanks largely to the media—has become a legend in his own time and an idol of millions of Americans. A recent article in *Fortune* speaks of Nader as follows: 'The passion that rules in him—and he is a passionate man—is aimed at smashing utterly the target of his hatred, which is corporate power. He thinks, and says quite bluntly, that a great many corporate executives belong in prison—for defrauding the consumer with shoddy merchandise, poisoning the food supply with chemical additives, and willfully manufacturing unsafe products that will maim or kill the buyer. He emphasizes that he is not talking just about "fly-by-night hucksters" but the top management of blue chip business.'"

Notably, Powell didn't quote Nader himself, but a caricature of him by *Fortune* magazine. It was a classic smear tactic. For Powell the demand for safe products and accountability was akin to Marxist revolution. This is a vital history lesson for those interested in progressive investing. As we put money in businesses that aim to do no harm and leave the world better, we still work in the cultural and regulatory hangover of an era where constraining big business in any way was considered dangerously radical or "socialist."

What did Powell propose? He urged business leaders to join forces and finance the influence of policies, elections, culture, and regulation, with the Chamber of Commerce as a major base of operations. He advocated heavy funding of right-wing think tanks. He proposed a pro-business speakers' bureau and a "staff of scholars" to evaluate and challenge high school and university textbooks (and teachers) critical of capitalism and US policies. He encouraged the Chamber of Commerce to "enjoy a particular rapport with the increasingly influential graduate schools of business."

Big money began to flow to once-obscure organizations like the Hoover Institute and the American Enterprise Institute, and to new policy shops like the Heritage Foundation and the Institute for Contemporary Studies. These were part of a larger constellation of think tanks churning out policy recommendations, critiques, and academic articles that included the Manhattan Institute, the Cato Institute, Citizens for a Sound Economy, and Accuracy in Academe. Most of these were funded through the Business Roundtable, a group founded in 1972 whose mission was "the aggressive pursuit of political power for the corporation."[14]

By 1974 the Roundtable's 150 members included 90 of the largest 200 companies in the United States, accounting for almost half the American economy, who were spending $900 million annually (about $4 billion in today's dollars) to influence political leaders and promote various forms of libertarian, anti-government, "free market" ideology.[15,16]

I've always felt "free market" was a red-herring term. What its advocates usually mean is state socialism for corporations in terms of subsidies and benefits, and unassisted, dog-eat-dog capitalism for most citizens. The aftermath of the 2008 Wall Street crash, in which fantastically wealthy corporations were bailed out with hundreds of billions in public money, is a good example.

This is only a sampling of Powell's comprehensive map for takeover of the direction of society, and much of it came to pass. Perhaps the most alarming outcome was the creation of a generation of downwardly mobile, angry people, who through crass manipulation and fear-mongering have become the core voting base for right-wing political candidates who fulfill Powell's objectives. The anti-government and anti-tax movements that grew out of these Nixonian strategies haunt us and drain the commons to this day, as we saw in the 2016 United States election of President Donald Trump.

In 1977, Carter's first year in office, ten CEOs from the Business Roundtable met with leading congressional Democrats to lobby them for the group's priorities. "The conventional wisdom is that they're extremely effective, for the very reason that they put themselves together," commented one legislative aide at the time. "When they come in here, it's not some vice president for public relations, but *the* president of GM, DuPont or another corporation coming in themselves. That has a hell of a lot more impact than some lobbyist."[17]

Conservative business leaders took Powell's advice to heart. "If our system is to survive," wrote Powell, "top management must be equally concerned with protecting and preserving the system itself.... Strength lies in organization, in careful long-range planning and implementation, in consistency of action over an indefinite period of years, in the scale of financing available only through joint effort, and in the political power available only through united action and national organizations."[18]

Forty years later, we are living in the world that these powerful conservatives helped create with their ideas and money. Paul Weyrich, cofounder of the Heritage Foundation and the Moral Majority, also helped found the American Legislative Exchange Council (ALEC) in 1973. ALEC's sponsors have included Coors, Kraft, Exxon, the Koch brothers, Altria, and Johnson & Johnson.[19] The organization helps members craft "model bills" for legislators to pass that advance pro-business agendas.

"To understand the magnitude of its influence," wrote *Washington Post* columnist Katrina Vanden Heuvel in 2014, "consider that of the more than 100 bills introduced between 2011 and 2013 to repeal or weaken minimum wage laws, 67 of them related back to ALEC."[20]

Vanden Heuvel noted that in 2009 alone, 115 of ALEC's 826 model bills were signed into law. The success is partly through the dark arts of bill-bundling, as Rep. Mark Pocan—a Wisconsin Democrat who joined ALEC to monitor it and critique it—noted in 2012: "It's very concrete advice that they give: 'Don't just introduce a single piece of legislation, introduce 14.' That way people can't oppose any one bill, which is actually very good strategic advice."[21]

It may seem a bit shocking that such bills are able to pass without voter backlash. Shouldn't a vision of a permanent, well-oiled patrician oligarchy ruling a perpetual underclass be a tough sell to most voters? They pass now, as they did in the 1970s, by being hidden in legislative bundles the size of a phone book—and thanks to rivers of money that pour into politics via lobbying and campaign contributions. But they also succeed because of a popular base of people who want to erase the complexities, failures, and vulnerabilities of the post-World War II era. So many people still want turn back the clock to a dreamy and mostly fictional Hollywood past of rugged individualism, patriotic parades, and home-baked pie. This longing for simple myths—like the patriarchal icon of the frontier hero who pulls himself up by his own bootstraps—has helped right-wing interests from Ronald Reagan to the Tea Party sell the public on cutting off their own public services, benefits, and power.

"Real power," as Gautam Mukunda wrote in an essay on Wall Street in the *Harvard Business Review*, "comes not from forcing people to do what you want but from changing the way people think, so that they *want* to do what you want."[22]

Reagan himself used the bogus concept of "welfare queens" bleeding taxpayers to justify his right-wing agenda of slashing social services—while quietly signing off on massive tax cuts for the wealthy. (Between 1981 and 1986 the tax rate on the highest bracket of earners was cut in half, from 70 percent to 34 percent.) Reagan also reduced the government's share of estate tax and cut corporate tax rates. These cuts in revenue were not accompanied by the supposed reduced spending upon which genuine conservatives pride themselves. Reagan is renowned for his Cold War spending spree that racked up about $4.5 trillion (in 2015 dollars) in defense budget expenses over eight years.[23]

Tax cuts to the wealthy have continued under successive presidents. Nobel-prize winning economist Joseph Stiglitz has commented that investing in anti-tax lobbyists gives the highest ROI to certain wealthy elites. "It's a vicious circle," said Stiglitz. "The rich are using their money to secure tax provisions to let them get richer still. Rather than investing in new technology or R&D, the rich get a better return by investing in Washington."[24]

As for deregulating the financial industry—and we all know where that led—that also continued in other administrations, even under Democratic President Clinton. This shows how successful Powell's social engineers were at shifting culture and politics to the right.

A 500-Year Calling

That brings us back to the storm-swept Cortes Island visioning session that opened this chapter. Much of my experience with integrated use of capital has come from my partnership with Carol Newell, one of the heirs to the Newell Rubbermaid fortune. We met through the Threshold Foundation. Our mind-expanding conversation with friends around that glowing wood stove followed the 500-year anniversary of the arrival of Columbus on the North American continent. Sitting on an island named for a notorious conquistador, we reflected on five centuries of genocide, exploitation, and ecological destruction brought on by European colonization.

Of course there were also constructive outcomes of the meeting of cultures, but we felt it was time to acknowledge and deal with the whole legacy, including the ugly sides. Genocide and exploitation were systemic. What could we do in our lifetimes that would influence the next 500 years for the better? It was a thought experiment. A way to reframe our goals and intentions to a "seventh generation" approach. Thinking in generational terms is a valuable exercise in a culture where businesses and politicians are focused on quarterly bottom lines and two- to four-year election cycles. With a generational vision, the results may not be seen by you, or even your grandchildren, but only by people far into the future. The payoffs are distant and you'll probably never get credit for them.

When I began sharing this 500-year concept publicly, I was fascinated to see it appear in Canada's conservative newspaper, the *National Post*—a publication that specializes in disparaging environmentally and socially progressive ideas. The columnist noted my long involvement with Hollyhock, a leadership and learning institute on Cortes where my wife, Dana Bass Solomon, served as CEO for 18 years. In particular he focused on our work bringing together diverse change agents at the Social Change Institute (SCI). "Coordination, cooperation and collective power is precisely the point of the Social Change Institute," he wrote. "And not just the institute: it's the point of all the efforts Mr. Solomon has brilliantly co-ordinated into a breathtakingly enterprising strategy." [25]

Your greatest praise sometimes comes from those who oppose you.

The *National Post* columnist latched on to our 500-year vision idea, ending his piece with the lines: "There are still 480 years left in Mr. Solomon's revolutionary plan. And this is only phase one."

As people who want to invest in change, what would it look to plan now for a 500-year impact, or even a 50-year impact? This is the kind of question, and intention, I love. It provokes imagination and creativity. You can see the power of such thinking in Powell's 50-year plan for a conservative American revolution, which has left such a tragic political and environmental legacy—not only in the United States but in Canada, the United Kingdom, Australia, Europe, and many developing countries.

As progressive investors and entrepreneurs, what we can take from all this is how much a long-term plan and combined efforts can accomplish. Abandoning a sole focus on the quarterly bottom line in favor of the long-term future is to break a spell, a hypnosis. If we believe the playing field is unfairly tilted against a regenerative economy that can restore the planet and bring social justice, then we need to play bigger—not only in the world of business but in the corridors of political power.

The place to start is with a more generative vision for long-term resilience. Enough of the winner-takes-all mentality. We can blend the best of the service and helping professions with the ingenuity of the marketplace. Business can be designed and led for complementing and collaborating with the public sector, creating a harmony of intelligent stewardship and innovation. Values melded with sophisticated strategy can accomplish great things.

While in my twenties in the 1970s I was just catching glimpses of these ideas. When I was helping mobilize the youth vote for Carter, I thought I might build my career in politics—partly because it was a way to dodge the family mall business back in Tennessee. I was done with the South, or so I thought, and my father would have approved of my leaving the business behind for the White House.

But when Carter won, I wasn't ready to commit to a political career. I needed time to think about who I was and what I really wanted to do. Why did my life matter? What was my path? What would I contribute?

Later these questions became more urgent and complicated. Mall business or not, I learned I wasn't going to escape a different type of link with my father. My father's family carried the gene for polycystic kidney disease (PKD), where multiple cysts grow on the kidneys. The cysts gradually crowd out kidney function, with an inevitable outcome of renal failure. My grandmother and aunt had died from it, as had many other members of that side of my family. I'd been tested as a teen, and showed no signs yet. But this possible "death sentence" was haunting me. If I turned out to have that shortened life gene, I wanted to know more about myself, and the world—and the best way to live meaningfully.

Don Shaffer

served for ten years as the President & CEO of RSF Social Finance in San Francisco. He is now cofounder of a new venture called Jubilee, which is "joyfully reimagining our financial system, based on the principle that all of us are interconnected." Jubilee provides advisory services, learning journeys, and co-investment opportunities to those who are new to impact investing.

How did you get into this work?

I grew up outside of Princeton, New Jersey. It was a community where lots of Wall Street traders and bankers lived. My first job, when I was fourteen, was caddying at a golf course where these people played. It was clear to me they had a lot of power and wealth in society, so I'd ask them what they did to make their money.

My dad was a sheets and towel salesman; he worked for a textiles company. That was pretty easy to understand. But from these guys I got wildly variable answers. It's hard to explain to a 14-year-old kid about derivatives and leveraged buyouts—and about using lots of borrowed money to invest in high-risk stuff, not to mention explaining who's left holding the bag if you don't get the money back.

Their explanations were completely unclear to me and it was frankly jarring. I said to myself, "So how does this actually work and who does it ultimately serve? And what is money anyway?" Since then I've basically been obsessed with how the financial system operates and how we could reimagine it. My work is trying to find innovations that make our financial system more direct, transparent, and personal—unlike typical Wall Street innovations, which generally make things more complex, opaque, and anonymous.

What are the risks we face if we continue with business as usual?

The stakes are extraordinarily high. In terms of risks and stakes you could talk about increasing income inequality, you could talk about climate, you could talk about all these major kinds of things that are at stake and most of us are aware of. Instead of waiting for that to happen, why not start doing things differently?

There are several root systems in our society. One of them is agriculture. One of them is energy. Another is capital itself. If we can't figure out how to reimagine the current financial system, we're going to keep getting the results that we've been getting recently, which is extraordinary volatility. Go back to 2008. Is that something that we want to see again? I am not really an Armageddon-type person, but what's at stake is that we continue on with highly centralized, top-down gigantic organizations that don't even know how to govern themselves. The banks are only bigger now than they were in 2007. If the Dow average goes from 17,000 to 3,000 we're talking about 30 percent unemployment across the board—as opposed to just African American men.

Why do so many good-hearted, ethical people ignore the true impact of what their wealth is doing?
One reason is that given the choice, people would rather not deal with their money at all. To say that people are money-averse is a gross understatement. So A) people don't want to deal with it, because there are lots of more fun things they could do with their time and B) the system is set up to reinforce that inertia. The approach of the banking and financial services industries is to create inertia and intimidation.

The inertia is that these industries actually make it relatively hard for you to switch out of something once you've put your money in it. On the intimidation side, you get the army of guys in blue blazers who pat you on the head and say, "Honey, we'll take care of this for you. Just chill out." And while you're there they give you a whole bunch of glossy reports that have seven thousand words on them that you've never seen before, and your takeaway will be: "God, I thought I didn't want to deal with my money before, now I want to deal with it even less!" And you'll want to say, "Yeah, Joe, yeah, why don't you just take it from here. Let me know how it goes next quarter and I'll just wait for my statements."

Do you have suggestions for solutions?
We should do more from the grassroots perspective, because that's what's going to lead to real, lasting change. It's really around changing hearts and minds. One item, for each of us as individuals, is to think through where your banking relationship is. Whether you're a high net worth person or a small investor, think about who you bank with. If you have a chequing account at Bank of America, you have no idea if that money is being used to make loans in your community to organizations that you would feel really good about—or if it's being farmed out to hedge funds to clear-cut rainforests in Malaysia. As Vince Siciliano at New Resource Bank says, "Where does your money spend the night?"

That's solution number one. Number two would be to do the same in terms of your investments. Even if you don't want to make it your day job like it is for me, I feel people are obligated to think it through. If you're a sustainable agriculture supporter or activist, you cannot own Monsanto stock in your retirement portfolio. That is just not okay. It's too much cognitive dissonance to not pay attention to the stocks you own and the system you're participating in.

If people feel their banks and portfolio managers are working against their values, what do they do?
There are viable alternatives. For problem number one, you can bring your money to a community bank instead of Wells Fargo. You just have to get over the inertia and do it. Sure, the online bill pay system may not be as snazzy as your big bank. Deal with it. At least you're voting with your dollars and standing up for something. And on number two, there are way more options than there were even ten years ago to construct a portfolio, even as a small investor, that ensures your investments are at least closer to not directly conflicting with your values.

The very first thing to start with is clarifying what you're absolutely the most passionate about in life. What is the world you'd like to see? Start investing in those things. Then—as Leslie Christian says, a financial adviser who I think is the most innovative in the United States right now—you can actually have a shot at developing what she calls a "beautiful portfolio."

Instead of getting your statement at the end of each quarter, and hoping it went up by 0.7 percent and then throwing it away—and ignoring the damage your money may be doing—you could actually get your statement and it would reflect a beautiful portfolio. It would show you all things that you are so happy to own, and how they're doing, and you'll be part of that. You'll want to read the stories. You'll want to connect with the people behind it. Those are the benefits of what she calls a beautiful portfolio.

Quest for Purpose

JIMMY CARTER won the election. Young campaign staff spruced up their resumes and watched for signals from those who would win senior positions in the government. The spoils of victory were playing out. Future careers were unfolding.

My father had been a major fundraiser for Carter. He was eventually appointed to a sub-Cabinet position as head of the General Services Administration (GSA), a multi-billion-dollar agency with 45,000 employees. He regularly sat in cabinet meetings with the president.

The campaign had been one of the great experiential learning opportunities of my young life. I attended the glamorous inauguration parties in Washington. They were fun, but the intrigue was thick. I was unsettled. The ruthless competition for assistantships to cabinet leaders or White House desk assignments disturbed me. The passion and intensity of the campaign had shifted into the power dynamics of governing. There was an open pathway into the power structures of my country, but I wasn't ready. I was 22 and had my life to figure out. I stood apart at the parties and thought to myself, "I'm going to do something else."

Meanwhile, family business elders were circling. They had big plans for me. The shopping mall business was now part of a Manhattan-based national conglomerate. There was a gauntlet I was expected to run. A command performance ushered me to a penthouse boardroom on Central Park South, where elder male chieftains firmly let me know it was time to get serious and begin training for future business leadership, and perhaps ultimate control of the empire—if I were good enough.

But my restlessness to break out had only increased. In university and in the campaign, I had lived a mostly mental and intellectual life. I was hungry for physical experience. Family genetics were also a factor in the back of my mind. The fear of PKD was still haunting me. What would I do if I found out I had inherited the gene? I ended the Manhattan meeting saying, "I'll think about it. I need to do a few things first. I'll let you know later."

I'd grown up through the '60s era of questioning everything. At 14 I'd been riveted by TV coverage of the "police riots" of the 1968 Democratic convention in Chicago, where I saw hundreds of thousands of protesters chanting "The whole world is watching!" I'd seen Jim Crow and civil rights laws change. I'd seen the assassinations of the Kennedys, Martin Luther King, and Malcolm X—along with the Kent State killings, the "summer of love," and the rise of Cesar Chavez and the Black Panthers. Singing along with Joni Mitchell's 1970 pop radio message—"They paved paradise, and put up a parking lot"—shot to the heart of a shopping-mall heir.

So much was churning inside me. Conventionality was looking more and more like a trap.

For those who have such opportunities presented to or thrust upon them—the "right" school, the high-paying job, the role of CEO or wealthy scion—discernment can be strangely difficult. There are big pressures to conform, in spite of the voice inside us that says (or yells), "I don't really want to do that!" Often our family and those closest to us can't give us the advice we need at those turning points. As our society, culture, and economy dramatically transform in the years to come, more and more young people will be called upon to trust their ideals and instincts over the propulsive inertia of the expected ways of doing things.

To all young people who feel there is a better way of living and working: trust yourself. The twenties are the seeking years. They're when we define and imprint values that will last our lifetime. Trust your instincts that there is a better, more fulfilling frontier waiting for you. Go for it, even if it means leaving behind the known and comfortable.

A great example is from Adam Braun, who founded the school-building and education organization Pencils of Promise in 2008 at age 25. When he was feeling stirrings of dissatisfaction with the career path laid before him—amid the "top shelf liquor and flowing champagne" of pre-2008 Wall Street—he had a conversation with his parents, which he recounts in his book *The Promise of a Pencil*.

> When I sat with my parents, I told them, "I want to work on things that I'm more passionate about."
>
> "You can't. First you need real-world experience," they said. I was on a safe path to financial security, and they didn't want me off it.
>
> "But I don't feel like myself," I complained.
>
> "That's what it means to do a job!" yelled my dad. "Grow up, and stop being such a baby." [26]

In the end, Braun trusted his own vision. He left a lucrative "dream job" at global consulting firm Bain & Company for full-time social entrepreneurship. He started something that fed his true dreams. As of 2018, Pencils of Promise has now built 462 schools in countries like Ghana, Laos, and Guatemala and served 86,000 students.

The Dreaded Diagnosis

I headed West. Rather than White House meetings and writing reports, my first post-election job was as a ranch hand and cattle wrangler outside Jackson Hole. Next I was the delivery boy for Bru's Bagels in Jackson Hole, Wyoming. Then I shovelled snow at Grand Targhee ski resort near Driggs, Idaho, and learned the finer arts of ski bum culture. It was a magical time. My pals and I would climb mountains at night on cross-country skis, then glide down deep snow fields bathed in moonlight.

During the glorious freedom of that Idaho winter, I saw an ad for a "French intensive biodynamic gardening" course at the Farallones Institute (now the Occidental Arts and Ecology Center) in Sonoma

County, California. The chance to go to mystical California and put my hands in the soil, to learn more about growing food, lured me to the "Left Coast."

West Sonoma County, north of the Bay Area in the rolling golden hills of California, relaxed my whole being. The hard physical labor of gardening was deliciously tangible and satisfying. I felt blessed with new awakenings. The Farallones gardening ethos emphasized diversity, complexity, interplanting, beauty, hard work, and respect for the soil—as well as galactic forces like the cycles of the Moon. This all imprinted a pattern for making sense of the world. My life's journey was changing. My perspective moved from the prevalent patriarchal model—mechanistic accumulation for the smartest and most dominant—toward balance with more feminine principles. Shared abundance, love, relationship, and generosity.

One afternoon my father called the single campus payphone while I was working in the garden. He said he needed me to rejoin him in Washington, D.C. He was uncovering massive spending scandals at the GSA and, because of my relationships with campaign workers who were now in the White House, wanted my help in connecting with people and navigating the politics. Senate investigative hearings were calling him to testify at length. Despite the new life unfolding for me, I still had a taste for political drama. I agreed. My father had coaxed me back, as savvy parents can do. I suspect there was craftiness in my father's asking me to join him. I'm sure I was helpful, but he was also hunting a way to reel me back to his ambitions for me.

It was alluring and confusing to return to Washington, D.C. I managed to keep balance by working a half-time job on an organic vegetable farm in West Virginia. The role included selling vegetables once a week at a farm stand two blocks from the GSA. Half the week I put on a suit and worked at my father's side. The other half I was weeding, harvesting, and selling vegetables.

Then I received the dreaded PKD diagnosis. Odd physical symptoms had led me to seek medical tests. I had hoped the results would be routine. They weren't.

While PKD was generally a longer, slower deterioration than, say, a diagnosis of brain cancer, for me it was earth-shattering news. There were three possible outcomes: dialysis, transplant, or death. Transplants were relatively new, and post-transplant drugs were in their early stage. Dialysis meant running one's blood through a filtering machine for hours every few days. Most people with PKD died on dialysis while waiting for a kidney donation and transplant.

Western medicine is a miraculous tool, and a kidney transplant was a best-outcome solution. But in the early '80s transplant methods were nascent.

It felt like a death sentence. Just about everyone, including me, assumed I would die young. This was tough to absorb in my mid-twenties. I was shaken by a mix of sadness, fear, anger, confusion, and anxiety.

Faced with mortality, certain life choices became clearer. No shopping malls, no lifetime career in politics for me. In fact, no known, structured conventionality would do. I became a motivated seeker. I explored spirituality and alternative health pursuits of many kinds: the *Tibetan Book of the Dead*, Jewish mysticism, Zen, macrobiotics, yoga, Ram Dass, Starhawk.

Death's visit had grabbed my attention. I needed to find the purpose of my life.

A stroke of luck was finding Andrew Weil, the Harvard-educated doctor and ethnobotanist, who was an emerging authority on complementary medicine. I'd stumbled upon his first book, *The Natural Mind*, while scanning a health food store bookshelf. Seeking an alternative worldview about health, I contacted Andrew's publisher with a request to meet and ask him about the kidney diagnosis. To my surprise he agreed. He invited me to visit him in Amagansett, on Long Island, where he was sequestered writing his next book.

The doctors at George Washington University Hospital had given me minimal advice about how I might slow the disease. PKD progresses unpredictably. "Keep your blood pressure low, and don't eat too much protein," they said. "Have your blood and urine checked regularly to monitor your condition as it deteriorates."

That was about it. I questioned the doctors. What about diet? Lifestyle? Stress? Alternative medicine? All unproven, they said. They cautioned me about esoteric alternatives—predictable skepticism from Western doctors, but also valuable. Sadly there is indeed plenty of quackery out there. People who fear for their lives are ripe for exploitation.

That's only half the story, though. There is a vast world of healing wisdom beyond what conventional modern medicine offers.

Andrew's advice was more nuanced than the opinions of the doctors, and immensely helpful. Use Western medicine for what it does well, he told me. Learn more about your body, mind, spirit, emotions, and life purpose. Sample credible alternative methods that work for you. Understand stress and how to ground yourself. The psychological, emotional, spiritual, and relational aspects of life are integral to enduring health.

Put clean, non-toxic food in your body, he counseled. Clean food equals cleaner blood, vital for anyone with compromised kidney function. There are many other ways to damage yourself. Understand them, he advised, and make conscious choices. Moderation is valuable—including moderation itself. Cut loose sometimes too. Living life well is the cure. Extend your life as much as possible through mindful living and let go of anxiety about death. You will die. Live a meaningful life while you can. Be happy. Be fulfilled.

What is a happier life? What would that mean? It's a deep question to ask oneself over the years. Considering and embracing mortality is an ancient wisdom, one our culture tends to hide from. Think about your death bed. Who will care when you're gone? What was your contribution? Will you feel good about how you've lived?

I often reflect on these questions. They turn my attention to what is real and has meaning beyond pure ego satisfaction. It's possible to trick the ego into aiming for a healthy, meaningful goal. Ambition can become a force for collective good. Instead of aiming to be a billionaire of dollars, how about a billionaire of good deeds?

As unfair as life is for so many, we know countless stories of those in the most challenging circumstances finding beauty, grace, compassion, and peace. You would think having more affluence, safety, and ease in life would guarantee happiness. Ironically, some of the wealthiest people on Earth are lost, confused, unhappy, and self-destructive. Money can help a lot. A lot of money can cripple.

Like a visit to a sage on the mountaintop, I soaked up Andrew's guidance. It set me on a new life course. It was permission, a blessing, to follow my instincts while seeing life as an adventure. I concluded that meaning, purpose, and loving my life were the magic I needed. Work on the type of person I want to be, and live authentically. Be my best self.

The diagnosis turned out to be the best thing that had ever happened to me. It was the awakening moment I needed. In Andrew's advice, merged with holistic gardening principles of interdependence and diversity, I saw a unifying theme that would weave my life together. Clean blood required clean food. Clear mind, honest and healthy relationships, emotional integrity, and "clean living" were cures as well as life tenets. Career, money, and health, must be connected.

Better health through cleaner living gave me hope. If clean food was better for my blood, might clean money also be profoundly important, even to one's physical health? What is clean money? How does capitalism work? Who wins? Who loses? Is there a connection to our health? Might the health of life on the planet depend on clean money?

I had a lot to contemplate now. I sensed the answers were waiting to be discovered.

Pollution, Poverty, and Responsibility

My hometown of Chattanooga was a heavy-industry city. Its air and water quality were notoriously poor, even dangerous. Chattanooga Creek, a tributary of the Tennessee River that snaked through the downtown industrial zone, was a dumping ground for chemical plants and metallurgical coke foundries. It was so polluted that the

EPA proposed it as a Superfund site in 1994. Under-regulated emissions from the city's factories, coal fires, and railroads were trapped by the surrounding mountains and atmospheric inversions. Air quality was so bad that in the '60s it was said that on some days you needed your headlights on at noon when driving through the city. In 1969 the federal government declared Chattanooga "the dirtiest city in America."[27]

Thirty-five years ago there was already evidence linking growing cancer rates in North America with lifestyle and ecological factors. Minimal and weak environmental legislation surely played a part. As I continued researching alternative health approaches, I pondered the connection. My kidney had to process everything that went into my blood. Wouldn't cleaner food, water, and air, make a difference to me and so many others? Could allowing bigger loads of toxins in our bodies be anything other than foolhardy? Why was no one saying anything?

My exploration of clean food, air, and water began as a personal issue of survival. But as I saw big companies lobby against regulation—then try to hide the toxic damage so they could continue making more money—I found a larger quest. Helping to promote clean organic food, healthy environments, and a just society would become my life's work.

There's a strong social justice aspect to money that gets real very quickly. Wealth buys shortcuts to cleaner air, water, and food, along with better services. Where there is poverty, on the other hand, there is usually pollution. Poor communities routinely suffer from limited access to quality food and green space. Underfunded health care, education, and community services are common. Many environmental justice leaders have presented at Hollyhock. Van Jones, Reverend Lennox Yearwood, Adrienne Marie Brown, Caleb Behn, Eriel Deranger, Katrina Pacey, Aqeela Sherrills, Andrea Reimer, and Nikki Henderson all speak eloquently about how toxic waste, public policy, and unhealthy foods disproportionately affect the poor, particularly people of color.

As Van Jones and Keith Ellison wrote in a 2015 *Guardian* article called "Pollution Isn't Color-Blind":

African-Americans are more likely to live near environmental hazards like power plants and be exposed to hazardous air pollution, including higher levels of nitrogen oxides, ozone, particulate matter, and carbon dioxide than their white counterparts. The presence of these pollutants increases rates of asthma, respiratory illness, and cardiovascular disease. It puts newborn babies at risk. It causes missed days of work and school. We can't afford this. Black kids already have the highest rate of asthma in the nation, and our infant mortality rate is nearly double the national rate.[28]

The affluent may thrive financially by investing in the "cheap food" industry while ignoring its reliance on monoculture, fossil-fuel intensity, and low-wage labor. For budget-constrained consumers, the outcome can be nutritionally denuded food options. Obesity, diabetes, cancer, heart disease, malnutrition, and addiction to alcohol and other drugs are only a few of the spiralling "lifestyle illnesses" afflicting North Americans, most of all the poor. These assist in bankrupting public health care and drive more people into deeper poverty, homelessness, or prison. Avoidable lifestyle diseases cost society unfathomable billions. And they silently create mass suffering.

We know these issues. Are we thinking about how our own money choices contribute to them? More of us are keeping our litter off the streets. We recycle our soda cans. We make our homes, offices, and cars more energy efficient. We waste less food, make energy from the sun and wind, and turn yoga and meditation into big industries. But do we know where our money is right this moment?

What is it doing to workers, neighbors, citizens everywhere? What is it doing to other people's children? What is the legacy we are creating with our money?

We, not our wealth managers, bear moral responsibility for our investments and profits. We employ them. We sign over authority

Deborah Frieze and Meg Wheatley are the coauthors of the 2011 book *Walk Out Walk On* from which this excerpt is taken. Deborah is cofounder of Boston Impact Initiative and Old Oak Dojo. Margaret Wheatley is an author, speaker, and cofounder of the Berkana Institute.

All systems go through lifecycles. There's progress, setbacks, seasons. When a new effort begins, it feels like spring. People are excited by new possibilities, innovations and ideas abound, problems get solved, people feel inspired and motivated to contribute. It all works very well, for a time.

And then, especially if there's growth and success, things can start to go downhill. Leaders lose trust in people's ability to self-organize and feel the need to take control, to standardize everything, to issue policies, regulations, and laws. Self-organization gets replaced by over-organization; compliance becomes more important than creativity. Means and ends get reversed and people struggle to uphold the system rather than having the system support them. These large, lumbering bureaucracies—think about education, healthcare, government, business—no longer have the capacity to create solutions to the very problems they were created to solve.

When a system reaches this stage of impotence, when it becomes the problem rather than the solution, we as individuals and communities have a choice. Either we struggle to fix and repair the current system, or we create new alternatives. New alternatives can be created either inside or outside the failing system. But if we choose to walk out and walk on, there are two competing roles we're called upon to play: We have to be thoughtful and compassionate in attending to what's dying—we have to be good hospice workers. And we have to be experimenters, pioneers, edge-walkers. Playing these dual roles is never easy, of course, but even so, there are enough people brave enough to do so.

Skilled hospice workers offer comfort and support to those at the end of their lives far beyond attending to physical needs. They help the dying focus on the transition ahead, and encourage them to see what their life has taught them—what wisdom and values shine clearly now that the distractions are gone.

Walk Outs need to do this kind of hospice work on ourselves. Even as we stop struggling to fix things, even as we reject the status quo, we don't leap empty-handed into the future. We need to consciously carry with us the values and practices that feel essential. What have we learned, what do we treasure as the means to create good work, fulfilling lives, meaningful relationships? From our many experiences—the battles, victories, disappointments, successes—we need to glean our hard-won wisdom and preserve it at all costs. This is what we'll most need as we walk out and walk on to give birth to the future.

Inside dying systems, Walk Outs who "walk on" are those few leaders who refuse to work from the dominant values that permeate the bureaucracy, such things as speed, greed, fear and aggression. They use their formal leadership to champion values and practices that respect people, that rely on people's inherent motivation, creativity and caring to get quality work done. These leaders consciously create oases or protected areas within the bureaucracy where people can still contribute, protected from the disabling demands of the old system. These leaders are treasures. They're dedicated, thoughtful revolutionaries who work hard to give birth to the new in very difficult circumstances.

for investment strategies. We drive them for a "higher return rate." Do we know how that higher return happens, and what its consequences are?

The ubiquity of values-blind finance gives us no absolution. Alternatives exist and choices can be made. As the clean money imperative grows through awakened understanding and growing demand, new financial products are emerging. There are many wealth managers testing new strategies. Tomorrow's products will follow the growth of market demand. Our priorities will create that demand.

Do business and investments the same way you do food and personal health. You are what you eat, and you are what you invest in. The side effects of how we make money live in us. They *are* us. We drink the water, breathe the air, and eat from the food chain that our choices are creating. Like chemical toxins, toxic investments create internal burdens, a kind of soul pollution, similar to the repeated pollution of the Earth's living soil. Even the healthiest kidneys can't clean that poison.

How we use money is an expression of who we are and all that we believe. We may choose to be unconscious, as in the past we have ignored the truth about cigarettes, coal, slavery, cultural genocide, and so many other issues.

But ignoring things is less and less of an option for those of us in the world of business and finance.* The move to a more just, post-carbon economy is gaining momentum through increased transparency and communication speed. Bad practices are exposed sooner and more widely. Irresponsible operations in remote locations are more visible. Information spreads globally in seconds. Institutions are pressured for better behavior, and there is a growing clamor for stringent punishments for financial criminals.

---

* There are already many inspiring examples of people and organizations that are moving from inquiry to action. In 2018, the organization Divest Invest estimated that 845 institutions and approximately 58,000 individuals across 75 countries—representing $6 trillion in assets—had committed to divesting from fossil fuel holdings. As Justin Rockefeller succinctly put it: "Given that we fight climate change, to us, investing in fossil fuels is somewhat akin to a cancer-fighting foundation investing in tobacco. It just doesn't reconcile." [29]

Start with your own moral sniff test. Then divest steadily from anything you know it is wrong to make money on. Personal and societal transformation is a process. We start that process by becoming clear about what matters. Then we can locate people, organizations, institutions, and political leaders we want to support. Our actions help move bigger forces.

The first step in financial detox is inquiry. Where is my money? What effect does it have? Who and what is harmed? Would I want everyone to see how I make my money? Can I change that?

Once you are aware of what your money is doing in the world, the next steps will appear. Put your money where your heart is. Give yourself permission to invest in what you care about. Acknowledge and honor who you are in the world, what matters to you, what you believe is nourishing.

Money is intimately connected to our personal and collective health. The clean money revolution is you, me, our friends, and our neighbors, all honoring our highest purposes. We know so many of our human and ecological systems are sick and suffering. Considered wisely and reoriented, money can be their most powerful cure.

 ## Janie Hoffman

is the founder and CEO of Mamma Chia, a food and drink company based in San Diego that makes all its products with organic chia, a plant in the mint family native to Mexico and Guatemala. Named a *Beverage World* "Disruptor of the Year" for 2016, her mission is to sustain Mamma Chia as a "conscious and sustainable company that honors and uplifts both the soul of humanity and the soul of the planet." The company is a certified B Corporation, a member of 1% for the Planet, and a founding member of Slow Money. Janie is also the author of two books, *Chia Vitality* and *The Chia Cookbook*.

Why do you do what you do?

Chia seeds changed my life! I struggled with multiple autoimmune issues for almost 20 years. I dealt with the challenges that lupus, scleroderma, dermatomyositis, and others presented and continually searched for ways to heal. My husband noticed that my rash flare-ups were less active when we ate fresh organic food from the farmers' market. But it was when I was turned onto chia—this powerhouse of nutrition that has eight times the omega-3s of salmon, six times the calcium of milk, and tons of antioxidants and protein—that I became symptom-free. I mean not just going into remission, but no longer testing positive for any of the issues I had.

Having experienced the magic of chia firsthand, I wanted to share it with the world. It is truly a superfood with so much to offer. We still eat it every day! We start with scrambled egg whites and chia seeds, and boost our meals and snacks throughout the day with chia.

What particular challenges and advantages do women have in business?

I have personally experienced the challenge of being underestimated—not only because I am a female entrepreneur but also because I was new to the food and beverage world. But I quickly learned to turn it to my advantage. I asked a lot of questions early on and found many generous souls willing to share their wisdom and experiences. We created the first-to-market chia beverages, a whole new category. So being underestimated became a gift. I often flew under the radar of the so-called competition and was able to make strategic moves more effectively.

Can for-profit business be a real driver of change for the massive ecological and social challenges we face?
Absolutely! It is time for all hands on deck. The old paradigm of accumulating wealth and *then* giving back is outmoded. It is essential that individuals and businesses focus on doing good all along the way. From the beginning we were a certified B Corporation and a member of 1% for the Planet, meaning that 1 percent of our gross sales right off the top are donated. That's not net profits but gross sales, so it's a real commitment. We're helping to shift the old paradigm of accumulating wealth, waiting until you have millions or even a billion dollars and then giving back—to one of giving every step of the way.

In terms of changing economy, ecology, and culture through business we are certainly very proud that there is more organic chia in the world because of Mamma Chia. There was virtually no organic chia being commercially grown when we started. That goes back to our mission: uplifting the soul of humanity and the soul of the planet. We believe that organic farming is one of the ways to do that. All our foods and beverages are USDA certified organic, meaning they are produced without the use of toxic pesticides and fertilizers, antibiotics, synthetic hormones, genetic engineering, sewage sludge (yes! that's a conventional farming input), or irradiation.

By supporting businesses that use organic farming methods, we all help reduce the amount of chemicals that get into the environment, disrupting the ecosystem and damaging human lives. Chemical inputs from farming don't just end up in our food supply. They also end up in lakes and streams, forests and grasslands—essentially, everywhere—and they wreak all kinds of havoc, adding carbon dioxide to the air and killing and causing odd physiological changes in fish and animals, to say nothing of the effects on farmworkers and people who live near farms. Supporting organic is a very powerful driver for positive change on many fronts.

How should people with more than enough money invest?

I would love to see more folks invest time and resources in their local communities. First one needs to figure out where their interests and passions lie. For me it's local food systems, which can include being a member of a CSA, which is community-supported agriculture, and supporting farmers' markets. Or it could also be fueling entrepreneurs in your community with low-interest loans to help them build out the local food system.

Of course, that passion could be something different for someone else. If you believe education is key to shifting folks out of poverty, then give back to the schools in your community. Know what you relate to, what connects with your soul.

What advice do you have for entrepreneurs who have a vision for a business that can change the world?

Go for it! Don't wait for your plan to be perfect before you start, and don't think you need to know everything. Trust that as you do the work in front of you that the appropriate resources will come at the right time. Continue to hold onto your vision even in the face of adversity, while also allowing room for things to unfold that expand your vision.

No one knows the heart and soul of your company better than you do. So you become a steward for your company, where it's your responsibility to be able to birth and protect your company's soul mission. I believe that every company has a soul purpose and that we're the guardians of that as the entrepreneur. When we truly align with divine order, there are no limits to our ability to serve.

Discoveries on the Edge

FROM MY AMAGANSETT meeting with Andrew I journeyed far, to the islands off the British Columbia coast.

I was lured there by a fellow gardening student from the Farallones Institute, Nori Fletcher. Nori had written to me from an intentional community called Linnaea Farm, on Cortes Island* in BC. Nori painted pictures of a magical paradise. The weather was suited to year-round gardening or foraging, and summer ocean swimming. The soil was mineral-rich and fertile. Sockeye salmon, wild mushrooms, oysters, and berries were abundant.

The back-to-the-land, simple-living dream! It sounded attractive and soothing.

The corruption my father had unearthed at the GSA led to dozens of indictments that pointed up the chain toward a senior leader of Congress. Dad resigned from the GSA under pressure from the White House to quiet the scandal. My Washington, D.C. work was over. Now my PKD diagnosis compelled me to step back and search for my life purpose.

I took Nori up on her invitation. In the winter of 1979–80 I pared down my belongings and hitchhiked to the West Coast, visiting friends along the way. In March of 1980 I took a ferry from Seattle to Victoria, and two more ferry crossings brought me from

---

* The island has a rich history of attraction for utopian idealists (more on that in Chapter 9). Ironically it was named by an 18th-century Spanish explorer for the ruthless conquistador Hernando Cortes—a key figure in bringing disease, devastation, and untold violence to Mexico in the 1500s.

Campbell River to Cortes. I had crossed into Canada for the first time. Little did I realize how momentous that would turn out to be.

I had come out of curiosity and whim, and because I was drawn to the kind of agrarian self-sufficiency that is lost for most Westerners. I wanted to rely as little as possible on the industrial, petrochemical-dependent food complex. If there was a way to opt out of the traditional commerce system, consume lightly and waste little, I wanted it. Are "back-to-the-land" ideals only armchair utopianism? For some, maybe. I think they're a natural impulse to be rooted in the land, self-sufficiency, and connection to authentic life cycles.

With my pals at Linnaea I gardened six days a week. It was hard labor, as anyone who has spent time weeding, digging a bed, and planting a large garden knows. It was also our fun and our passion. We lived on near-zero cash earned from occasional odd jobs. Foraging, harvesting, drying, canning, bartering, and fixing broken tools felt like freedom.

Our crew was called the "gypsy gardeners" because on Sundays, we used our tools and strong backs to give makeovers to the gardens of elderly or incapacitated island residents. They showed their gratitude with smoked salmon or jars of local wild berry jams. We also received the gifts of stories, history, and tips about Cortes, which then had a population of five hundred people. Breaking into the community took steady patience.

Linnaea was an early model of money transformed by intentional "cleaning." The founders and funders were Robert and Penny Cabot. Robert's family descended from early American settlers, and was known for wealth and philanthropy. The Cabots later introduced me to the Threshold Foundation—a group of high-net-worth individuals, mainly inheritors, whose members and organizational offshoots would be immensely influential in the clean money revolution.

I met Drummond Pike at Linnaea. Drummond is an early-adopter social entrepreneur who started the Tides Foundation in San Francisco in 1976. Tides was a financial services organization that helped to advance unique forms of change-making philanthropy. The Cabots were clients. Rather than raise donations and compete with other not-for-profits working on social change, Tides charged fees for services to meet its own budget. Drummond pioneered this idea of an intermediary financial institution whose service was to solve challenges in progressive philanthropy outside the usual norm of charitable giving. It was an early social enterprise long before the term was used. Drummond's example was formative for me when I partnered with Carol Newell later in the '90s.

The Cabots wanted the Linnaea land in permanent protection, kept as a working farm with resident farmers and a community of peers. This was very out of the box. It was legally complex to create land protection in such a context, and at the time Canada had no existing framework for land trusts. Linnaea helped kick-start the land trust movement in BC and Canada.

An OrcaLab "Masters Degree"

I was 25 with long hair and a bushy beard. I rarely wore shoes. It was a good time. My mother, who travels the world as an artistic photographer, came to visit in 1984. "I've never seen people living this way by choice," she said, shaking her head as she surveyed our scene. We looked like quintessential hippies, but I was learning natural systems, diversity, and practical skills. (I am still a gardener on Cortes, 35 years later.)

I would later see the relationships between gardening and investment. Single-crop monoculture is as bad in a portfolio as it is on a farm!

But eventually I became frustrated at Linnaea. Intentional communities get entangled in power struggles all too similar to those in Washington, D.C., and Linnaea in its early years was no exception. They say the two necessary poles for spiritual growth are community and solitude. After many months of interpersonal intensity, solo time had a strong allure. I wanted answers about life. I had found some in Linnaea's community, and now I was hungry to be alone.

When I heard from a visitor to Linnaea that a cetacean research facility to the north needed a caretaker, I jumped at the chance. It was OrcaLab, the only human habitation on Hanson Island. Hanson was about 45 minutes by boat from Alert Bay, home of the 'Namgis First Nation. I wrote a letter expressing interest to its founder, Paul Spong. He was a New Zealander who had a degree in neuroscience from UCLA and in 1967 had been hired by the University of British Columbia to study captive orca whales at the Vancouver Aquarium. After months developing relationships with the orcas, he became intimate with their personalities and intelligence.

"Eventually, my respect verged on awe," Spong wrote. "I concluded that *Orcinus orca* is an incredibly powerful and capable creature, exquisitely self-controlled and aware of the world around it, a being possessed of a zest for life and a healthy sense of humour and, moreover, a remarkable fondness for and interest in humans."[30]

Spong advocated publicly for the release of captive whales. Not surprisingly, his contract was not renewed by the aquarium. At that point in the early '80s, whales were still widely slaughtered for dog food, heating oil, cosmetics, and human consumption. Paul persuaded Greenpeace, recently birthed in Vancouver, to adopt a "Save the Whales" global campaign. It famously succeeded to a dramatic degree. Images of courageous activists placing their small rubber boats between the harpoon and the whales were seen around the world. One powerful clip showed a harpoon shooting over the head of a protester in a tiny Zodiac and into a sperm whale, whose blood gushed into the ocean. These powerful images helped accelerate the near-elimination of global whaling.

OrcaLab is on a narrow passage between open ocean and northern Vancouver Island. Its purpose is to study whales in the wild, recording their voices and songs by hydrophone. Paul called as soon as he received my note. "How about next week, matey? I'm leaving for three weeks." A few days later he was showing me around the facility: buildings for sleeping, living, and laboratory work nestled against the most dramatic old-growth fir—hemlock—cedar forest I'd ever imagined. We hauled drinking water from the tiny spring beneath a massive old-growth cedar that would take at least ten people stretching arms to encircle it. Below the caretaker loft was the laboratory of tape recorders, receivers, and other tracking devices. The equipment was generally second-hand and rigged together from the always-sparse budget.

My job: "Turn on the tape recorders when the orcas come, feed the dogs, and don't burn down the house."

After my first solo test drive, Paul invited me to stay. I said yes. His relentless commitment profoundly inspired me. I admired his work as researcher, gadfly, activist, and lobbyist. He became another unlikely hero to me, someone able to achieve world-changing objectives through passion and sheer cussedness. First was Jimmy Carter, a two-year, one-term governor of Georgia who took the most powerful office in the world thanks to a well-executed plan. Then there was Paul, an aquarium researcher appalled by the slaughter and captivity these institutions condoned, who became a world authority on cetaceans and helped catalyze a global whaling moratorium.

OrcaLab was a good fit for my life direction. Andrew's book *The Natural Mind* suggested that every culture on the planet had consciousness-altering methodologies, from vision-inducing plants to multi-day rituals. This broke open patterned thinking. I longed to similarly "walk through a looking glass" of conventional perception and explore the roots of my thinking and choice patterns. That seemed key to a good life pathway, guided by death's inevitability.

Paul's estimates of how long he'd be away inevitably doubled, stretching to seven or eight weeks at times. He and his wife Helena would attend global gatherings on whaling, lobbying nations to protect whales using their field research showing the intelligence, language, and advanced social systems of orcas. Early hydrophone technology was central to their research. That was where I came in. When orca vocalizations came through the sound system strung through the lab and main building, it was my job to record them.

Those eerie, otherworldly undersea sounds became the backdrop to my life. At any moment my daily routine might be accompanied by the serenades of whales. For a few years orca communications were more familiar to me than human voices. Hearing them echo through my living space gave me a felt experience of sentient beings more advanced than most humans in their displays of protective compassion, nurturance, generational culture, language, and play.

One day I was out in a kayak, watching orcas hunt salmon in the bottleneck of Blackfish Passage. (Blackfish is a translation of the 'Namgis word for orcas.) As their dorsal fins glided by both sides of my boat, I heard and felt the vocalizations through the kayak, amplified by its hull. My own hydrophone! I was treated to a full-body sonic massage of orca voices.

Hanson Island was a wonderland of such experiences. It was a perfect backdrop for a self-directed "advanced degree" in philosophy, history, anthropology, human potential, and emergent culture. I combed Paul and Helena's fascinating library, and during my three-year tenure added boxloads more books from occasional city visits. I read hundreds of them: Aldous Huxley and John C. Lilly on consciousness; Alexandra Morton and John Ford on whale biology; fiction by Margaret Atwood; essays by George Orwell and Germaine Greer; Hazel Henderson's *The Politics of the Solar Age*; and *The New City States* by David J. Morris.

Hazel Henderson's 2006 book, *Ethical Markets: Growing the Green Economy*, opens by questioning how we measure national progress: "Today, more and more groups—from environmentalists who value nature, to women who perform most of the world's unpaid work, as well as those concerned with social justice—are critiquing Gross National Product (GNP) and Gross Domestic Product (GDP) and a host of other indicators. They ask common sense questions that are difficult and embarrassing for economists. Why do they focus on money and factories as capital and so often ignore human and social forms of capital, as well as ecological assets like rainforests and biodiversity? Why does GNP treat education as a cost instead of a vital investment in our future while not accounting for its quality? Why does GDP go up when people are sick and have to pay for health care but doesn't include ways to measure wellness?"[31]

Euro-colonialist history became clearer to me, and framed my ideas of contribution. How might I be a peaceful warrior for a better future, rather than blindly following prescribed patterns? I also read many perspectives on the temporal and spiritual qualities of life from different traditions. Carlos Castaneda's advice to "keep death on your left shoulder" resonated with my post-diagnosis reality. *The Tibetan Book of the Dead* suggested death as a consciousness shift. The philosophy of land-based traditional cultures that emphasized the value of ancestral responsibility fed into my solo studies. Shouldn't decisions be made with a time horizon that looked seven generations into the future? It was a simple, radical idea that made so much sense.

I spent time with my girlfriend Louise, and long periods completely alone. The days were physically active, from towing in floating logs by kayak for firewood, to hauling giant kelp from the low-tide line for compost. I took long foraging walks through the dense forest and dug rich soil from it for our vegetable and flower beds. Silence and nature were great teachers. I found a life infused with good energy, meaning, purpose, and contribution. I decided it didn't truly matter how long I lived. Living meaningfully became my goal.

On Cortes I had been immersed in agrarian life. On Hanson Island I went further back in time, to a more primordial, hunter-gatherer type of existence. Most of my calories came from the ocean or the forest. I'd fish from the kayak with a hand-line for lingcod and snapper, and comb the beach for limpets, urchins, and seaweeds. With the help of Euell Gibbons' 1964 book on tidal foraging, *Stalking the Blue-Eyed Scallop*, I sampled nearly all the edible food off that beach, with the exception of starfish gonads. In the temperate rainforest were salal berries, huckleberries, and mushrooms—mostly chanterelles, boletes, and the treasured matsutake. Occasional feasts followed when I found giant "cauliflower" mushrooms, up to three feet in diameter and weighing several pounds—a full armload to trek home with. (They make a choice, pasta-like meal.) I got pretty good at baking bread, warm slabs of which accompanied wood-stove feasts of seared lingcod, steamed nettles, and sautéed mushrooms.

Nature is the sustenance of species, the provider, the rich soil of our being. It's a great mystery laced with the hidden mycelial roots of spirit and deep secrets of complexity, diversity, and interdependence. (This is why Dana and I call our holding company Interdependent Investments.) During years immersed in silence and nature—rubbing up against it, swimming in it, foraging from it, building with it—my affection and loyalty grew.

Life was punctuated by Paul and Helena's bustling returns with news of their exploits for the whales, and by sporadic deliveries of mail and dog food from their friend Michael in Alert Bay. In long stretches of solitude I lost touch with normal clock and calendar time. It was hard to remember the day of the week. My patterns moved to the cycles of the Sun, Moon, and tides. I read, explored, recorded the whales, and made occasional returns to Cortes for social fun. I got glimpses into the rich history of the 'Namgis—formerly one of the wealthiest potlatch-based nations on the coast—and the ongoing revival of their once-outlawed practices.

I saw other friends occasionally. Andrew Weil came to visit to experience the orcas. A variety of unique characters showed up, including early Greenpeace friends of Paul.

During extended periods alone, I did start to lose it a little bit. Paul returned to OrcaLab in his motorboat one gray day during my second year as caretaker. He spotted me hand-lining in the kayak, blankly jigging for a fish in the steady rain. As he pulled the boat up next to me, he took one look at my face—shaggy, salty, wild-eyed—and said, "I'm taking you into town. Come on."

We went back to his house in Alert Bay. There he turned on the television and the stereo, gave me a shot of whiskey and a beer and told me to call a friend. I called Bill Wheeler, one of my garden teachers from Farallones who had traveled to Cortes with me on my very first visit (and lives there today, more than 35 years later). Bill came out from Vermont to be co-caretaker with me in my last season, which helped save me from bush fever.

It was a wise suggestion on Paul's part. Too much going it alone, as many entrepreneurs know, is a good way to crack up.

Early Clean Money: Hollyhock and Stonyfield Yogurt

In those years I was immersed in critiques of modern Western culture. The books I read and conversations I had with disaffected colleagues on Cortes and Hanson convinced me that we needed to chart a new course. Even on the edge of the continent, it was impossible to escape the ripples created by business and politics, which continued to ravage the Earth's beauty and resilience. Damage to indigenous culture was obvious and ongoing. Escape wasn't solving things for me. I was suffering low-grade depression: often thick in my emotions, sullen, and harshly critical.

My father had done his best to keep me abreast of his business while I was growing up. Our family began building their fortune through movie theaters, but after a tornado in the late 1950s destroyed one of their drive-in movie screens, a high-rise office developer offered them big money for their one Atlanta theater. They then gambled on a new enterprise: shopping centers. They built the first one in Tennessee. This became their mainstay, and they traveled the South building strip malls. For a brief period my family was the largest mall developer in the country. They were part of the trend that drained many small city downtowns of commercial vitality. It took me many years to understand why my family went into shopping centers: it was a reaction to being excluded. As Jews, members of my family were not welcomed into downtown business culture. As malls later bled business out of many urban cores, the unintended, ironic effect was a kind of delayed revenge upon the downtowns that had rejected them.

Dad would take me on long car trips to the small towns of the Southeast. From the back seat of his Chevy Impala or Pontiac LeMans (the fanciest cars we ever had) I eavesdropped as he courted the reps of stores like JCPenney and Sears. I learned the secret was the big anchor stores. With them signed, it was easy to fill the rest of the space with tenants. Voila: a money-making model.

Though shopping mall development was dull stuff for a boy, I liked the time riding around with my dad. The influence his business life had on me was deeper than I knew. It planted a seed that was waiting to sprout as I lived out my hunter-gatherer-agrarian lifestyle on the BC coast.

In 1983, while I was still at OrcaLab, my sister Linda and I each got a $50,000 distribution payout from one of our fathers' investments. Years before, in a tax-planning move, he had put us in a sliver share of a property partnership. Now that we had received the money, we had to decide what to do with it. This is a pivotal moment for many kids of affluent families. The next step is usually the parent-accompanied visit to a wealth manager, and the indoctrination of old-school capitalism begins.

Ever since coming to social and ecological consciousness as a teenager in the late '60s, I'd felt uneasy about the mall-building that was making my family's fortune. The money originated from something contrary to my beliefs. I'd rejected the career that had made my family's fortune and was uneasy about to how to handle this windfall. What now? How could I translate this money from a source I rejected into something I could believe in and be proud of? This was the first step of my personal clean money journey.

My friends on Cortes had purchased the old Cold Mountain Institute property on the island and hung a shingle as Hollyhock Farm—now known as Hollyhock. The place had been an oasis for me, first as a gypsy gardener tending the soil during its defunct Cold Mountain days, and later as a kitchen volunteer in exchange for massage and tai chi workshops during my "be with people" holidays from OrcaLab. I admired the eccentric, accomplished collection of phenomenal people who had gathered together to buy Hollyhock. These included Shivon Robinsong and her then-husband, artist Lee Robinsong, who recruited author and Greenpeace cofounder Rex Weyler. Rex was another early and crucial mentor. Shivon would later save my life by giving me her kidney.

Hollyhock is today a renowned not-for-profit leadership learning center, but it started as a private business. Shivon, Rex, and the other founders had scoured their contacts across the continent to assemble a down payment. A year later I offered to invest half of the $50,000 I'd received from my father and became the first partner after the initial founding investors. This clinched what is now my

Rex Weyler is an ecologist and author of *Greenpeace: How a Group of Ecologists, Journalists, and Visionaries Changed the World* and *Blood of the Land: The Government and Corporate War Against First Nations.* He is a lifelong activist, author, photographer, and mentor for many. He writes for the "Deep Green" blog at Greenpeace International.

Humanity is in a state of ecological overshoot, which occurs with every successful species. Nature teaches species how to grow and flourish, but does not teach species how to stop—so everything overgrows its habitat capacity. Everything. Plants in a garden, wolves in a watershed, algae in a lake. Humans have been so successful (ecologically) that we have now overshot the productive capacity of our ecosystem. That is normal—and is the fundamental ecological challenge. Now, *all* genuine solutions to overshoot involve contraction—plants crowd each other out, wolves die off until the prey recovers, algae die off until nutrients are restored. That's pretty much a law or pattern of nature. No escape. Technology and efficiency don't buy us a pass.

Starvation, disease, and predators are some of nature's default "solutions" to ecological overshoot. We can add our own contribution of warfare. But as intelligent, ingenious creatures, we want to devise better ways to contract, and create a mature, stable culture as opposed to simply growing bigger. *That* is our challenge. But our economic system—capitalism—is fundamentally based on growth, and few governments (outside of Bhutan, perhaps) are willing to discuss the end of growth capitalism. Few environmentalists are willing to discuss it. So we're in a deep dilemma. We have to learn to talk about it in adult conversation, without freaking out, and then we have to actually act on this knowledge.

How to contract as a species and reduce consumption to suit our finite habitat on Earth—how to do this creatively, intelligently, minimizing suffering as we do so—is the work that lies ahead.

35-plus-year involvement with Hollyhock. I have learned so much there about values, mission, and purpose. (Hollyhock shifted to a not-for-profit in the early 2000s. Along with the rest of the partners, I donated my full ownership stake back to the organization.)

There was still the other $25,000 to steer to meaningful use. I contacted my wise friend Chuck Matthei, then director of the Institute for Community Economics (ICE) in Greenfield, Massachusetts. ICE helped to develop the modern community land trust in the United States, as well as community loan funds for economic development projects rooted in social justice. One of ICE's many innovations was low-interest loans from affluent donors to help low-income residents purchase trailer parks and other affordable housing. This enabled residents to build wealth and better control their own destinies as owners, through (hopefully) appreciating property values.

Chuck was a prominent draft resister during the Vietnam War, and he was articulate, principled, and "intransigent" (as Denise Levertov's poem about him put it). Chuck passed away in 2002. He always carried a Levertov poem in his pocket. On the back of the poem he had written his own words, summing up his personal philosophy, which read in part:

> This is your only life—live it well! No one man can bring about a social change—but each man's life is a whole and necessary part of his society, a necessary step in any change, and a powerful example of the possibility of life for others.

Chuck was a human clearinghouse of meaningful enterprises. I asked him for a place to lend my $25,000 "to clean up this dirty money." He introduced me to a New Hampshire not-for-profit focused on proving the viability and necessity of small family farms as alternatives to the industrial food system. With seven cows they were making exquisite, old-world style organic yogurt and selling it to a few local stores under the name Stonyfield.

Demand was intense. It flew off the shelves. It might be hard to remember, but in the early '80s, few North Americans had even *tasted* natural yogurt. Even fewer had encountered organic. Rich with probiotics, it was a living food well known to those from rural agrarian life, where it extended the life of fresh milk. Commercial yogurt at the time was industrially manufactured, loaded with sugar, chemicals, stabilizers, modifiers, and that familiar list of mystery substances that remain primary ingredients on supermarket shelves.

With my soil-freak background, I was in. I sent my check. Soon a phone call came from Gary Hirshberg, one of the two founders. Gary had been the executive director of the New Alchemy Institute on Cape Cod, a sister organization to Farallones. New Alchemy built and tested human-scale alternative technologies for renewable energy, fish and plant farming, integrated waste systems, and many other ideas that are now becoming tomorrow's industries. On the phone Gary told me that he and business partner Samuel Kaymen saw that yogurt sales were growing too fast for a not-for-profit to finance and were thinking of becoming a for-profit business. Would I convert my $25,000 from a not-for-profit loan into an equity investment in Stonyfield?

I agreed. Later I added additional modest funds to the investment as Stonyfield grew for ten years while losing ever more money. My goal as a smaller investor was to provide value and try to be helpful. That became a lifelong preference and passion: to invest as a minority owner in a variety of enterprises, rather than be in control.

In one of those surprising life coincidences, it turned out that I already knew Gary's wife, Meg Cadoux Hirshberg. I'd recruited her to the Carter campaign while we were classmates at Vassar. At UC Santa Cruz she had also studied the Alan Chadwick "French intensive biodynamic" gardening philosophy I'd learned at Farallones. (I recommend her 2011 book *For Better Or for Work: A Survival Guide for Entrepreneurs and Their Families*; inside are powerful insights into raising a family while married to a fanatical entrepreneur!)

I periodically visited the Hirshberg family, riding with Gary on long car trips around New England to stores, suppliers, and buyers.

I kept him awake at the wheel by asking endless questions, and often helped him talk through the latest crisis. There were lots of crises!

Stonyfield served as a type of business school for me. This private equity investing approach gives access to many inside stories and invaluable learning. It is immensely rewarding. Gary has been an important mentor with his seasoned advice about startups, financing, and growing successful "clean" businesses. (The full Stonyfield natural yogurt success story, including how Orthodox Jews in Brooklyn taught them to make it, is detailed in Gary's great 2008 book, *Stirring it Up.*) When Groupe Danone, one of the seven largest food companies in the world, bought Stonyfield in 2001, the deal was estimated at $180 million.

Stonyfield was a lucky first investment for me. I put in further dollars over time, and decades later the sale enabled Dana and me to build a beautiful home on Cortes Island, which we use regularly for hosting Hollyhock conference social evenings. Hosting is a wonderful way to share resources and support unexpected, valuable connections.

My experience with Stonyfield contains many takeaways for clean money investors. One is about selling businesses to larger corporations. Gary watched other natural food icons sell to big food companies and lose too much of their mission. He knew colleague entrepreneurs unhappy with their buyers. He shopped carefully and extensively, and determined that of the multinational food companies in a position to buy Stonyfield, Europe-based Groupe Danone had values that were best aligned with his.

There is plenty of controversy over the ethical purity of selling mission-based companies to larger conglomerates, and whether it is "selling out." Passions run strong. There is no black-and-white answer. The world is complex. The enlightened vanguard is always well ahead of the mainstream, and many steps are needed to achieve long-term resilience. We each must determine where we fit best on the spectrum. Then we can make room for divergent viewpoints. We should do our best to build on the learning and changes created by those who came before us, and to keep advancing toward the ideal.

Progressives turning on and denigrating their allies for choosing less "perfect" strategies is a repeat motif in history. We should remember the bigger forces that benefit when do-gooders battle with each other over ideological purity. Rigidly held principles risk elitism. Major change takes many steps. When is a compromise a sell-out? How do we build strategic partnerships that advance "very good" even if they fail to reach "perfect"? In the clean money revolution we should work to be allies in always getting better and cleaner, rather than moral militants ready to take each other down for perceived imperfections. Regressive forces love watching idealists turn upon their natural allies.

Big dividends from investing in "clean" business are lucky but not impossible. We are in the middle of massive market shift toward regenerative business, and such big dividends are more and more common. There is vast wealth in the world that needs better uses, and those uses can be very profitable. Stonyfield was an early example. If you're looking for a meaningful career, consider the world of social ventures, or mission venture capital (the term I prefer).

I'm a mission venture capitalist by profession. People entrust our Renewal Funds team with their money alongside us, as we have our own resources invested in the promising clean economy companies we pick. As intermediary professionals, we handle the research, relationships, and hands-on oversight work, then aim to bring the investor a good return rate. For those new to investing in private companies, intermediaries are the safer, easier way to move wealth into cleaner uses.

You can do it yourself. Just know that it is a serious profession that must be learned like any other. If you want to learn, first experiment with smaller dollar amounts. Take your time and never bet bigger than you can accept losing. If you find you like it, make it your career. Transforming capitalism into a regenerative force needs many hands.

Stonyfield's story demonstrates the power that private equity investments have to leverage massive change to a sector. Gary vowed to shift the world of industrial food after seeing the Land Pavilion at Disney's Epcot Center in Orlando in 1982. It was sponsored by Kraft Foods, and as Gary describes in his book, displayed "rivers of chemical fertilizers, herbicides and pesticides swooshing around the naked roots of anemic-looking plants grown hydroponically in plastic tubes. In this paean to fertility, there was not a single grain of actual soil. Natural farming is all about creating great dirt, rich with nutrients. This was a cartoon scene of chemistry gone mad."

Twenty-five thousand people paid to see the Kraft pavilion every day, more than visited the New Alchemy Institute in a year. Needless to say, this disturbed Gary's organic soul. But the experience led to a "eureka flash" in which he realized he needed to "become Kraft." He wanted to have their resources and reach. Gary succeeded beyond what anyone could have predicted. Stonyfield is a renowned story of the pioneer period of organic food. Organic dairy products are now a $5.5 billion industry in the United States alone, with yogurt sales making up a fifth of that at $1.1 billion. That may still sound small. But thanks to the blood, sweat, and tears of many entrepreneurs like Gary, organic foods have gone from near zero market share to become the fastest-growing part of the entire food industry.

A 2008 article in *Fortune* magazine told the story of Gary's sister bringing him a package of Kraft Singles Organic American Slices—the sort of not-really-cheese slices that turn up on fast-food hamburgers. This gave Gary a different kind of eureka moment. "I was trying to become Kraft," he said. "Now Kraft is becoming us. You couldn't write it as a movie script."[32]

Gary uses his resources and stature now as a strong advocate for transforming the largest food companies in the world into manufacturers of cleaner, healthier, more honest products. He invests widely in promising young entrepreneurs, helping speed growth of the clean economy. Money is a high-value nutrient. As Joseph Mailman—businessman, philanthropist, and father of clean money pioneer Josh Mailman—is often quoted: "Money is a lot like manure. If you pile it up, it stinks. If you spread it around, it can do a lot of good."

The groundswell of conscious consumption, and the hard work of innovative entrepreneurs, is forcing adaptation on big multinationals. Take Campbell's Soup for example. The company owns many well-known brands: Pepperidge Farm cookies and cakes, Pace salsa, Goldfish cheese crackers, V8 Juice, and many more. A recent analysis by *Fortune* noted that Campbell's "has found itself grappling with big changes in consumer behavior, in particular growing interest in fresh food and consumers much more keen to know what impact what they're eating is having on their health and where it's from." Campbell's profit margins have been hit, as have those of other major food corporations: Kraft Foods lost market share in 40 percent of its brands in 2014. As Campbell Soup CEO Denise Morrison put it in 2015, there is "mounting distrust of so-called Big Food, the large food companies and legacy brands on which millions of consumers have relied for so long."[33]

In 2016 Campbells launched a new $125-million fund, Acre Venture Partners, to invest in early stage organic food innovators. Breaking ranks with typical funds, they take only minority positions in front-edge products. They realize they need to access nimbler entrepreneurs, earlier. They get an "inside look" at new products and how they develop. Then Campbells is positioned to become the purchaser of the company at the right time. It's another example of the fringe moving to the center and transforming it.

My Stonyfield experience confirmed what can be achieved as a "sprinkle investor" holding a portfolio of small private-equity investments in promising mission-based companies. That's what I call my approach with Stonyfield and many other enterprises. I love the learning, pleasure, and connectivity of relationships that comes from involvement in numerous cool companies. Outright control is rare; I prefer to be a valued minority owner of as many innovators as possible. That reduces the stresses of responsibility while still allowing me to contribute to improvements and evolution in various companies.

It's a privileged position! While the entrepreneurs may be up all night struggling to keep the business alive, I'm available when

I can be for advice, introductions, and a trusted ear. The sprinkle approach offers the protection and strength of diversity—and being on the inside with these entrepreneurs is highly satisfying. I learn a lot. When a business distributes money to investors, I replenish my pool and do it again.

There is an explosion of entrepreneurship underway across the globe in which clean money investors can take part. Incubators, accelerators, angel investment clubs, crowdfunding, loan funds, social entrepreneur fellowships, young presidents' organizations, and crafted gatherings like the Social Venture Institute and Toniic are all contributing to the new economy culture.

The sprinkle method is a great way to start as a clean money investor. You can have lower-risk involvement, then go deeper when it feels right to do so. You can be proud of a wide portfolio of small investments and lose less sleep worrying. You gain a lifelong education in real-world entrepreneurship and develop a knack for knowing what works and what doesn't. And you help build a web of relationships, interconnections, and symbiotic alliances that increase trust and love in society. This strengthens the regenerative economy in more diverse ways than big empires can.

Are you dreaming of controlling a business empire? I caution you to consider what that entails, and question how it will affect your life. Empires take big walls and big armies.

For those intent on attaining massive wealth, first ask yourself: Why? How much is enough for your needs, sense of safety, and ability to fulfill your dreams? Go for that. What will you do with bigger money? Will you give it away? Will you drive the regenerative economy? If you need to win the money race, do something meaningful to the future.

Aim for enough money, while making your primary goal to be a billionaire of good deeds. You can still make money. And if giving is your goal, give now. Why wait? Invest only in what you are proud of. Invest as an expression of who you are, of your values and beliefs.

Because your investments *are* your values and beliefs. They have your name on them. We are our money.

Sallie Calhoun & Esther Park

Sallie Calhoun worked in the high-tech sector for 25 years as an engineer, manager, COO, and CFO. In 2001, Sallie and her husband Matt Christiano purchased the 7,600-acre Paicines Ranch in California's Central Coast. Sallie is rejuvenating the property and its grasslands as a working ranch, farm, and event center. In 2014 she formed Cienega Capital to invest in building regenerative ecosystems, improving soil health, and bolstering local food systems.

Esther Park is the CEO of Cienega Capital. She spent several years in community and economic development finance for low-income communities, primarily with ShoreBank in Chicago. Esther went on to direct the lending program at RSF Social Finance and eventually serve there as vice president of strategy and business development.

Sallie, how did you end up at Paicines Ranch?
What is it, and what is it intended to do?
Sallie: I spent the first half of my career in Silicon Valley as an engineer, and in operations and finance. We bought the ranch after we sold our company, with no plans for really being big ranchers or farmers. Then one day after we'd bought it, I was at a cattle branding, sitting across a picnic table from a woman who introduced herself to me as the former owner of Paicines Ranch. She said to me, "There's this book you should read. Because if I had read this book, I would still own this ranch and you wouldn't."

It was Allan Savory's book on holistic management, which is a pretty hard read. But I went home and read it and it made a lot of sense to me. I was like, "Wow, if it's maybe possible to restore California's grasslands by grazing cattle, I want to see if this will work."

**What is the connection between
Paicines Ranch and Cienega Capital?**

Esther: Cienega Capital is the investment entity that funds different business-driven strategies around soil health. We have some direct loans to farmers. We also invest in some food companies that are working with smallholder farmers and diversified farmers. The relationship with the ranch is one of constant communication. There's so much innovation there.

**Many people are trained to think only about achieving
market rate returns. Can you talk about your more holistic
philosophy about returns, and how it relates to Cienega?**

Esther: We've been trained and brainwashed in this generation to look for what we call market-rate return without really understanding where those market-rate returns came from. So if you look at the average investment return over the last, let's say, fifty years, you also have to understand that that was a period of unprecedented economic growth in this country. That was a very unusual period in which those returns were able to be given to investors, and looking back now, we can say that they were gotten at the expense of ecological capital and human capital. We severely degraded our landscapes and our natural resources to achieve those kinds of returns. We've also exploited human resources both in our own country and in others. And so we have to ask ourselves: Is this really a model of sustainable growth?

What's the alternative?

Esther: If we want to bring financial capital back into line with ecological and human capital, we need to readjust our expectations of return. And so at Cienega we talk about the work that we do as being more of a regenerative approach, because we're taking a whole-system view of investing. It's not just about the financial return. It's about making sure that we're also fostering ecological return and human return. Financial return is not the top of line thing for us—it has to be in balance with the other two. This is very different of course than most approaches to capital these days, but we're trying to foster a new model for how that's being done.

Why is a whole-system approach to investing in agriculture so crucial?

Sallie: One thing that all humans have to do multiple times a day is eat. We all eat. All the food that we eat is derived in some way from the soil. It's either a plant that grows in the soil or it's an animal that ate plants that grow in the soil. So our food supply and its nutritional value depends on soil health. It's not only humans; that is true of every animal and every plant on Earth. Our whole survival hinges on healthy soil. Globally, we only have something like sixty or seventy years of topsoil left. We've been degrading it through agriculture for twelve thousand years or so, and we have seventy years left if we keep going at the rate we're going.

That's pretty alarming, given that it can take five hundred to a thousand years to create one inch of topsoil.

Sallie: There's another side of soil loss that isn't much talked about: climate change. Massive amounts of carbon in soil have been lost to the atmosphere. Grasslands are part of the solution to climate change because they sequester carbon. Another is economic sustainability. We really just devastated rural America over the last fifty years with industrial agriculture and consolidation, you know, the whole "get big or get out" thing. Communities are just gone. So what we're trying to do is to demonstrate that you can do agriculture responsibly. You can support people while making ecosystems better and making communities stronger and more resilient. And—if we do a really good job—you can probably also mitigate climate change.

Your advice to those who want to follow your investing example?

Sallie: My advice is to think about how much you're paying your financial advisor, and think about using some of that money to get help—a different kind of help. Find someone who shares your values and has a background in this work. Go find your local Slow

Money group or regional network. And then go out and make a loan to somebody who is doing something that you care about. I know that is kind of heretical advice in most financial circles. But I say, just go do it. Manage your risk but put some money into something that's relationship-based, based on what you care about, and see what happens.

There's no way to dip your toe in the water without dipping your toe in the water. There are certainly more measured approaches that you could take: you could find an intermediary like RSF Social Finance or another type of fund that will help you deploy that money. But, again, you're not in a direct relationship with that project and that borrower at the end of the day.

Esther: Our strategy is not prescriptive—it's really based on the emergent. If we support enough folks out there that are doing this emergent work, they're going to establish relationships and find ways to connect with each other, and they're together going to build a system that we could have never prescribed. The players have to do it themselves. And so our work is really to encourage the emergent changemakers that are out there—to support them and give them the resources that they need to effectively do the work that they're already out there doing. By doing this, by supporting them in this approach, these will form catalytic points of connectedness that in turn will form a new system.

Sallie: That's the way we look at ecosystems too. They're emergent in the same way. If you want a complex beautiful ecosystem, you don't really know what it's going to look like; you have to let it develop on its own. You have to stand back, get out of its way. You're not in control of what happens to them.

Nashville Calling

4

WORLD NEWS rarely reached me at OrcaLab. There was no Internet with billions of social media postings, no desktops, laptops, or handhelds. But I still knew enough about politics back home in the United States to be alarmed.

Ronald Reagan was in the White House. He had beaten Jimmy Carter, partly thanks to suspicious backroom deals around the Iran hostage crisis. Once they'd moved in, the team around him began rolling out a Lewis Powell dream come true. The Reagan administration oversaw a concentration of power around a "trickle-down," supply-side economic agenda, with tax cuts for high earners and legislation that enabled corporate growth. The economic genius at work! Republicans slashed EPA enforcement, dismantled social programs, and angled to undo the Clean Air and Clean Water acts— while spending billions on nuclear weapons, "Star Wars" defense systems, and illegal wars in Central America.

That was the reality of the mid-1980s—tax and regulatory cuts for the powerful and reduced safety nets for the many. In 1986, in a dark and symbolic moment for the nascent clean economy, Reagan even took the trouble to remove the 32 solar panels Carter had placed on the White House roof. Attorney General Edwin Meese is said to have felt solar energy didn't suit a superpower like America.

In Canada, dark influences of the past were still present and visible. Hanson Island was in the territory of the Kwakwaka'wakw group of First Nations, neighbors to the Coast Salish group to the south. They all had withstood colonization but suffered its devastating racism, near-genocide, land theft, disease, and forced residential schooling. Indigenous families and communities on the coast and across the country continued to deal with the trauma.*

Five years on Canada's western edge exposed me to BC's indigenous cultures and their history of oppression, survival, and rebirth toward an era of new empowerment. I was also meeting visionary pioneers on the cultural fringe: organic farmers, community organizers, and some of the world's greatest environmental activists. I'd absorbed a rich blend of wild nature, alternative philosophy, and West Coast culture. Now I was about to be called back to my origins, closer to the mainstream.

The Outhouse Blessing

Hanson Island gave me many valuable epiphanies. An unexpected highlight came thanks to the OrcaLab outhouse that sat amidst the giant trunks and filtered sunlight of the rainforest. Someone had placed a single, tiny "New Age" book there. As the only reading option, I opened it frequently. I was just as frequently annoyed by its homilies, which went something like: "Your thoughts affect your reality. You can change the course of life by shifting your attitude. Notice negative thoughts and consciously reframe them to positive." The daily ritual kept putting that little book and its aggravating messages in my hands.

Months of silent days in this primordial setting, and long dark nights of many books, were opening me up. Now 28 years old, I saw that I'd developed a toughened posture of criticism, cynicism, and anger. I was angry at life. I was angry with my death diagnosis. I was angry at the institutions and individuals that were destroying

---

* Today Canadian First Nations are working ever more successfully to reclaim land rights and territories, as in BC's landmark Delgamuukw case, and to create functional liveable economies on their own terms. One example is the 'Namgis people from Alert Bay, close to OrcaLab. The nation recently launched Kuterra, one of the world's only land-based salmon aquaculture companies, to create jobs and help reform the poorly regulated salmon farm industry. Tides Canada has played a large role, helping international funders as a local, trusted financial intermediary.

As the Executive Director of the First Nations Technology Council, Denise Williams works to elevate the voice of indigenous people in the technology and innovation space, providing equitable opportunities for access and leadership.

In Canada's short history, a legacy of colonization, intended elimination, and eventual oppression of indigenous people is so prevalent and recent that it will resonate for generations to come. In our lifetime we have witnessed the rise of exploitive capitalism and the degradation of our collective understanding of what "wealth" is. In parallel, we've seen a degradation of our responsibility to the natural world and to one another in the pursuit of an overly simplified understanding of wealth creation that comes at the expense of all else.

An indigenous approach to modern global crises provides insight on the principles we must return to in rebuilding a sustainable economy. We need a renewed understanding of local and global responsibility and our ultimate interconnectedness to all things. Terms like *green economy*, *circular economy* and *sharing economy* all reflect elements of these principles, and a modern expression of indigenous belief systems in an increasingly conscious society.

The clean economy is evolving within a country that has tremendous responsibility and work to do in advancing reconciliation and learning to walk beside indigenous people and nations, as the power dynamic equalizes and our nations advance the economy in the way that respects ancient principles in a modern context. There is much to be shared with economic ecosystems that have come to realize that indigenous economies are a constant and always will survive any challenge, as we always have.

The principles that provide the foundation of these systems are what allow for this resilience. These principles must be foundational to our movement forward together, in our coupled liberation from a structure of exploitation, racism, and patriarchy and toward one of shared prosperity and a clean economy.

the Earth. I now realize I was ultimately angry because I was in my twenties, and that's often part of the package.

The little book started to get to me. I realized I was seeking strength from being a negative critic. So long as I could point out the flaw in everyone and everything, I could numb over my insecurity, my self-doubt, maybe even my self-loathing—feeling those painful emotions less and gaining an upper hand as an armchair asshole.

So many of us are stuck in that posture of critical anger. Shock-jock radio and TV talk show hosts, hell-fire televangelists, and ranting conspiracy theorists all grow their audiences through derision, attack, and trashing others who think, live, or love differently than they do (or purport to). There is power in being "against" and acting smarter, and angrier, than everybody else. It's a type of bullying, which might be the most cowardly form of power there is. The ultimate victim is the bully themselves, who becomes a slave to negativity.

Was I going to settle into life as a bully? Did I need to pick apart everything outside my comfort zone and beliefs? What a bleak choice.

The core message of that little outhouse book—"your attitude and outlook shape your reality"—started to get through. It didn't happen overnight, but days alone and time in nature prepared the ground. Examining my own mindset was an unsettling and radical step for me. It can get more difficult with age and experience. Never underestimate the power of a spiritual cliché! Keep your mind open to seemingly simplistic advice when it comes your way, and give it a fair look. Life is full of opportunities for insight.

At many points in life we must reassess who we are and what our calling is. Doing so maximizes potential for our highest service. I was fortunate in the silences of OrcaLab to have had time to detox, question myself, and clear up a lot of inner turmoil. It made me more positive, constructive, and open to possibilities. Voluminous reading helped me to a fuller sense of the mess our civilization had created, and lent me historical perspective, ecological insights, and hints about the transcendent nature of being.

It all helped prepare me for a return to the world of privilege and power my family was part of—even if we were small players—and begin charting a path for me as a change agent.

Nashville Calling

My sister Linda telephoned me in the summer of 1984. Our father's kidneys were now all but destroyed by PKD. He was on dialysis, dying of renal failure. Our parents had divorced, and Linda was tending our father as his deterioration advanced. I packed up my belongings and flew to Nashville two days later.

Near his final hour, Dad pulled me to his side. He knew I was not interested in carrying on the mall business. He mustered the words: "Son, your grandfather and I worked our entire lives to create something for your sister and you. Please don't reject it. I don't care what you do with it...but please do something with it."

On the edge of death he wanted his achievements to have meaning and be useful, to go on and seed a future. I think that building a successful business was his way to show his love to his family and to express his creativity. Malls were only a means. Now he was closing his final deal, bringing me back into his legacy. His plea touched me and resonated with what I was already feeling. It was time to "go back in" and work with the base he had built. My rebellious resistance and earlier words of rejection—"I don't want your dirty money!"—had been transformed. His deathbed words went straight to my heart.

I knew my way would be very different. By no means was that way clear to me. The goal was to find how his legacy could serve a higher meaning and purpose. The task was daunting. There was so much for me to navigate and learn.

Money scared me. I saw how much damage it had done. It could confuse, distract, and destroy. It could numb me, dumb me down, cost me my balance.

Watching my father die was a glimpse into my own future, my own deathbed. In those last moments, what will matter? What will our life have been about? Will our children respect us for our life work? How will we have contributed to making their world safer, more loving, more resilient?

Will we be satisfied that we lived our true meaning and purpose?

Threading the Business Needle

I had no idea what I would do after my father's estate was sorted. All that time marinating in the salty West Coast air had changed me. My experiences investing in Hollyhock and Stonyfield had warmed my curiosity about money and business. I knew these two forces dominated the world. They were central drivers of so many problems I'd encountered, from cultural genocide and industrial whaling to corrupt political bureaucracies and gutted environmental legislation.

My activist friends were dedicated to highlighting atrocities. Rather than the either/or of "business vs do-gooder," I wanted to find a synthesis. I saw many activists make tremendous gains but ultimately hit brick walls, in part due to inexperience with the mechanics of money, business, and power. For some there was simply no access. Others saw those worlds as too crass and dirty to engage with. Why did doing good in the world require outright rejection of power, money, and business?

I believe that is a big mistake. It limits possibility, and makes well-meaning people vulnerable to attack. The purist can appear arrogant and self-righteous about the concerns of hardworking people supporting their families. This makes them easy to beat politically, through simplistic accusations of being "job killers" or "anti-progress."

But I could identify with why my friends rejected money and power. I had been born into the world of money and business, and embracing it felt variously like a compromise, a sacrifice, and a hopeful opportunity. Was I another "sell out"? How *does* one maintain integrity, consistency, and authentic contribution while dancing with a devil like modern capitalism? Those questions live with me. They should live with all of us, whether we are purists or pragmatists. They are especially important for those transforming entrenched systems from within.

I was unwilling to enter the business world if it meant giving up a life of meaning, or abandoning my incredible friends who had dedicated themselves to protecting people and planet. I needed an eccentric model that blended both realms. I wanted to activate the not-for-profit activist world with more enterprise savvy and access to money and power—and bring more values, purpose, and meaning into the world of business and deploying capital.

At about the same time in the early 1980s, many clean money pioneers were thinking and feeling the same things. I would go on to meet some of them in the Threshold Foundation and the Social Venture Network. Like me they were determined to transform money and business into forces for regenerating the world rather than destroying it. Clean money. A thriving, just, ecologically conscious economy. A new meme began bursting forth across society, like mushrooms after a good autumn rain: Money could be a force for good.

That was the very beginning. We are still in the very early years.

Now in my sixties, I see how successful the forces of domination and "power to the few" have been. The rapid overhaul of our economy is a moonshot endeavor. Success is not guaranteed. But we have to try. More people with high ideals need to go into the financial world to bring a new ethic and vision about what really matters. Any of us called from within to do so should give that initially quiet voice our time and attention, and cultivate it. Money must be realigned with positive, long-term outcomes. That remains a dangerously under-tested solution.

Consciously choosing one's direction is the root of a meaningful life. Making big choices is one of the deepest privileges of existence. Consider them carefully. If the clean money revolution succeeds in building a truly regenerative global economy, it will be because of individuals who have heard this call and chosen self-inquiry, love, purpose, and courageous action.

I'm encouraged to see a million seeds of change growing steadily into broad acceptance. Fringe innovations steadily grow and move to the center to become major industries. Cultures advance and adapt.

Human emotions and struggle continue. It's the best of times and the worst of times.

The task of infusing love and responsibility into the long-term future of civilization is a big one. It needs millions of us, and ultimately billions. We need every willing hand, heart, and mind.

The "One-Mile Radius" Strategy

My father died in 1985. I moved to Nashville, cut my hair, bought a suit and a Saab, and made my first business card. My sister was engaged on her own soul search elsewhere, and I began to assess family business needs. There were millions of dollars of real estate holdings to contend with. When all was said and done, I inherited $3 million in real estate assets, most of them in Chattanooga. I wanted to use the assets to become a changemaker and social entrepreneur. Nashville would be my first learning arena.

My friend Mark Deutschmann arrived in Nashville in 1986. I had met Mark while I was caretaking OrcaLab. He was working at a research camp across the Johnstone Strait from Robson Bight Ecological Reserve—home of the famed "rubbing rocks" where orcas scraped barnacles off their skin. Our first meeting was memorable. The engine on Mark's Zodiac had caught on fire, and to avoid being swept into the open ocean he'd rigged up an improvised sail. With it he steered his way into our little cove on Hanson Island.

Louise was with me at OrcaLab at the time, and in truth I wasn't all that happy to welcome a castaway onto our island, especially one as charming as Mark, who took to singing duets with her around the campfire. In the end, we all became great friends. And I got better at singing.

Mark and I shared a love of orcas and an interest in business. He's one of the best salesmen I've ever met. Soon after his arrival in Nashville, Mark began selling futons to earn money. They were a novelty at the time. He placed fliers on telephone poles and used his own bedroom futon in our home as a showpiece. His father was connected to a futon factory in Minnesota, and Mark managed to survive for over a year taking orders and making $100 per sale.

We took long night walks around the neighborhoods of old Nashville, and often to Radnor Lake park with its ridges overlooking the city. On those walks we explored the meaning of life, big ideas, and how to make business a force for good within Nashville. We dreamed up various entrepreneurial ventures, the first of which was a typing services business that failed quickly—my first, and very lame, business idea.

Late one night at Radnor Lake, listening to haunting waterfowl sounds, I turned to him and said, "You're a great salesman making barely a hundred bucks per sale on futons. Why not try real estate, help protect the old historic neighborhoods of Nashville, and make thousands on a sale?" I argued that he could improve the city, restore quality of life to residents, and make dramatic environmental gains over the suburban sprawl that was chewing up the countryside of middle Tennessee.

Mark agreed. He studied for and earned his license, and began working his way up the real estate ladder in Nashville. Our late-night walk-and-talks became a thirty-year tradition. We crafted fun marketing messages playing off his first name: "The Mark of excellence. Marketing genius. Re-Mark-able skill." There was a new alternative weekly newspaper I'd put a minor investment in, *The Nashville Scene*. At that time, no realtors were advertising in this new publication, and we saw an opportunity for Mark to become the dominant real estate voice in the weekly. We persuaded them to add a category for "Best Realtor" in their annual "Best of the City" awards, and year after year Mark would win based on his skills, reputation, and out-of-the-box thinking.

By 1996 Mark had a broker's license enabling him to start his own firm, Village Real Estate Services. I invested as a minority partner. We raised capital from our friends on a formula that gave the investors the lion's share of dividends until they recouped 100 percent of their capital. After that point Mark gained majority control of the business, and the investors continued to earn dividends into the future. This type of arrangement is a good method for an entrepreneur to raise money for a new idea and end up with control of their business.

Mark and I were on fire about real estate for its potential contribution to a better city. We lived in the Belmont-Hillsboro area of Nashville and loved it. We wanted to rejuvenate declining urban neighborhoods like ours that were facing bulldozers. We saw potential in small-business commercial districts, too. A new era

Mark Deutschmann is a Nashville developer focused on urban revitalization through smart, mixed-use planning. He is the founder of Village Real Estate and Core Development, which support local efforts in affordable housing, social justice, and the arts through the Village Fund.

Cities create the most environmentally friendly conditions for human existence. By reinventing core neighborhoods with infrastructure, density, walkability, and urban greening we reduce our carbon footprint, slow sprawl, and save planetary resources. We work in urban edge neighborhoods, bringing in the spark that lights the fuse.

My manifesto for building livable cities includes the following:

- Create affordable workforce housing near the urban core. Mixed-use, mixed-income urban centers are essential to the future fabric of the city.
- Excellent affordable housing already exists. Retrofit homes and buildings for energy savings across the country.
- Densify corridors for effective public transportation and affordable housing.
- Incentivize, plan, and build walkable neighborhoods. We are obese nationwide, and green walkability improves our collective health.
- Help seniors "age in place." Existing housing offers multi-generational opportunities.
- Set tax increment financing (TIF) districts that create proper tools for affordable housing.

of indie entrepreneurs was just beginning, a counter-trend to the shopping mall, big-box trend that had crushed the prior generation of independents. It seemed no one in Nashville really looked at the emerging urban landscape that way. It was an untapped opportunity. Thoughtful development was a purposeful tool that could make money for us, the agents, our investors, and the city's entrepreneurs.

As one of the only firms located in the old part of the city, we stumbled onto a major regenerative trend that has since transformed cities across the continent: the return to the urban core.

This work was also a family legacy cleanup. My family's shopping mall business had drained the cores of cities across the Southeast and fueled the move to car-dependent, cookie-cutter suburbs, where community fabric was dispersed and weak. Walkability, bike-ability, and denser neighborhoods make healthier places to live. Areas where everyone is isolated in their own car—looking at every other driver, walker, or cyclist as an obstacle to avoid or get past—do a poor job of creating happiness, care for others, and good citizenship. They're bad for the heart. And the kidneys.

As Charles Montgomery said in an interview about his recent book *Happy City*,

> The shape and systems of cities really can boost or break happiness, although they do so in ways that most of us never imagine. In an age when people spend so much time and money on self-help, what we really need is city-help: programs that build health and well-being by understanding the relationship between our minds, our bodies and the places we inhabit....
>
> I also found a surprising link between human and environmental well-being. The doomsayers who insist that we need to sacrifice happiness to take on the urgent challenges of our time are wrong. The happier city can be not only easier on the planet, but a more convivial, empowering, healthy and fun place to live. So if we want to save the world, we should be focusing on building happier cities.[34]

According to the World Bank, cities account for 70 percent of global carbon emissions. From a clean money perspective, helping the shift to green, low-carbon cities with excellent transit, walkability, and density is a big opportunity. As part of my friendship with current Vancouver mayor Gregor Robertson, I've been fortunate to have an inside view as the city develops its "Greenest City in the World" platform. Vancouver's push for zero waste, 100-percent renewable energy, green buildings, access to green space, and aggressive climate targets has put it at the leading edge of sustainable urban development. At the Paris COP21 climate talks, the plan earned Vancouver a world prize from the global alliance C40 Cities.

Nashville is where I first learned the concept of the livable city. We called Village Real Estate's approach to the historical neighborhoods our "one-mile radius" strategy. Working with business, city government, artists, and community groups, we were able to help bring forth lively, walkable, and creative districts. One of Village's successes in the early '90s was the rebirth of 12 South, which at the time was a rapidly declining area about two miles square just south of downtown. It's now one of the most popular areas in the city.

Since then Village has sold over 15,000 homes, helped preserve and revitalize many of the remaining urban neighborhoods, and built or renovated over a thousand multi-family dwellings. Inspired by Ben & Jerry's "1 percent of profits" aspect of their business, we donated 5 percent of the ownership of Village to the Tides Foundation, so that the business would bake not-for-profit donations into its business model. As of 2018, Village has given away $2 million to dozens of grassroots groups across the city.

"The Nun Bun"

Joined by partner Martha Burton, we also invested in and advised small, new-to-Nashville ventures that are now familiar everywhere: cafés, yoga studios, event spaces, public art, and thriving not-for-profits who needed office space.

One creative entrepreneur from those years that I'm still in business with is Bob Bernstein, a former journalist from Chicago.

Bob bemoaned the lack of relaxed, comfortable gathering places for writers, readers, and neighbors wanting conversation and a sense of community. Coffee was the centerpiece. He needed capital and other help to open the business he named Bongo Java. This eclectic coffee shop called itself "Just too weird to franchise" and "Nashville's finest mix of organic, junk, and gourmet food." It brought the city its first taste of café culture. Now with eight unique variations in neighborhoods across the city, it's a beloved and dependable haunt for the "creative class" that Richard Florida highlights as a central generator for better communities.

In 1995 Bongo achieved international fame as home to a cinnamon bun that bore a likeness to the face of Mother Teresa. Some people said "the Nun Bun" looked more like Jimmy Durante than Mother Teresa, but I liked to take it as a little wink from the universe that we were doing good work in our Nashville investments. Nothing on the moral scale of a Catholic saint, but on the cinnamon-bun scale of urban social enterprise, we did pretty well.

This may sound like small potatoes in the grand scheme. But Bongo Java also exemplifies a certain facet of clean-money investing, one that supports local economies, knits the social fabric, and creates resiliency. The impact of such ventures in the long term shouldn't be dismissed too lightly. You never know what grows from such enterprises.

Bob's venture was another step in my move from the shopping mall world to the one-mile radius strategy. My passion grew for boutique entrepreneurs and eclectic cultural enterprises, far from the reality of big-box chain stores. I helped kick-start several Nashville restaurants. One was Cakewalk, the city's first chef-driven, local-and-organic-when-possible lunch venue designed for women professionals. Another, Tin Angel, is still in operation more than twenty years later.

Small businesses need tools and help as well as money. They need a trusted lawyer, an accountant, maybe a business coach, real estate support, branding, marketing, hiring skills, and much more. I was able to deliver these types of teams to Village, Bongo, Tin Angel,

Cakewalk, and others. This "trusted team" approach helps entrepreneurs on multiple levels. The financial model encourages them to raise money from friends and family, which supports integrity in the business relationship. Through their tireless work, entrepreneurs gain a substantial ownership stake. Having personal and transparent relationships with one's investors means a better chance for fair treatment for everyone.

As with Village Real Estate, the model also gives the owner-operator incentive to repay original investor capital promptly. Investors might get 80 percent of all dividends until fully recouping their cash. Then the operator shifts to 51 percent ownership, dividends, and voting control of the business. It's a good self-balancing formula for first-time entrepreneurs with a great idea but minimal cash. They receive a fair salary agreed upon in advance, and their sweat equity earns them full control of the business and a majority of future profits.

My team became a one-stop shop that helped change the cultural, economic, and political landscape of Nashville. Of course, several investments in restaurants and music and film businesses failed. That's part of experimentation and risk—and why the successes, when they come, are so sweet! If you have more than enough money, there is a vast opportunity to move capital from stock markets and massive corporations to dynamic small businesses that generation innovation, relationship, and community.

An Ecosystem Approach

Mark and I worked in a single-city model. I later experienced a more regional model in my work with Carol Newell and Renewal Partners. There is a strong underlying economic case for this approach, whether you call it clean money, social enterprise, or the "fourth sector." You can make money doing meaningful things with your time, skills, and creativity. That said, the gains to entrepreneurs and investors in building an interrelated ecosystem can be measured in a longer time frame, rather than a quick big hit. I believe this is a good thing. It might mean less money up front, but the social and financial results continue to pay out over a longer term. The strong relationships mean everything.

Our one-mile radius strategy was an example of building a healthy business ecosystem. It's similar to the principles behind every main street "business improvement association." If you want your coffee shop, restaurant, or neighborhood redevelopment project to succeed, you need to look beyond your own operations and bottom line to ensure that the surrounding social fabric is healthy and that people's needs for community and accessible services are met. To this end we worked with restauranteurs, real estate firms, and newspapers, as well as not-for profit community groups and politicians.

Compared to the typical dominate-the-competition model of big business, this natural-system approach to local economies spreads benefits more generously. Then and now I've sought out ecosystem approaches like this. It's the difference between building a skyscraper or cultivating an organic farm. In the one, you have to control every single detail to the maximum in order to reach the sky. In the other, you collaborate with others in helping a garden of opportunities grow. Individual creativity, rather than monolithic uniformity, flourishes. Local charm evolves from the eclecticism of independent entrepreneurs. People crave this kind of authenticity, where many diverse flowers bloom. Cultural resilience, neighbors helping each other, and more distributed financial success are the result.

When you cultivate such a garden, the dividends aren't narrowly concentrated to accrue so vastly to a few dominant owners. Many people get to join you at the harvest feasts.

In my small corner of the clean money revolution, I've been interested in positive influence and better practices alongside reasonable profit. These early experiences convinced me that by combining social purpose, financing, and pragmatic business fundamentals, powerful culture shifts could follow.

Our purpose can no longer be simply to amass and hoard ever-larger amounts of capital, whether for ourselves or for shareholders.

There's no good future in that. There is a great future in basing our economy on making a contribution, and using some of the better elements of capitalism to spread positive results. Key to this is fair and appropriate taxation on profits, which ensures strong communities and social services.

The question I ask entrepreneurs, investors, and high-net-worth individuals is: How much is enough?

If you've got a million dollars, do you need two? If you've got a billion, do you need two billion? A lot of people will say: "Well, I'm making more money so I can give away more money." That's an easy but often evasive response about motivations.

You need to ask yourself, "What am I really doing this for?" And then look at what it costs the world, and you in your life, to make that extra money. It's the deathbed question. Will making more money than you already have really mean anything to you at the end?

Good intentions don't always justify ends. There is no sense making a billion dollars in a business that pollutes just to ultimately donate those funds to a charity treating symptoms of some other damage. "Philanthropy is commendable," said Martin Luther King, "but it must not cause the philanthropist to overlook the circumstances of economic injustice that make philanthropy necessary."[35]

We need to minimize externalities as we co-create prosperity. This is the revolution. Its success is a truly regenerative economy: a web of enterprises that create a more resilient, fair, and safe life for everyone.

In Nashville I saw four interrelated aspects I believe are essential to systemic change. The long game, with a seventh-generation viewpoint, needs each of these four elements.

+ Profitable enterprises
+ Not-for-profit enterprises
+ Power and politics
+ Leadership and inner skills

Whether in a coastal rainforest, a French intensive garden, or a mid-size Southern city, diversity and interdependence are critical to resilience. I've already talked a bit about for-profit investing, and how our work with Village Real Estate helped boost not-for-profits. I'll talk more about leadership and inner skills in Chapter 9. So here's a note about power and politics, which are crucial to long-term culture shift.

Progressive businesspeople trying to create social good need political forces aligned with their vision—or at least not actively working against them. That's true locally and nationally. With Village Real Estate, we knew that redevelopment of urban neighborhoods into mixed-use areas with denser residential development and eclectic commercial space would be foreign to a city council that had mainly presided over Nashville's suburbanization. A city council's primary power is often over land use and zoning.

Our interests, therefore, naturally aligned with progressive politics. A mayor who set a tone of support for strong neighborhoods would be inherently better for us. Politicians elected on urban restoration agendas generally have better policies on social and environmental issues. Such representation is a win-win. Mark and I helped a local candidate, Stewart Clifton, get elected to council. Stewart was involved in neighborhood preservation, and wasn't exactly pro-development. He was an old-school progressive, skeptical if not outright suspicious of investors and businesspeople. But he saw that we were interested in protecting and enhancing places like Belmont-Hillsboro, rather than razing them and selling them to the highest bidder. He was intrigued with our point of view, and when he got onto council he was a strong advocate for our vision of restorative development. Years later he told Mark and me that we were the first people who helped him understand that business wasn't all negative, and could be powerfully constructive, when it has the right values.

Small, important victories! The example translates to bigger venues as well.

The City of Nashville moved with history, and kept shifting its infrastructure investments toward improving urban neighborhoods. Now instead of settling for suburban sprawl, chain stores, minimal street life, and a bleaker cultural setting, there is an inviting, eclectic magic in Nashville. Through the sophistication of the entrepreneurs, small businesses, civic organizations, makers, and artists who have since flourished there, Nashville has become a Southern city to brag about, and be studied as a success formula. Having watched thirty years of evolution, I'm deeply moved by the vision and risk-taking of smart people across the socioeconomic spectrum who could see what was ahead, and who stepped up to the responsibilities.

Business with Friends— and the Imperfections of "Good Business"

One advantage of the world of clean money is the many opportunities to partner with people who share your values. This raises another principle that contradicts traditional business wisdom: choosing to work with friends, or people who could be friends.

Close friends can be hard to find as we age. Everyone is busy, and isolation is all too easy. Friends who work together well can become very close. My pals at Guayaki are now twenty years in business as six partners from early life. They work and play together, often with their families. They intend a multi-generational business. What a beautiful goal in this era of flipping your company as fast as possible to satisfy investors looking for maximum returns.

Business with friends is a much-needed trust exercise that deepens relationships and actively cultivates love in the world. It's a deeply satisfying, ongoing practice of personal growth in working out disagreements, annoyances, and selfishness. Be sure there is a good agreement documented in advance, outlining how the arrangement can end peacefully. (That part is often neglected in the buzz of early "dating.")

It can also be smart business. In doing business with friends, or those with whom I could be friends, I've found mostly long-term successes and only a few disasters. It's when I've gone into business with people whose values or personalities make me uneasy from the beginning that things often end badly.

A related takeaway from my Nashville years relevant to social entrepreneurship is about cultivating a practice of inquiry. This means curiosity about new opportunities and conflicts, and also about the effects our enterprises have for good or ill. As an example, one serious downside to our Nashville neighborhood revitalization successes is the displacement of low-income residents who live in those areas.

Gentrification is a vexing issue. It can be seen as another form of (or a later phase of) colonization. Young creatives and entrepreneurs move into lower-cost areas to open small businesses, along with people with more money than current residents. As they buy deteriorating houses and renovate them, they raise home values and attract people with yet higher incomes. Tax rates rise. Longtime residents are displaced.

There are many positive outcomes of "fixing up old neighborhoods": vitality, economy, jobs, more property tax revenues, improved services, a greater sense of safety on the streets, and the upgrading of eyesores and abandoned properties. It all creates wealth and community—at least for the new home and business owners.

But where do the people go who were living there previously? What happens to affordability, and decent safe housing for those with less money or low-paid jobs? What happens to the race, ethnicity, and class mix of the area? As rents or housing costs increase, the culture changes. It looks good to those who arrive, but it can be a disaster for those who already live there. The city of Vancouver is struggling with these very issues today; most cities are. There can be negatives sides to a city's success. The trend is global. Population growth contributes, as does the move toward urbanization, as incoming migrants seek better services and better lives in the city.

My success as a Nashville entrepreneur—creating better restaurants, cafes, housing, streetscapes, and amenities for residents—helped raise many people up. But it also displaced others. I believe our work in Nashville has been important and valuable to the city as a whole and to most of the people whose lives we touched. But the less-visible negatives remain.

We were not able to solve the problem of gentrification. We continue to throw big support into important public amenities like protected walking and biking routes, and work closely with neighborhood groups in alliance for supporting better developments. We lobby the city for additional services and infrastructure. Village also invests in community organizations that work on housing issues like homelessness and affordable homeownership, including Habitat for Humanity, Room in the Inn, and Urban Housing Solutions.

If you want to invest in positive change as a social entrepreneur and clean-money investor, it's important to recognize all dimensions of success, and to seek solutions for uncomfortable consequences. My argument is not for "pure" or "perfect" solutions, but for ever-better, wiser outcomes. When human ingenuity is pointed in good directions, with responsible behavior, many improvements happen. It takes far more than businesspeople to shape the world, but business is powerful for its ability to create jobs and revenues and influence public policy. Success in a clean money context implies a responsibility to get involved in public policy and make things better for everyone, often against the values of the conventional business community. These realities are part of changing any system. If you engage with them, the results can be inspiring and amazing.

Power comes with the responsibility to use it for the good of the whole. To ignore that is a great tragedy.

Jose Corona

is Director of Equity and Strategic Partnerships under Oakland Mayor Libby Schaaf. Jose was CEO of Inner City Advisors (ICA) and led ICA to becoming a nationally recognized organization, scaling small businesses to create good jobs for those in need. Jose is a BALLE (Business Alliance for Local Living Economies) Fellow and serves on the boards of several organizations, including Fund Good Jobs, Net Impact, SPUR Oakland, and the YMCA of The East Bay.

What's your current role in helping the shift to a more just, restorative economy?

Oakland is booming. We see a lot of businesses come here because real estate is cheaper than San Francisco, with their employees commuting in and out. My work is making sure that the economic development and prosperity coming here benefits all Oaklanders: people with low income, people of color, and people with other barriers to opportunity, such as the formerly incarcerated and people with disabilities.

What motivates or excites you in your work?

Oakland is a community that's really standing up and putting its values forward. The business community, the activists, the organizing community, the public sector—everyone is rallying around this idea that Oakland and being an Oaklander needs to be different. We want to be a model city where increasing prosperity and investment don't push out the local people and culture that makes the city great.

What are some of the solutions or lessons for people interested in equitable, prosperous outcomes for inner cities and other communities?

People tend to hire people that have the same values as them, or that look like them. So in that sense, lack of diversity is no surprise. We all see it every day. But in Oakland now there's a real opportunity for a new approach. One example is something we call TechQuity. You can start a tech company here in Oakland and really figure out how to infuse those positive, equitable values at start-up. Companies are looking at diversity in hiring and at leveraging supply chains, buying power, employee engagement, and volunteerism efforts, and of course their philanthropy.

We want to lead with our values: nurturing diversity, the artist community, the non-profit community, the whole spectrum. The solutions are about bringing businesses and government together on that. At the mayor's office we're working with a group of high-level CEOs—people like Marc Benioff of Salesforce, and the CEOs of Clorox, Pacific Gas and Electric (PG&E), and Beneficial State Bank, a B Corp here in Oakland. We're leveraging their private investments to advance what we care about here. Equitable jobs. Creating and maintaining affordable housing. Building a safe, holistic community. Those are all things that business cares about.

We're saying, "We want to maintain that, and we hope that you use the power of your business to help us invest in that." In turn the City of Oakland, the public sector, will commit to make sure that your talent is well housed, that you have a safe place where your employees can live, work, and play. And that you have a government you can trust—not an annoying, ineffective, inefficient government.

What are some challenges or pitfalls funders and investors should be aware of when working to assist community and urban development?

My biggest advice for those interested in driving change in inner cities and other places is that as you come into a community that you may be unfamiliar with, come with really big ears. Really try to listen to what people say about their needs. I've seen well-intentioned high-net-worth individuals come into communities thinking they have a solution ready to go because it worked somewhere else, and it totally backfired. So whatever mission you're trying to drive in social justice or equity, be a good, strong listener first. Then determine whether you can assist through your capital or through your connections, or both. The social networks many wealthy individuals have are very unique—not many of us have them—and these sometimes go farther than dollars in supporting a community.

What would you do if you had $100 million to deploy?
There are two angles I would take. First, I'd make a concerted effort to ensure that a lot of this capital would be available to minority entrepreneurs in the Bay Area, mainly Oakland. I'd be creative about how we invest our money. I wouldn't make it a granting organization. Grants are great, but not sustainable. I would look at investing this one hundred million in a way that provides flexible capital to businesses—everything from loans to convertible notes—as a way to advance justice and equity. Convertible notes are great tools for entrepreneurs. They're flexible and allow business owners to grow their businesses without worrying about starting to pay them off next month.

Second, I'd invest in a robust workforce pipeline to feed these businesses quality employees. I want to create pipelines of people for good jobs in sectors that are creating them, like technology, digital arts, healthcare, transportation logistics. The actual entrepreneurs must help shape workforce training. Rather than just handing out random jobs, we need a pipeline of jobs that leverages people's real strengths and interests.

And we need to drive our training toward the jobs of the future. Major companies like PG&E have around 50 percent of their workforce eligible to retire within the next four to five years. That's hundreds, maybe thousands of jobs that pay $80,000 to $100,000 a year, but very few of the people in our community see them as an opportunity because they're not exposed to them. They say, "Oh, I'm going to become an entrepreneur and be the next Mark Zuckerberg, or I'm going to be an engineer or a coder and make tons of money." But those jobs are far and few between.

That $100 million would also be a major opportunity to leverage public sector involvement. You could say, "Look, here's this chunk of private capital that we can leverage, and if you put some skin in the game and philanthropy comes in, we can go from $100 million to $1 billion." And that's where you'd really start to make some large-scale systemic change.

Through the Looking Glass

WHEN YOU'RE IN over your head, the first thing to do is seek help.

The executor read my father's will to the family, and I inherited a portion of his estate. It was far more money than I'd ever controlled. The emotional effect was intense and confusing. I needed to get my head around this new wealth. The responsibility to steward it challenged my rhetoric about purported values. How would this money express my beliefs?

While I was living at Linnaea Farm on Cortes Island, the farm's cofounder Penny Cabot had invited me to meetings of the Threshold Foundation. My response was along the lines of, "No freaking way." Going to sit with a bunch of people to talk about money sounded downright weird.

In retrospect, that was fear talking.

My return to Nashville highlighted my need to learn to manage wealth in alignment with my beliefs. Suddenly you have money, more money than you've ever had, more than you think you need. What do you tell your friends? Do you tell them? What are your responsibilities? Should you work? Give it all away? How will it affect the way people think of you? What about dating?

There were many vexing questions. I needed to talk about these questions with people who shared my values. I contacted the Cabots, and they readily agreed—I'm sure with knowing smiles—to sponsor me to the Threshold Foundation. My first gathering in 1985 was at the Omega Institute in Rhinebeck, New York.

Dollars to Donuts

Threshold was founded by Joshua Mailman. Josh is the son of deceased New York businessman and philanthropist Joseph L. Mailman, who founded the Utica Knife and Razor Company in 1920, at age 18. This later became the Mailman Corporation, an early major conglomerate in North America. Josh started experimenting with clean money while in university in the '70s, via his involvement with the Haymarket People's Fund, which has awarded grants for social justice initiatives across New England for more than forty years.

He received a significant inheritance in his twenties. Rather than grapple alone with the questions the new money raised for him, Josh wrote a letter to fifty friends and acquaintances around the country. He invited them to gather to talk about money and the meaning of life. The recipients were people, Josh says, "with both personal wealth and a commitment to decreasing ecological destruction and human suffering."

Twenty-one people answered Josh's call and gathered in Estes Park in the Colorado Rockies in September 1981. Most of them were young inheritors. A taste for spiritual questing was part of the culture. As Josh said of Threshold in an interview for *Fast Company*, "We were part of the generation of people interested in meditation, Buddhism, Shamanism, rainbow gatherings, and Burning Man. It was a mystical, non-Western way of looking at the world." [36] It was also made up of people who didn't take themselves too seriously. Threshold members called themselves "Donuts"—nuts with dough—a nickname that stuck when someone spotted a donut-shaped cloud in the blue sky overhead.

The Estes Park gathering began a long-running inquiry into how money can be deployed in a spirit of service, rather than simply to make more money. The vision was to create a supportive community of peers sustained by periodic gatherings, as well as a public foundation to give away money together. The foundation was organized around a central principle: "Everything is alive, everything is interrelated, and all life is sacred."

In Rhinebeck in 1985 I reveled in meeting over a hundred others who were struggling with the personal and practical questions of owning money. At first glance it seems simple. It isn't. Who do you trust? When do you talk about it or share your doubts? Where and when do you invest, give, spend, hoard—and why? These questions were the core of Threshold. Dozens of newly wealthy oddballs like me found a place to learn amidst the relative safety of peers. It's a community of practice, a learning circle for the outliers in the "1 percent" who see money as a privilege to be used for the highest purpose. Tough issues surfaced and people shared their most poignant, painful stories. Having a safer place to break the great taboo of talking about money was golden.

I watched Josh with fascination and awe. I was moved by his activist relationship to money. I was excited by his quick decision-making and risk-taking. He understood that our wealth is a demonstrative statement of our values, that vast change was needed, and that if people like us could get our act together, we could help reduce suffering and destruction and increase restoration and justice.

Entering that community was like walking through an Alice in Wonderland looking glass into a new world I'd never imagined. I tried to bring my full self to the table, talking about subjects I'd never broached elsewhere. I was rewarded with a wide range of practices around group process, spirituality, artistic expression, and individual responsibility. The goal was to pass beyond the conventional guard posts and rethink money, with its indelible roots in colonialism, domination, and patriarchy. Looking into these realities is fair game at Threshold. It was a big twist on the assumptions I'd made about the self-indulgence of "people sitting around talking about money." It was profoundly meaningful, a mystery school of exploration. My world grew much broader. I'm part of Threshold to this day.

Roger Milliken Jr. is an heir to the family-owned textile firm Milliken and Company. He is now the company's director and also runs the Baskahegan Company, a sustainable forestry products enterprise that owns and manages 120,000 acres of forestland in eastern Maine. He wrote about Threshold:

It's about holding tenderly the mystery that binds us together, which is hard to articulate but unmistakable when we feel it—be it rumbling with a belly laugh, sobbing with pain, or quietly feeling the attunement of our grants committee with a larger purpose. It's about a radiance which increases as we come closer to who we can be and what we can do as individuals within our own communities of family, friends, and work outside the Network; as a community of loving, committed friends within the Network; and as a foundation dedicated to using our inner and outer wealth to help our hurting world heal itself.

Can you imagine a Chamber of Commerce member saying that? They may in the future!

The Opposite of Dark Money

For more than thirty years the Threshold community has helped hundreds of influencers learn basics and innovations in philanthropic giving, all with an eye to shifting culture and sparking lasting social change. As mentioned previously, most traditional charity dollars go to hospitals, disease research, private education, churches, and religions—along with beautiful museums, university halls, and football fields that memorialize the names of donors. These are generally worthy enough goals. But only a tiny percentage of the money given away supports a just, secure world. It's easy to enjoy the warm glow of social-status giving. It's harder to catalyze ripple effects for a better world, to invest in social justice, the biosphere, and long-term progressive initiatives.

Throughout the long era of regressive neoconservatism spawned by the Powell Memo, I was repeatedly inspired and strengthened by the examples of my fellow Donuts. They continually reached beyond conventional giving to explore a less comfortable, more transformative philanthropy. Though relatively small in dollars, Threshold and its colleague organizations exemplify the opposite of the dark money that has degraded environmental and social protections and built a reactionary anti-tax movement to further concentrate wealth for the few. The Threshold approach to giving money was early DNA for the clean money revolution. Threshold showed me what money can do when we look it squarely in the eye for what it is, where it came from, and why it must be used to help the future and society as a whole.

Organizations with a systemic approach can effectively leverage relatively small amounts of capital into accelerating change. Threshold has been doing this since the beginning. From 1988 to 1989, as example, Threshold granted over $1 million to dozens of organizations in peace, social justice, environment, and arts and media categories. A sampling:

+ Economic empowerment programs for women in Texas, Honduras, and the Ramah Navajo Indian Reservation
+ A documentary on the export of hazardous waste
+ A campaign (led by local radio DJs) raising awareness about teen pregnancy in inner-city neighborhoods
+ Community theater in Hell's Kitchen
+ Agroforestry projects in Antigua
+ Leadership and job-skills training in Harlem and the Dominican Republic

Money is a form of energy. There is so much more money can and should do than simply enrich shareholders and erode legislation designed for the common good. Money should help quicken our evolution toward a truly secure world, where ecosystems are protected and safe food, shelter, health care, education, work, and support for those in need are readily available.

The Threshold board once spent three days on the Onondaga Reservation in central New York State, invited to a ceremony led by Oren Lyons. Oren is a Faithkeeper of the Turtle Clan of the Seneca Nations of the Iroquois Confederacy. He helped create the Traditional Circle of Indian Elders and Youth.

We arrived on the reservation near Syracuse well aware of our role as heirs and beneficiaries of colonialism. Some Threshold

Oren Lyons has for forty years advocated for international indigenous rights and sovereignty issues. A cofounder of the Traditional Circle of Indian Elders and Youth, he is a distinguished services professor emeritus of the University at Buffalo. This excerpt is adapted from an interview with Barry Lopez in the Jan/Feb 2007 issue of *Orion*.

Sovereignty is probably one of the most hackneyed words that is used in conjunction with Indians. What is it, and why is it so important? It's a definition of political abilities and it's a definition of borders and boundaries. It encapsulates the idea of nationhood. It refers to authority and power—ultimate and final authority. It's such a discussion among native peoples in North America, I would say, because of our abilities at the time of "discovery"—and I use that term under protest, as if to say that before the advent of the white man in North America nothing existed...

The ideas of land tenure and ownership were brought here. We didn't think that you could buy and sell land. In fact, the ideas of buying and selling were concepts we didn't have. We laughed when they told us they wanted to buy land. And we said, Well, how can you buy land? You might just as well buy air, or buy water. But we don't laugh anymore, because that is precisely what has happened. Today, when you fly across this country and you look down and you see all those squares and circles, that's land bought and sold. Boundaries made. They did it. The whole country.

We didn't accept that, but nevertheless it was imposed. They said, Let's make us a law here; we'll call it the law of discovery. The first Christian nation that discovers this land will be able to secure it and the other Christian nations will respect that. What does that do to the original people, whose land of course they are talking about? We just weren't included. They established a process that eliminated the aboriginal people from title to their own land. They set the rules at the time and we were not subjects, we were objects, and we have been up to this point.

And so it goes on, this idea of private property, this idea of accruement of wealth. And now we have corporate states, corporations that have the status of states—independent and sovereign, and fealty to no one, no moral law at all. President Bush said, "Let the market dictate our direction." Now if that isn't about as stupid as you can get. What he said was, let the greed of the people dictate the direction of the Earth. If that's the basis of a country, then it's really lost what you would call a primary direction for survival.

This is really the danger today—this empty, senseless lack of leadership. But it doesn't mean that responsibility isn't in the hands of the people. To come down to the nut of the whole thing, it's the people's responsibility to do something about it. Leadership was never meant to take care of anybody. Leadership was meant to guide people; they take care of themselves. People should be storming the offices of all these pharmaceutical companies that are stealing money from them. They should be dragging these leaders, these CEOs, out into the streets and they should be challenging them. They're not doing that. They're just worried about how they're going to pay more.

It's the abdication of responsibility by the people. What was it that they said? By the people and for the people? That was the Peace Maker's instruction: of, by, and for the people. You choose your own leaders. You put 'em up and you take 'em down. But you, the people, are responsible. You're responsible for your life; you're responsible for everything.

People haven't been here all that long as a species on the Earth, and our tenure is in question right now. Do we have the wisdom, do we have the discipline, do we have the moral rule, the moral law, are we mature enough to care for what is our responsibility? That question can only be answered by the people.

members can trace their ancestry back to the *Mayflower*, while others of us are from more recent immigrant families who lived "the American dream" and built thriving businesses. Our intention was to learn, reflect, and get guidance. We wanted to help bridge a divide, face deep cultural wounds, and imagine our future legacies. We knew that meant being part of the reconciliation process between settler descendants such as ourselves and the people our elders had devastated and stolen from.

Chief Lyons and his allies were generous to welcome us as sincere. Our time there led to some Threshold members investing in indigenous businesses or finding lifelong commitments to indigenous causes—language and culture preservation, access to opportunity or clean drinking water, battling the exploitation of Native reserves as sites for dirty resource extraction and toxic waste dumping.

When you bring money together with vision, strategy, and love, things move. Evolution happens. I served as Threshold's president from 1988–89, and in the 1989 annual report, I wrote, "Since its inception, one of Threshold's clearest missions has been to stimulate the unleashing of held wealth into immediate use in the world." That's still true. Since 1981 Threshold has given over $50 million to hundreds of projects. Far bigger money was leveraged through this work, perhaps in the billions, as the ripples of its work influence families, institutions, colleagues, and networks.

While all Threshold participants come from privilege, an equally deep uniting factor is a determination to grow as agents of change. Donuts discover personal purpose, then find smart ways to put their energy, influence, and resources to work in the world. Threshold gave me an ongoing setting for self-reflection and informal therapy, a place to step out of the day-to-day, and challenging material to immerse myself in. When I served as president, I suggested to my fellow members that "Threshold is a school for dying." My meaning was that learning from spiritual traditions about the fleeting nature of life and the inevitability of death could show us how to live a legacy that matters. Who do we want to have been when we look back from our death bed? How did we leave the world better?

Clean Money Roots: The Social Venture Network

In the 1980s and '90s, more Threshold members wanted to move beyond philanthropy into investing for-profit capital in social good. That was a big moment in the history of clean money. And it was a big question: How might we shift our investment dollars to encourage growth of socially conscious, regenerative businesses? As with most movements, this thinking was sprouting all around the world about the same time. Those mushrooms sprouting up again!

Once again, Josh Mailman was out front. In 1987 the Threshold community made a clear choice to focus on philanthropy and members' personal growth. Josh and his friend Wayne Silby seeded a second organization, the Social Venture Network (SVN), by gathering do-gooders who wanted to mobilize business as a potent force for change. This was a big advance on charity alone, requiring top to bottom activation of business design. Forty entrepreneurs attended the founding meeting.

Like Threshold, the first SVN was in the Colorado Rockies, this time at Gold Lake Ranch. I traveled from Nashville with one of my best friends from high school, Jon Kinsey. (Jon later became a successful mayor of Chattanooga. He attended only one SVN meeting, but I think it influenced his progressive values when he took over leadership of my hometown.)

I met many inspiring people and lifelong friends at Gold Lake. One was Gifford Pinchot, grandson of the founder of the US Forest Service. He is now an author, businessperson, and founder of Pinchot University, now Presidio Graduate School, which in 2002 launched America's first MBA in Sustainability program. Today MBA degrees in sustainability are in high demand, and universities are scrambling to offer more space for them.

"We decided to build a new paradigm," Josh has said of SVN, "in which business operates to add value to society—without compromising the well-being of future generations."[37]

Josh shows up everywhere at the nexus of "doing good" and finance. He arguably defines the early era of private equity impact investing. He continues to make fearless risks on important trends.

Through his robust Serious Change fund, Josh invests tens of millions into mission-based early-stage ventures, including Alter Eco, Grameen Telecom, Stonyfield, Ethical Electric, and digital media hub Upworthy.

In these and so many other ways Josh is helping remake the modern economic landscape. His audacity, conviction, and extraordinary instinct have led the fusing of business with social action, turbocharging the clean money revolution. His epic entrepreneurial courage was an essential early model for my own "ecosystem gardener" approach. Watching him, and those drawn to ideas and networks from his legacy, inspired me to experiment. His work helped me act quicker and go further, acknowledge imperfections inside and out, keep my eye on the big picture, seek role models, and commit to my meaning and purpose. Josh's openness with his stories and insights helped me find a career I never knew existed.

"I didn't have any experience or training," Josh says. "I just figured if you have more money than you really need—do something!"

One of his many impressive commitments was to hire Kesha Cash, a young African American who grew up in economic hardship and was her family's first university graduate. She studied math at Berkeley and did her MBA at Columbia, where she later advised the trustees on social and ethical issues related to the university's endowment. Josh wanted to broaden impact investing into more diverse communities, and put up funds for Kesha to co-manage Jalia Ventures, an initiative focused on mission-driven entrepreneurs of color. There she deployed $5 million and built a portfolio of ten companies while supporting Josh with Serious Change. She went on to found the Impact America Fund and be named a "Top Five Gamechanger" by *Forbes*.

Wayne Silby is another leading light pioneer. Most Threshold members were inheritors, but Wayne, founder of Calvert Funds and ImpactAssets, made his own money. He launched Calvert in 1982, he says, to get rich. "It wasn't a crusade. Actually we got kind of lucky, we were one of the first money market funds... And so in my twenties we were already managing over a billion dollars."[38]

During a period of exploratory world travel, a conference on the Buddhist tenet of "right livelihood" got Wayne thinking about how to give back. His mulling of these concepts ultimately inspired him to help move the rudder of global finance. "We were the first fund to say, 'Well, we want to set aside a small part of our monies for social justice issues.' We weren't sure if it would capture other people's imagination, but it felt true to our values. It got a lot of notice in the press, but a lot of Wall Street was like, 'These guys are still on drugs!'"[39]

Calvert was an early giant of SRI or socially responsible investing, a screened stock product. (I have a small retirement fund there, one of my rare engagements with public markets.) Such screens were virtually unknown in the early 1980s, other than several obscure, small, ethical and church-based funds.* Offering SRI products required researching stock exchanges and evaluating companies for best and worst practices. This gave stock pickers and wealth managers a tool to "offer better companies" for clients. A new choice was birthed. SRI ratings and funds became a foundational influence at the roots of the clean money revolution—the first big, values-based product for the financial industry. (More on SRI in Chapter 8.)

Josh and Wayne's SVN achievement remains a watering hole for creative characters in the emergent clean economy ecosystem. Thanks to them, we gained a place to hear stories from private companies, not-for-profit social enterprises, professional advisors, young people considering career options, socially motivated artists, media moguls, investors, and a few at-large magicians. SVN has powerfully influenced thousands of careers and new industry subsectors, and begun changing the definition of the purpose of business.

Mentors and friends there gave me a practical landscape of vision and hope, disruptive stories, form-breaking norms, and a fertile soil to grow my nascent sensibilities into tangible strategy. Hilarious laughter, surprising tears, and wicked good parties were all part of

---

* Two very early examples: Quaker Friends Fiduciary, founded in 1898, and Boston's Pioneer Fund, launched in 1928.

the mix that confirmed my path of reinventing business as a driver of social change.

Vermont's Finest: Ben & Jerry's

I met Ben Cohen and Jerry Greenfield at SVN in the late '80s. They were a charismatic partnership. I loved their outlandish, irreverent behavior and their deep commitment to social and environmental causes.

Ben & Jerry's took the guilty pleasure of ice cream and brought it back to its pure-ingredient roots, minus the additives and chemicals. In person they were down-to-earth and authentic. They were industrious hippies who used the allure of deluxe organic ice cream to advance progressive ideas and causes. They gave 7.5 percent of their pre-tax revenues to charitable groups. They were anti-war and pro-renewables (before most knew energy alternatives existed). I first heard about their business when it was very young. That I knew anything about a small ice cream company was a testament to their ability to generate major publicity from brash and colorful stunts.

Their goal was to influence the world with big smiles, strong messages, and local jobs in their Vermont backyard. It worked. They defied traditional rules while mastering the daunting challenges of rapid growth, product excellence, and the loyalty of fickle customers. The result was a legendary change-agent business tool. Ben and Jerry proved something important: business could make the world better. Nothing pleased them more than inspiring a generation of younger activists and businesses with their clean and zany model of capitalism.

In 2001 Ben and Jerry sold the company to Netherlands-based Unilever, one of the largest global food conglomerates. They did so after exhausting their hopes of finding values-aligned investors with the financial scale that could have kept the ownership closer to home. (Therein lies one of the obstacles still being resolved in the mission and money sector. With success comes size, and size means big dollars are required. Big dollars often means only institutional investors or very large corporate entities are able to acquire you. The coming decade will hopefully see new solutions to this obstacle.)

They regretted aspects of the decision to sell, and shed some tears. But they have managed to keep much of their progressive brand features inside Unilever. The power of their groundbreaking ideas lives on.

The clean money revolution is made up of billions of ideas, innovations, reforms, successes, and disappointments. Early visionaries are essential. They break the paradigm so others can then perfect things. Gary Hirshberg's later sale of Stonyfield to Groupe Danone, for example, built upon lessons he'd learned from the Ben & Jerry's transaction. Both of these iconic acquisitions created heated discussion among do-gooders about "selling out"—and whether it was possible for a mission-driven company to fold into a major conglomerate without losing the soul of the founders.

Increasingly, big buyers of cool and meaningful brands realize the gold of an acquired company is in its forward brand essence. That's the early clean money revolution showing its disruptive character. Entrepreneurs are going deeper into developing brand authenticity, making it essential to company success. Big Food is now facing slowed growth as demand booms for healthier, more holistic products.

Ben & Jerry's demonstrated how to convert common consumer products into drivers of better social and environmental practices. Michael Kieschnick, an SVN member, took the concept further with his partners in Working Assets, now called CREDO Mobile. They sell phone services to drive money into progressive causes, while educating members and using participatory decision-making in grant decisions. CREDO has invested in election law reform, and organized opposition to climate-damaging megaprojects. (CREDO gathered civil disobedience commitments from nearly 100,000 people opposed to the Keystone XL pipeline.) It's an integrated model of activist business that inspired the rapid spread of next-generation, political-change focused companies such as Mosaic, Ethical Electric, and social enterprises like Blue State Digital and As You Sow.

Ben and Jerry are heroes who led with their values. They stand for peace and inclusion, justice and political fairness. They continue as icons, role models, and advisors for young entrepreneurs. At SVN gatherings and beyond, they—along with Josh, Wayne, and inimitable SVN executive director Chuck Blitz—brought fearless fun to the ethical business community. Other SVN luminaries emerged as important characters of the clean money movement: Rebecca Adamson, Nikhil Arora, David Berge, Karl Carter, Cheryl Contee, Ram Dass, Ed Dugger, Adnan Durrani, Bernie Glassman, Reed Glidden, Rha Goddess, Linda Goldstein, Alisa Gravitz, Denise Hamler, Amy Hartzler, Janie Hoffman, Jeffrey Hollender, MaryAnne Howland, Van Jones, Si Kahn, Scott Leonard, Jared Levy, Linda Mason, Jeff Mendelsohn, Deb Nelson, Sherri Pittman, Anita and Gordon Roddick, Mike Rowlands, Greg Steltenpohl, Denise Taschereau, Rob Thomas, and Nina Utne, among others.

These great mentors helped me embrace the value of cosmic humor. Early SVN meetings were a great training school. Like Threshold, SVN cracked open the emotional, vulnerable side of businesspeople, and tears were common amidst the laughter.

This kind of community is more important than meets the eye, especially for entrepreneurs and activists who spend their lives pushing against entrenched interests. Swimming upstream all the time is tough, and emotions can pile up and weigh you down. You need a chance for shared laughter and emotional release. In the old-school patriarchal business world, emotional vulnerability is assumed to be a weakness. Leaders are taught to block emotions. Unfortunately that snuffs empathy and becomes the source of much trouble. Modern science is catching up with common sense and ancient traditions, acknowledging that contemplative practices and emotional intelligence are essential skills. More on that subject in Chapter 9.

When asked (in this interview with the founders of the Usual, a Montauk-based creative agency) what he thinks makes a good company, Patagonia's founder Yvon Chouinard answered:

"Responsibility. During this last recession our company has experienced the highest growth it's ever had. I think it's because during a recession people stop being silly, they stop buying fashion stuff that will go out of fashion in a year or two. If they think it'll last a long time, they'll buy better quality things they need rather than things they just want, and that's the kind of stuff we're making. So our business is really strong.

With the Millennial generation, they really appreciate what we're trying to do to 'cause we do the least amount of harm in making our product. The Millennial generation has had some environmental education. They know what the problems are, they know we're destroying this planet, they want to do something about it. And they want to support the companies that are doing something about it.

In fact we're trying to tell our customers: think twice before you buy a product from us. Do you really need it or are you just bored and want to buy something? Then we're taking responsibility for our product forever. If it breaks down, we promise to fix it. We're going to come out with little booklets and videos showing people how to repair their Patagonia stuff themselves and when you're finally either tired of the product or you've outgrown it or whatever, we're going to help you get rid of it."

The Ripple Effect

I remember other indelible moments from SVN gatherings. Some were alarming, like Van Jones being accosted by conference hotel security who thought he looked "suspicious." That revealing and troubling event opened up race and privilege topics in the most direct and emotional way. Others cut to core paradoxes, like Judy Wicks debating Gary Hirshberg about whether we ought to sell off companies to change multinationals from within (Gary's position), or stay smaller and locally owned (Judy's). The debate rages on.

At one SVN conference a senior military officer mapped out why climate change is the largest, most pressing threat to global security of our times, and shared how the military was focused on understanding its threats. At another, spoken-word poetry by Rha Goddess of Move the Crowd masterfully wove painful messages of bias into a fabric of love and mutuality, bringing the room to joy and tears. George Soros once defended his investment in a highly profitable land mine company, based on the once-unquestioned theory of "make as much as you can in order to give away more" (I suspect he has evolved that thinking by now). This was the early days, but he was already a multi-billionaire financial genius. He has since been instrumental in fighting reactionary politics around the world, and his funding priorities are cutting-edge and controversial, including open democracy in Eastern Europe, rights for Roma people and the LGBT community, and reforming welfare, drug, and prison policy.

The idea of separating profit-making from social consequences and contribution remains dominant, but it is showing cracks. It will change. We will soon reach an era where big money commits to "social change investing" using integrated capital strategies to shift huge systems in the world, from food to energy to infrastructure. This is a radically better role for the power of capitalism.

Are you invested in, banking with, or purchasing from companies that contradict your values? It's worth looking deeper, because you almost certainly are, even if only in retirement funds or by the bank you use. Our financial system is ubiquitous in its hold on those of us who are not monks, nuns, or saints. The future depends on reinventing this system with long-term thinking. There will be no soft landing for us without it.

We must each do so some personal accounting. If you're becoming more conscious of these contradictions and less willing to continue them, stick with it. You will be vindicated soon enough.

And your financial returns may be stronger than those of traditional investors.

There are many networks and resources to help guide your personal clean-money transition. SVN has long provided a space for innumerable effects on participants' careers—and on their employees, customers, transactions, and supply chains. This type of work has a ripple effect on the economy and society in general, affecting the lives of people unaware of the origins. Many great organizations have spun off from or were inspired by SVN, which itself was birthed from Threshold.

A sampling:

Business for Social Responsibility (BSR)

BSR began as a conversation among SVN members who wanted to influence big corporations from within. Josh Mailman, Judy Wicks, Chuck Blitz, Arthur Hiatt, and Mal Warwick all worked to bring the vision into reality. I participated in a heated hotel-room strategy discussion and donated to a start-up pool for the initial launch of BSR in 1991. It was first led by Harvey Wasserman, a noted antinuclear activist, but lost momentum. Chuck Blitz—entrepreneur, activist, and then-executive director of SVN—recruited former Levi-Strauss Foundation executive Bob Dunn to relaunch it in 1992, which he did with great success.

That year there were 51 member companies, and the inaugural kickoff event featured Ben Cohen, Anita Roddick, and Gary Hirshberg. It is now a globally successful not-for-profit working to reduce negative environmental and social impacts at over 250 major corporations, from Microsoft to Walmart. For example, BSR's Clean Cargo Working Group has 85 percent of the players in the ocean shipping industry tracking, reporting on, and working to improve their environmental performance.

Net Impact

Net Impact was started in 1993 by entrepreneur Mark Albion, an early SVN member, as Students for Responsible Business (SRB). It was a joint project between SVN and Business for Social

Responsibility. The intent was to embed ethics and social responsibility curricula in MBA programs, and organize values-aligned career opportunities for grads. An early SRB mission statement summed up their goals this way:

> SRB believes that companies no longer are only responsible to their shareholders, but they are also responsible for the well-being of their colleagues and employees, the communities in which they operate, and the natural environment that we all share. As future leaders, SRB members believe that they can and should be in the forefront of changing the role of business in society. But to do this, they need role models, documented evidence and tangible experiences that demonstrate that it is possible to combine business success and societal good.

Now as Net Impact, it is represented on almost every business school campus. With 80,000 student and professional members in three hundred chapters, it empowers "a new generation to drive social and environmental change on campus and throughout their careers." It's a hotbed for new leaders of the clean money revolution.

Investors Circle (IC)

IC began as a means for private investors and funds to meet emerging mission-based entrepreneurs from diverse sectors. Started in Chicago in 1992, it was a collaborative forum to find, share, assess, explore, and make investments in mission companies. IC was founded by Susan Davis, a former board member of SVN, and assisted by Wayne Silby, John May, Josh Mailman, Phil Villers, and Artemis Joukowsky.

IC's mission is to "catalyze the flow of capital to for-profit companies that provide social and environmental solutions." It has helped place over $200 million into 300+ companies over 20 years. It catalyzes regional angel-investor networks across the mission investment sector.

BALLE (Business Alliance for Local Living Economies)

Judy Wicks started the White Dog Cafe in Philadelphia in 1983, as a muffin shop in the bottom floor of her house. It eventually grew into a city landmark: a 200-seat restaurant serving local and organic food. Judy was a pioneer in sourcing local ingredients from regional farmers and urging other Philadelphia restaurants to do the same. She joined SVN early on. As she told it in an interview on the BALLE website, "I was invited to join SVN by Ben Cohen. Ben discovered me, and connected me to like-minded business people. It was then that I realized I wasn't working alone and that I wasn't crazy. Other people, too, had unusual ideas about using business as a vehicle for social change. I learned many things at SVN, where we all inspired each other to do more in our efforts to make the world a better place."

At SVN Judy was vocal about local. She is a passionate and articulate advocate of developing resilient, self-sustaining regional economies. Judy founded BALLE in 2001, along with Laury Hammel, an SVN member who founded a Massachusetts tennis club chain called Longfellow.

They envisioned BALLE as a small-business alternative to the Chambers of Commerce and their conservative values, with the mission "to nurture and curate the emergence of a new economy." Their goal is gradually to displace our current destructive system of big-box, monotone companies with one "that supports the health, prosperity, and happiness for all people and regenerates the vital ecosystems upon which our economy depends."

BALLE is now led by Rodney Foxworth, founder of Invested Impact, a consultancy that assists investment in promising ideas, social change leaders and enterprises. The BALLE Fellowship Program supports the best "localists" across sectors, to strengthen diverse, generative local economies. They work on racial justice and reducing inequality, while supporting robust small entrepreneurs— who in turn go on to act as change agents, run for political office, and anchor important community issues.

The Local Economy Investors Working Group is another BALLE initiative made possible by the support of RSF Social Finance. The members (I am one) are "path-finders who are focused on a regional approach" to deploying capital with integrated strategies. We share best practices and build new approaches to local economy funding. It's an important initiative, sparking circles of local funders across many geographies. These test models and innovations help others with wealth find new methods for their own clean-money work.

As BALLE says: "We're all better off when we're all better off. With inequality, we miss out on good ideas and relationships, unhappiness increases, and eventually systems collapse. Rather than 'every man for himself,' we understand that real security comes from community. We need to rebuild the middle class, engage in fair trade, and decentralize power and business ownership."

The List Keeps Growing

There was a time when I thought I knew every single organization focused on aligning values with money. Today it's hard to keep up even in my hometown of Vancouver. So much is happening. Here are a few other groups and movements in the clean money revolution that have been seeded or influenced by SVN or its spin-offs:

+ **PlayBIG** was founded by Carol Newell, with Marian Moore. Adopting tools from the Threshold culture into a more intimate setting, PlayBIG gatherings support individuals of high net worth to "activate their whole portfolio to mission and purpose." Using story sharing, peer coaching, case studies, and one-on-one advisory sessions, PlayBIG motivates, empowers, and inspires wealth-holders to compound positive influence on places and issues: "How can every dollar be more closely aligned with what I most care about?"

+ **Divest Invest** supports the global clean-energy transition. Focused on large endowments or family wealth, Divest Invest encourages exits from fossil fuel investments because of the risk of stranded assets and the urgency for action on climate. In

2018, they counted 845 organizations and approximately 58,000 individuals—together holding assets worth $6 trillion—that had pledged divestment.

+ **Slow Money** is dedicated to countering the pace of high-speed global financial transactions. Founded by former Investors Circle CEO Woody Tasch, Slow Money is bringing money back to earth and urging people to invest "as if food, farms, and fertility mattered."

+ **B Corporation**, or B Corp, is "a global movement of people using business as a force for good." They offer an impact assessment process drawn in part from Ben Cohen and Mal Warwick's book *Values-Driven Businesses*. B Corp certification is now a gold standard in external metrics assuring strong attention to values and progressive business practices. People are already seeking out B Corps because of that certification of authenticity. Renewal was an early fund to become B Corp certified.

+ **Bioneers**, the "social and scientific innovators who are mimicking nature's operating instructions to serve human ends," was started by Kenny Ausubel and Nina Simons in 1990. Bioneers gathers people and ideas at the intersection between deep ecology, natural values, natural systems, indigenous rights, and visionary ideas. Bioneers Media, Bioneers Radio, and their big annual gathering are all superb learning and connecting environments for front-edge practical tools for living in tune with natural systems.

+ **The American Sustainable Business Council (ASBC)** is a coalition of mission-based businesses dedicated to building "a vibrant, just, and sustainable economy." Representing 55,000 businesses and 150,000 entrepreneurs, executives, and investors, the ASBC educates and seeks policy change on key issues: health care, financial reform, chemical regulation, global warming, and taxation.

+ **Toniic**—whose name is a playful riff on GIIN, the Global Impact Investing Network—is a global angel network for impact investors that offers access to mission-aligned deals, peer support, best practices, and online and in-person forums. Toniic provides guidance and support to social entrepreneurs and impact fund managers. Founded by Charly and Lisa Kleissner, Morgan Simon, Sean Foote, and John Kohler, the organization has also built the 100% Impact Network, a global group of investors who have committed to move their entire portfolios to positive social and environmental impact.

• **SOCAP** is the Social Capital Markets Conference, a three-day extravaganza where 2,500+ clean money people and organizations intersect annually in San Francisco. It's a mash-up of speakers, workshops, and networking events where everyone—dazed newbies, field veterans, and big Wall Street firms—show up to learn about the state of impact investing and changing the world with capital. SOCAP has become a "must do" for much of this booming sector.

I hope this gives a window into the explosion of clean money activities going on, and some of the history that birthed the movement. The diversity, values, and creativity represented in these networks form a magnificent kaleidoscope of opportunity. We have abundant resource sharing networks, intersectionality, potential access, and rich creativity. And it has only just begun! We live in a networked age, where the global is more local than ever—and the local can change the global.

There have always been business clubs and elite power organizations where people ate and drank and laughed together. But where once these were only conventional, secretive networks strictly focused on money-making and keeping hold of power, there is now a robust and aspirational culture that blends the personal and professional. It brings deep values to the challenge of making money. It's about winning for all: pushing hard for fairness, social equity, and taking care of people and planet.

For those of you early in your explorations of clean money, these kinds of networks offer a rich germination zone of opportunity and support. The art of convening, hosting, cross-pollination, generosity, fun, and love as part of doing business and building organizations is alive and well. What I've noted in this chapter is only a small slice of the vibrant sector inventing itself today.

I see something very large and profound underway. It's moving so fast it's hard to track it all globally. Success and expansion are outpacing research and cataloging. Start looking and you will uncover networks, peer circles, angel investing groups, advisory firms, LinkedIn groups, Twitter hashtags, podcasts, "mystery school" circles, certification programs, incubators, accelerators, study circles, books, and fellowship—more than you can handle. If you've had to invent your own pathway as a values-aligned investor or entrepreneur, or are a reform agent inside a more conventional business organization, there is a gold mine of opportunity waiting for you.

Are you part of local or national networks that help you learn to innovate? Do you have places to go for peer support? Do you attend events where you are immersed in new ideas, icons, and inspiring pioneers? It's all there for you. As fast as it is all growing, it's a very big world we have to remake. Your contribution is needed. By mid-century we need to collectively turn around the devastating challenges now facing us as a species. We are smart enough. The tools exist. And the will is growing.

We need more people to plug into learning and support networks that connect values with careers. We need people like you to step up and innovate—to push the boundaries, creativity, and capacity further, faster. Plenty of money will be made, and many new, successful businesses built. The really amazing stories are still to come.

"Seek and ye shall find." You may have to run to keep up, but it will be worth it!

Morgan Simon

is Managing Director of Candide Group, which is building a portfolio of social and environmental investments. She was founding CEO of Toniic, which has brought together 200 investors seeking to deploy over $4.5 billion into impact investment. Cofounder of Transform Finance and the Responsible Endowments Coalition, she is a professor in the graduate school of Middlebury College in Vermont, and author of the recently published book *Real Impact: The New Economics of Social Change.*

How did you get into the world of impact investing?
I grew up in Los Angeles, and worked extensively in East LA with mostly immigrant families. The relationships I developed, particularly with the children I was in community with, were so powerful they felt like family. When I saw the challenges these families faced, it felt deeply personal. And I very quickly understood the difference between charity and solidarity.

For a period of time I was directly case-managing sixty homeless families. Attempting to make a real difference in their lives seemed like an exercise in futility. Even if they had a Section 8 voucher, the best I could do was get them some bus tokens, because the system was just so incredibly broken. These experiences sparked a passion for the idea of policy change and systems-level thinking. When I went to Swarthmore College, which has a billion-dollar endowment, I joined their committee on investor responsibility. I saw it as an opportunity for real activism. The school in the past had voted on shareholder resolutions, but had never filed one. No American college had filed a resolution since the apartheid era.

I went to the administration and made the case for responsible investment. We ended up getting, and winning, a resolution with Lockheed Martin asking them to add sexual orientation to the non-discrimination clause and giving domestic partner benefits. We used this success to build momentum and leverage it with other Fortune 500 companies that also didn't have sexual orientation in their policies. In each instance, we were able to grab their attention with a simple question: "Did you see Lockheed in *The Wall Street Journal*, and do you want this to be you?"

The resolution got a lot of national attention. Students started reaching out from across the country asking how to do it. That was the start of the Responsible Endowments Coalition, of which I became the executive director when I was 23. I've now been in the field for over fifteen years, and feel there is still so much work to do.

What's your role in activating wealth for good?
My role is in two capacities. One is that there are lots of really smart, committed asset owners that want to ensure that their money is in line with their values, but either don't have the time or the background to know how to do that effectively—and they're humble enough to try to seek support in that journey. I think being an impact investor requires a unique set of skills, where you have to be equally competent on both the social and the financial side of the business. My business partner and I provide that support to a tremendously committed family and are proud to do so.

The second role I personally play is encouraging the impact investing industry—which is at a really interesting point of scaling—to be as thoughtful as possible about what impact means. It's not enough to just to say, "Oh well, this was in health or education or agriculture and therefore it's impact." You really have to be accountable to beneficiaries to determine what the *right* kind of impact is—which is really just a basic social justice principle.

Can you name examples where impact investing has created a structural systemic shift?
Absolutely. Uncommon Cacao is a company we love, that actually makes sure that farmers really do get a fair share of the proceeds. They've been able to triple farmer income, as opposed to just giving three cents over the usual price, which is, unfortunately, the

prevailing practice. There are funds like Huntington Capital that are being really thoughtful about making sure people earn a living wage and that there are employee ownership opportunities, rather than just counting jobs created. GAWA Capital is an investment microfinance institution that is working on not just providing loans, but also savings, insurance, and the whole suite of financial services that someone would need to have a successful life.

Is there a danger that impact investing could get diluted into a feel-good thing without substance?

Yes, and that's what a lot of my work is trying to guard against. We need to not throw the baby out with the bathwater, but we need to make sure to create, and scale, structures of accountability right alongside the industry. For instance, with investment and job creation in a developing country—is that impact, or do such jobs actually need to be well-paying ones that don't harm the environment? Is cleaning up a wastewater from fracking impact, or is that still a fossil fuel investment?

You don't want just the big banks making that decision. You probably do want them at the table in some fashion, because they offer some of the best financial expertise, but how do you make sure they're in conversation with the Greenpeaces and other watchdogs and local communities? If we can all get into that conversation, then absolutely, I think we can do amazing work. But that's not going to happen naturally on its own, because financial systems are very capable of scaling without accountability to anyone. An essential element in the growth of impact is demanding that accountability.

Do we need matchmakers who bring various actors and voices to the table—so decisions are informed by people aware of local context and negative externalities as well as by people with financial acumen?

Definitely. That's where Transform Finance comes in; in building a bridge between social justice and finance—from both sides. The Transform Finance investor network has brought together over

$1 billion of asset owners who are seeking to take a social justice approach to their investment. Its trainings provide civil society leaders—who so far touch over five million people—with background on impact investment. We help them learn how to leverage it as a positive tool for change, and how to hold it accountable. Notably, over 75 percent of people who have gone through the training are people of color.

What advice do you have for values-committed wealth-holders?
First, I would advise anyone to pay more attention to your social education: a knowledge of local communities, issues of poverty, and the complex dynamics of the "impact" area being addressed. Don't be so focused on what you need to do to be a great investor that you forget to make sure you actually understand the issues of the day. If I'm looking at improving job quality, do I know if people care more about an extra dollar an hour or about paid sick leave? Who are the organizations that I need to be in communication with to understand the issue? Try to understand those perspectives on a consistent basis, whether it's in a geography you care about or a sector, and prioritize that. These are equally critical questions alongside more common ones like, "How do I do this valuation, or accept this term?"

I'd also recommend the Transform Finance principles, which provide a framework for people committed to systemic change and not palliative change. We're working to provide people a roadmap of what can help them get to real impact.

The Story Machine

W HEN A MOVEMENT catches on, the growth can seem sponta-
neous, happening in many places all at once. It can be hard to
find a straight line of cause and effect.

Where did the civil rights movement begin? Who started the
organic food trend that by 2025 will be a global industry worth
$320 billion?[40] Determining who and what influenced whom, and
when, is complicated. Such movements can seem to "just happen."
Suddenly a lot of people are sharing similar ideas. When the right
conditions for a new paradigm come together, it can become huge—
almost as if it were simply the next step of evolution. Where the
seeds originated is a mystery we may never unravel. But when you
see that growth starting to explode all around, many opportunities
open up to step in and find your role.

The clean money revolution is the result of millions of hands.
There are so many important networks, organizations, relationships,
partnerships, and good works moving it forward. Collectively they
are influencing new approaches to responsible investment and social
finance around the world, from Australia to the UK, from Japan to
Brazil, from Indonesia to Bangladesh.

The fractal nature of this revolutionary inspiration carried into
my own life. The Social Venture Network was a direct inspiration
for the Social Venture Institute (SVI), a program I co-produce
at Hollyhock on Cortes Island. Like Threshold, SVI is one of my
treasured communities, the work of a lifetime. It's now in its twenty-
fourth year as a cross-sectoral, intergenerational, peer-learning

leadership conference and social network. SVI curates a dynamic mix of for-profit and not-for-profit social entrepreneurs, investors, artists, and promising young people.

One success begets the next. SVI has sparked creation of the Social Change Institute, Web of Change, Story Money Impact, SVI Vancouver, and Activate. A five-week series called Feeding Growth emerged after 2015 SVI, specifically for skills and connections in the Vancouver area organic food entrepreneur community. There is now an annual gathering for women entrepreneurs in the San Francisco region (SVI Women Bay Area), and SVI Alberta is launching in 2018.

All of these experiences I've had in clean money since 1992 may never have come about if a certain prospective member hadn't joined the Threshold Foundation. Her name was Carol Newell.

An Extraordinary Woman

Carol is an exuberant, visionary strategist. She was born in upstate New York to a wealthy business family: her father was CFO of the Newell Manufacturing Company, a third-generation family business that got its start making curtain rods. Her hometown of Ogdensburg is near the Thousand Islands area at the Ontario border, formed by the great St. Lawrence River. She spent her childhood summers at the family cottage on the shore of those waters, forming a lifelong love of nature. Devotion to ecological causes would have been a very good guess as to her future contributions to the world.

Carol and I have many things in common. Like me, she fell in love with the British Columbia coast but grew up far away. We both make our homes in Vancouver and on Cortes Island. We both believe in long-term thinking. We know that money is a powerful tool for making the world better, if used thoughtfully and with the right values and goals. We have faith that people will do the right thing with the right tools in the right conditions if given the right information.

When Carol was nine, her father died of a sudden heart attack. The tragedy prompted her mother to take his seat on Newell's board of directors. At 47, she helped to guide a major company as it planned to go public, and beyond for 16 years. By the time Carol was 16, her mother had introduced her to managing the family investment portfolio. Her first inheritance, of several million dollars, came when she was 21. She tended to her accounts, but didn't make too much of the assets at the time.

"The amount I first received back in 1977, in my early twenties, was significant, but I didn't pay much attention to it, other than to manage it as it came to me—mostly family stock and dividends," she says. "When I received my second inheritance, in my mid-thirties, it was much larger and thus a whole different ballgame. I knew more, and I had a sense of mission."

As with many inheritors, that new situation raised profound questions. "I suddenly began thinking of all the possibilities connected with that amount of capital."

Carol spent her twenties studying geology at college and afterward as a field assistant. She traveled abroad and tended to a home with her husband, who was a professional geologist. Field geology led to Carol tromping around the backcountry of various places, and the travel led her to consider the relationships between people and place. Those early influences furthered her growing passion for ecological protection and smart, efficient uses of resources.

In the mid '80s, while living in Middlebury, Vermont, Carol read about an unusual conference on socially responsible investing (SRI) in New Hampshire. It was produced by the same group that Josh Mailman had encountered as a student, the Haymarket Fund. One of the presenters, Amy Domini, founder of Domini Social Investments, was a leading SRI pioneer. Something mobilized in Carol when she heard Amy speak. "That was probably the first 'aha' moment," Carol says. "The conference awoke in me a whole new sense of what capital could accomplish. I realized that money could be used as leverage to reorient us away from rampant consumerism and back toward building solutions, connection, and regeneration."

Carol returned from the conference, signed up for Amy's monthly newsletter, and instructed her traditional financial advisor to look for companies that had an SRI component. When solicited, she agreed to make a small loan to help a new start-up called Earth's Best Organic Baby Food.

Carol has a knack for discovering pioneering strategies. Her instinctual turn toward this work and these companies were early, formative steps into what is now called impact investing—as one-mile radius entrepreneurship and the Stonyfield and Hollyhock investments were for me.

As President of Threshold I was relentless in membership recruitment. Identifying and screening new members was crucial to the organization's makeup, effectiveness, and ability to thrive, so I paid close attention to new prospects. By that time Carol had been living in British Columbia for a few years. When I saw her application I was intrigued by the BC connection and impressed that she was funding and strategizing the work of the Sage Foundation, which she had cofounded. Sage was becoming an influential organization working to reduce our ecological footprint. I leapt at the opportunity to travel to Vancouver to interview her.

Sage was ahead of its time. They developed programs to establish water, energy, and solid waste reduction initiatives for households, schools, and businesses well before the "reduce, reuse, recycle" norm. Carol funded the organization quietly. Besides their executive director and two other founders, none of her Sage coworkers knew she was anything more than a smart and committed cofounder—they had no idea she was also the organization's benefactor. This was classic Carol. For an entire decade she kept her generosity quiet, preferring to stay anonymous and behind the scenes as a person of wealth. "In many ways, anonymity can be difficult, because you are always holding something back," Carol admitted in a 2013 interview with *Montecristo* magazine. "It wasn't until I was in my mid-forties that I came out about my wealth. Until then, I was a woman walking around with a secret."

I met Carol in her modest Endswell Foundation office in Blood Alley in Gastown, part of Vancouver's old waterfront warehouse district. We saw that in addition to our love for BC, we shared

Carol Newell on her clean money goals and philosophy:

"My broad goal was to lighten our culture's environmental footprint. I saw philanthropy and business, both, as venues to address the issues—that I could utilize my wealth and influence to address things I really cared about: a healthy environment and vibrant, sustainable communities in balance with that environment. By that time, I lived in British Columbia, Canada, a remarkably beautiful place. As our regional strategy emerged, I noticed that investing locally multiplied the effectiveness of capital due to proximity and ability for relationships to build. I wanted to see the region—and the world—grow toward a future that values precious resources and thrives without stripping away essential life systems, the very systems essential for future generations and all life forms. I could see a new way of leveraging capital to accomplish this. It needed to escape the norm controlled by what I call the traditional 'Money Manners.'

I affectionately refer to them to illustrate the rules we are taught to think about money. Such rules state that we should 'Not talk about money,' 'Maximize profit at all cost,' and for goodness' sakes, 'Don't touch the principal!' Considering my capacity, these rules no longer made sense to me. In fact, I could see how they were preventing many others from making bold decisions—that folks almost needed permission to change the game. When the premise of sound financial planning has been exceeded so profoundly that those precepts really don't apply any more—when they have begun to wreak havoc instead of build security—it probably *is* time to change the game."

many passions around the intersection of money, social change, and ecology. It was clear that Carol and Threshold were a perfect match.

The two of us had many conversations about clean money and investing in change.

The Birth of Renewal

I was still based in Nashville, learning a new approach to social purpose real estate and community development. I stayed involved with the evolution of Hollyhock on Cortes Island, making extended visits there at least once a year. A new relationship in the Bay Area had me also encountering the leading edge of "social change meets money" in that forward-thinking region. During that period, Carol asked me to help with a few of her budding initiatives. Her top-flight lawyer and accountant were perfect for the first stage of building Carol's foundation, and for the initial management of a sudden 400-percent increase in capital. But Carol wanted to do more than simply let money make more money. She wanted to be bolder: to activate the majority of her wealth for maximum planetary benefit.

As a social change investor with a more limited inheritance, I saw a huge opportunity in working with someone as avant-garde, tactical, and determined as Carol. I had this clear feeling that we had important work to do together. I accepted her offer.

Carol initially asked me for consulting help on specific challenges, particularly in identifying businesses to invest in. In time she invited me to work with her team to create a long-term, ecosystemic approach to social change investing, with an "integrated use of capital" strategy. That meant a wide-ranging mix of money uses across sectors and legal structures in Vancouver and British Columbia. They were linked in values and vision, connected through themes of 50-year outcomes—all building the soil for the blossoming of a new creative economy, a progressive political ethos, and a modern, global city.

We later named the entire strategy Renewal. "Investments, grants, and collaborations" were our subthemes. The complete story, with all its diversity and complexity, is challenging to encapsulate. It was about much more than accumulating wealth. We saw the operation as Carol's "activist family office," with money deployed creatively into business, not-for-profits, and individual leaders. Carol was eager to test experimental strategies toward a regenerative model for the future. Few people broke the constraints of traditional investment and philanthropy at that time, leaving a surprisingly broad playing field for new approaches.

Models of integrated capital of integrated capital deployment at this scope were hard to find in '90s North America. We found pieces of inspiration and insight in various smaller examples. The multi-level right-wing organizing in the United States that followed the Powell Memo was a giant, national version of a similar strategy, though with a dramatically different vision for the future. Powell's was the corporate domination version, a modern return to oligarchy. Our vision was rooted in decentralized, collaborative, and progressive values, seeking a regenerative culture and economy—a return to the principles of natural systems.

Carol asked me to lead Renewal Partners, the private equity side of the initiative, in 1994. We searched for credible businesses with clear mission focus. We interviewed dozens of entrepreneurs who were looking for capital, selecting the best and crafting transactions that worked for both sides. By 1997 I'd also taken on leadership of Carol's Endswell Foundation, which became our vehicle for delivering philanthropic support, focused on environmental issues in British Columbia.

All of this required substantial accounting and legal backup. Critical to that was Martha Burton, our vice president. Since the early 1980s Martha had worked for my father, then me, in our respective Nashville businesses. She moved to Vancouver to set up the growing office and help build the team. Her tenacious abilities were essential in orchestrating our unique enterprise, in which Carol generously gave both Martha and me the ability to earn sweat equity ownership. Martha remains a valued friend and extended family member. She has a particular love of social purpose real estate, where she makes her mark today.

By fall 1992 Carol had received the bulk of her inheritance. Favorable cross-border exchange rates and wise tax management gave her wealth a big boost. Over the next sixteen years, by steadily divesting the majority of her Newell Rubbermaid holdings and reinvesting into screened funds and emerging cleaner businesses, the money grew significantly. We were assisted by a particularly exuberant stock market during our major divestment period.

Our heavy weighting in local business, community banking deposits, private loans, and steady moves to organic food and other rising "clean" sectors made our track record much better than conventional public equities options when major market plunges happened later. Clarity of vision, or just luck? Trends can go your way—but sometimes they don't. Luck is definitely part of it. We picked the right trends, and between 1993 and 2008 we were able to "recycle" additional tens of millions into the people, businesses, issues, and capacities aligned with our mission. The net result was one of those inexplicable and amazing good fortunes. We were simply betting on a regenerative, long-term vision, but it was easy to believe the higher powers were rooting for us to succeed.

Once you have a certain level of wealth, as global capitalism grows, so does your money. This drives increasing inequity. Wealth buys access to better returns, and the ownership of capital usually translates into more capital. Favorable tax treatment further grows the money. Through the labor of others and the ever-more-refined exploitation of natural resources, fabulous wealth can be made simply by making clever investment choices from your desk chair. More money makes it easier to make even more money. Influencing tax rates, regulations, and legislation through the power of wealth adds icing on the cake.

For our Renewal team, the additional wins were wins for the places we loved. We wanted to support our region and the people in it. We kept pushing gains out the door and into progressive causes and entrepreneurs. Our strategy for a generative future was focused on British Columbia. (We defined "local" to include our relationship networks as well as geography, a strategy I highly recommend.) Inspired by bioregionalism, deep ecology, slow money, ancestral responsibility, and good old-fashioned love of place and people, we were "all in" for the region we loved.

Renewal was able to help multiple organizations and leaders who were themselves already far along the path of cultivating the soil of a better, more resilient future. We avoided top-down control. We wanted to spread the manure of money around effectively like good gardeners, helping many plants sprout and propagate.

Our approach encouraged others. Carol's wealth helped unleash other people's money into protecting BC ecosystems and communities in turn. The resulting multiplier effect fed the growth of more smart people and projects than we would ever dream up on our own. Many remain unknown to us. We know only a fraction of the generative effects that Carol's money has had. We like that. That is the beauty of a distributed, generative model. No need to track or count it all.

We did track what we could, intentionally cultivating a "story machine." We hoped what we had learned and done would empower other change agents. Stories are resilient and have lasting impact, far more than numbers on a balance sheet.

Good Business Stories

Carol understood business as a tool for social change. Her goal was to invest in "companies that would be part of the solution, rather than part of the problem." Renewal Partners grew into a professional angel and seed capital firm that helped kick-start many enduring mission-based companies in BC and elsewhere. We were one of the first to systematically invest in organic, green, change-focused entrepreneurs in Vancouver. Once we had deployed the majority of Carol's dollars for the risk-taking that true innovation requires, we began to focus on a next chapter.

In 2008, led by Paul Richardson, myself, and Carol as lead founding investors, we launched Renewal Funds, a mission venture capital firm. We welcomed in other people to prove that venture investing could be done with a "mission first" strategy. By 2018 we had built the Renewal3 Fund, to be followed by Renewal4. More on those projects and what they mean for the clean money revolution in Chapter 8.

Renewal Partners put capital into for-profit enterprises, but our larger goal was to model money and capital as a tool for positive change in the world. What we accomplished stands as tangible proof of the potential of clean money and a generative economy. We played a role in helping the BC economy begin to move beyond resource extraction (often with faraway owners) as the economic base.

We put small "love money" amounts into dozens of companies. Many of them grew profitably, adding jobs and helping Vancouver become a national leader in green entrepreneurship and cleaner money. So much can happen when a visionary leader like Carol assembles an effective, turned-on team, drives a strong long-term vision, supports innovation and risk, and stays on course.

SPUD (Sustainable Produce Urban Delivery)

SPUD is an online organic grocery delivery service. You can find its HQ in East Vancouver—a full warehouse wafting with the aromas of celery, green onions, and ripe fruit. Dozens of employees fill customer bins for thousands of deliveries all over Vancouver. Given the notorious failure of over-funded digital groceries that crashed in the late '90s, sucking up hundreds of millions of investment dollars, this might seem a dubious bet. The logistics of grocery delivery are complicated. Perishable products and low margins add challenges. But SPUD's many positives—carbon reduction, climate, and local, organic food—compelled us to continue investing over many years. Once this type of platform is successfully established, the possibilities become huge.

SPUD had calculated the carbon-intensiveness of food products and grocery shopping and found an impressive reduction in carbon footprint through delivery vans. Their customers' response: "You mean I can sit at my computer and order my organic food, and it shows up at my door, with prices similar or better than health food stores? How cool is that?!" We saw multiple wins for planet and profit, and a solid new digital economy investment to test.

I met founder David Van Seters in 1996. He was leaving a sustainability position at KPMG, a big accounting firm, in order to start SPUD. In David I saw a methodical, hardworking entrepreneur with a deep commitment to the environment and a head for numbers. His previous work with senior levels of government and large companies—making the business case for adopting high sustainability standards—was impressive. David saw in us a sincere interest in a clean economy. He trusted our intentions.

"Because I had charted the company as a social mission business," I wanted to find investors and lenders who really shared that mission," recalls David. "It wasn't easy to find those investors then. Maybe I could persuade conventional investors, but I was concerned they would force me to water down the values to generate bigger profits. Soon we'd be selling Coca-Cola, Spam, and Captain Crunch."

The dot-com crash of the early 2000s wiped out the big-money, conventional grocer Internet delivery companies—including Web-Van, HomeGrocer, Hannaford Home Runs, Kozmo, and Streamline. But David was on the local and organic trend-line, just starting to take off in Canada.

There were about twenty other players in Vancouver using pickup trucks and garages to do roughly the same thing as David. His professionalism, ability to raise capital, and steady acquisition of exhausted, underfunded small operations enabled him to become the largest—and perhaps the only profitable—home deliverer of organics in North America at that time.

The 2007 recession hit hard, and SPUD began losing a lot of money. David was able to find new investors to buy a significant position in SPUD and update the strategy. Our Renewal Funds group took the opportunity of investing further at the attractive discount valuation. SPUD carries forward now under the leadership of Peter Van Stolk, with an omni-channel approach in four Western Canadian cities. With over double the sales, a group of small retail locations, fresh juice and prepared meal divisions, sophisticated on-line ordering, warehouse fulfillment and delivery, and Millennials moving to online food shopping, SPUD is poised for big gains.

Horizon Distributors:
From Worker Co-op to Strong Independent

In the mid-'90s, CRS Worker's Cooperative owned Horizon Distributors, moving "health food" and organic groceries across Western Canada. CRS also owned a second co-op, a successful organic bakery called Uprising Breads. CRS was the largest such co-op in Canada at the time, with 55+ working owners. Grocery distributors have big warehouses stacked high with thousands of local and international products, and truck fleets filling stores across the landscape.

Renewal Partners was asked to help when CRS was at a crossroads. More capital was needed for expansion to a cash-flow-positive level of sales. Like many smaller businesses, they were never able to borrow enough money from their bank or credit union to cover new purchases and operations.

Success—growing sales and orders—can actually damage a business if they can't perform on their promises. It can be a race to find capital to keep up with orders. Capital shortages cripple fast-growth companies.

CRS looked for a way for Renewal to invest in a business where workers controlled their own wages and benefits, as well as all decisions. Instead of purchasing ownership shares, the agreed solutions was a large loan, which was risky. If things failed, the credit union's debt was ahead of us in priority for payment. But loans are always a safer way than ownership to invest, as debt repayment comes first if a company tanks.

At the time, the CRS members were in soul-searching mode. They knew their model was a tough one with which to handle the fast growth they were experiencing in the still-young organic sector. Decision-making with over fifty owners was difficult. Nerves were fraying. Ultimately they chose to sell the company to a successful organic health products entrepreneur. They made sure Renewal Partners was able to convert our debt and be part of the private company going forward. I think we were considered extra insurance for the mission and purpose staying intact. Honored by the trust, we converted our debt and became minority partners. Many co-op owners took shares alongside us, while others cashed out.

CRS was renamed Horizon, and today sales are fifteen times larger and growth robust. They are a premium name in distribution in Canada, employing hundreds, and thriving through an era of large publicly traded American distributors. We later cashed out a part of our position, and held the rest. We are proud of the company's integrity, good practices, and success. A fair estimate today is that the co-op owners who stayed in alongside us will earn an upside probably thirty times the value of original cash invested.

I'm glad all the owners shared the financial upside, and that Vancouver is such a hotbed of organics today. I do wish the co-op had found a way to continue and to thrive. Worker-owner models are an important part of the clean money revolution.

Lunapads: Honoring Blood

At a holiday craft fair in Vancouver one year I noticed an animated young woman named Madeleine Shaw. At her small booth, she was selling handmade, organic cotton menstrual pads that were washable and reusable. I was moved by her passion for overcoming menstrual shame, and by her advocacy against toxic products used for women's monthly cycles. Here was a determined feminist riposte to millennia of patriarchal suppression. Fierce passion combined with intelligence, wisdom, and relentless determination can make miracles, and Madeleine's charisma was infectious.

Over twenty billion menstrual pads and tampons go into landfills every year in North America. Madeleine wanted to change that. Renewal Partners made a small "get to know each other" investment. We wanted to see if Lunapads could fly if given a boost. Like many entrepreneurs, Madeleine was a one-woman shop doing it all, and understandably apprehensive about who we were and why we were interested. Carol's philosophy and cultural-ecological goals were a comforting answer. We made further investments and loans over the years, along with expertise and introductions. Suzanne Siemens, a professional accountant, joined later and is now CEO. Almost twenty years later, this dynamic duo are stars. With seven-figure sales and modest profits, they are mastering digital sales around the world and again testing retail aisles to see if consciousness has moved forward enough in the consumer market.

Lunapads has steady growth, a loyal base, and creates employment. I'm convinced it is yet going to have its day of financial success. But there is so much more to this story and its triple bottom line.

Since 2000, Lunapads has been providing girls and women in developing nations with cloth pads and underwear so that they can attend school or work during their period, a program they call Pads4Girls. As many as 10 percent of African schoolgirls miss up to one-fifth of their education to avoid ridicule or exclusion. That is devastating to their futures as it increases the odds that they will drop out of school, get married, and get pregnant at a young age—all of which limits their career choices. Lunapads helped grow a movement where African women manufacture low-cost pads and lined panties. Along with this they help girls and women carry on with education and normal community participation, rather than be ostracized, during monthly cycles. The Pads4Girls movement has since grown into a small industry in Africa.

Back on this continent they launched G-Day, a series of celebration and empowerment gatherings for "tween" girls, to celebrate and affirm the adolescent rite of passage. They help normalize topics that are often repressed—resulting in shaming, bullying, and other negative experiences that can harm young women as they transition through one of life's formative times.

Lunapads diverts 24 million disposable menstrual products from garbage dumps every year. It's the larger gender issues raised where the truly big wins are. Who knows what these growing legions of budding teen women will do with the rest of their lives, supported with a healthier self-image? Renewal Partners has recouped debt, and seen the financial value of our shares grow nicely. The bigger mission win is dramatic, satisfying, and of unquantifiable value.

Organic incontinence products are next. All of us may end up wanting those.

Seventh Generation: Household Detox

Seventh Generation is a well-known success for its toxic-free, Earth-friendly household products. I met founder Jeffrey Hollender through SVN, when the company was small and struggling. His platform compelled me: landfills full of plastic waste, old growth forests decimated, cancer rates accelerating. He painted a disturbing picture of the household products industry, where a factory job could easily mean a high chance of an early death from chemicals used—all to serve North Americans living the good life of cheap, dangerous, disposable products.

Most of us ignore the ingredients in cleaning products. We are unaware of their sources, how they're made, or that manufacturing effluents released into the biosphere ultimately end up in human tissue and breast milk. The privatized American health care system and pharmaceutical companies all profit from this non-virtuous cycle.

A $50,000 early bet on Seventh Generation from Renewal Partners was an easy decision for Carol and me. The company name captured our point of view. Jeffrey's drive, vision, and smarts clinched the decision.

It was a tough, monolithic sector to break into as a tiny do-gooder. Seventh Generation was an early experimenter with the direct public offering (DPO), which is currently making a resurgence. A DPO is a tool for raising money directly from your customers and local citizens through small investments. Jeffrey did it successfully but company growth outran the model. He asked the investors to convert back to a private company. Some of my friends who had invested early were frustrated by the years ticking by, and sold their interest. Carol gave her blessing for us to stick it out. The mission meant too much to us to abandon. We gambled again, and stayed in.

When Renewal Funds launched in 2008, Carol put her Seventh Generation shares in as a founder contribution to kick off the $35 million fundraising for the Renewal2 fund. It was her "skin in the game" as an owner, paving the way for others to risk their money. By then we were at well over a 50-to-1 increase of our $50,000 initial investment. Our patience had paid off. In late 2016 Seventh Generation sold for an undisclosed sum believed to be between $600 and $700 million.

We cashed out part of our holdings when the company offered to buy back shares. Al Gore and David Blood's Generation

Investment Management later came in with a large cash infusion. Seventh Generation is now a well-known brand, with products on store shelves far and wide. The company likely has a long runway of growth and profitability ahead. Our investors will make good money on this success story.

Happy Planet: Juice to Politics

Happy Planet was the first company to bring the modern fresh smoothie and juice movement to British Columbia and Canada. The two founders wanted to shift from the orange juice base that American companies like Odwalla were using and use apples (which grow very well in Western Canada) instead. What captured my heart most about Happy Planet were the two outstanding founders themselves, Gregor Robertson and Randal Ius. Smart, tenacious leaders, they exuded vision, mission, and purpose.

They wanted children and families to have clean, organic, regionally grown nutrients. Reconnecting people with local soil through clean food would, they hoped, create a cascade of goodness for coming generations. We loved the big-picture thinking and the authentic practices of the company. We made a six-figure investment. Happy Planet grew, as did their capital needs. A strategic partnership was made with a larger organic food company that later bought the business. Happy Planet now offers healthy nourishment for growing kids with their line of soups and juices.

Cofounder Gregor Robertson's second act was a big one. Today he is in his third term as mayor of Vancouver. He leads a new municipal political party, Vision Vancouver, that broke across partisan political divides to unify center, left, and green voters, and holds a majority on city council. Gregor and Vision are leading Vancouver to the global stage, with goals of being the "Greenest City in the World" and a "100% Renewable City by 2050." This green economic push is combined with a serious commitment to reconciliation and alliance with the three First Nations upon whose land Vancouver is built. In 2014 city council acknowledged that Vancouver is on "unceded traditional territory."

Vancouver is currently one of the strongest regional economies in the country—a hotbed of digital, information, film, animation, and other sunrise industries. The success of Gregor and Vision Vancouver shows what engagement in power and public policy can mean to a long-term, purposeful agenda. Building a business is excellent training for political leadership. I hope many other entrepreneurs choose to enter public service to help manage the intensity of global challenges.

And yes, we did just fine on the financial investment as well!

Guayaki: Market-Driven Restoration

Another example of a magical micro-investment for Renewal Partners was Guayaki. Coffee is a dominant global commodity worth $19 billion annually, loved for its stimulant properties and taste. It's grown throughout tropical and subtropical countries, and along with black and green tea, holds a very large portion of the stimulant drink market worldwide. Guayaki's vision was to bring a lesser-known stimulant to the global consumer. Yerba maté is the leaf of a small, shade-grown South American rainforest tree, beloved and long ritualized ("sharing the gourd") in Argentina and nearby countries. Its natural stimulant mix of caffeinoids creates a more gradual, lingering alertness than coffee, with less post-caffeine crash. It's also healthy: it contains more antioxidants, bioflavonoids, and other active compounds than green tea. By partnering with indigenous people in Argentina and Uruguay, Guayaki's shade-grown yerba maté expands rather than depletes South American forests.

The company was started in the mid-'90s by two university pals, Alex Pryor from Buenos Aires and David Karr from Northern California. They were soon joined by other surfing buddies, including Christopher Mann and Steven Karr. Charismatic, down-to-earth, and passionate, they hooked us with their idea and pied-piper charm. The founders have spread the Guayaki gospel mainly through giving away their tea drinks at events, festivals, and universities. It is gathering a loyal following among young people. It will likely grow, grow, and grow.

Guayaki is at over thirty times the sales levels achieved when we invested, and momentum is gaining speed. Recalling my Coca-Cola roots, I believe that yerba maté could eventually displace the nutritionally useless caffeinated soft drink empires, while expanding native forest culture in South America. It has the potential to break the crushing monopolies that currently control a startling percentage of all liquid sold on the planet today.

Maybe it sounds like I drank too much tea! Those of you around in 2050, see what happens. My bet is that current giants like Coke and Pepsi will be scrambling to understand customer loyalty to authentic companies selling beverages as simple as natural leaf extracts. The disruption of industrial food giants is just beginning.

To Win Some, You Have to Lose Some

Investors in riskier, early-stage companies like these ones learn a lot. You make your best bets. It rarely turns out how you expect. Leading a business is like being a farmer: there are hailstorms, drought, locusts. It's real life. Human frailties rear their heads. There is more complexity than you could possibly predict.

Entrepreneurs, when you talk to investors about your business plan, their first thought is, "We know it will never happen that way." There's no certain map in growing a new business. Clean money investing doesn't fit a stringent, military-type plan of attack. What a plan can demonstrate is that the entrepreneur can think through things strategically. Investors want operating partners who make smart plans, can adapt to the unexpected, and have real integrity. We know the unexpected is guaranteed. Our question is always, "How will this person function in a crisis?"

Investors, you win some and lose some. Be willing to lose. Understand your relationship to money, ego, and self-esteem. Do you need to win every time? Can you lose money and keep your balance? Renewal had plenty of losses. Hard work, luck, being "on trend," spreading our bets, being good partners with companies, and a growing economy all helped us to more wins than losses.

Understand the basics of your sector. Groceries have brokers, distributors, slotting fees to rent their shelf space, special discount periods, and so much more. Is it better to manufacture your own product or to outsource? Happy Planet had their own manufacturing plant. They were purists and didn't think anyone else could meet their standards. In some cases owning a plant will kill you if you're also trying to be a brand-builder and self-distributor. More big orders means more cash needed. Customers can pay late. Being starved for cash is a legitimate fear.

Business is like any craft. There is no fixed formula. Do you strictly follow your analytics, or prioritize your passion? Both can work.

In my case, organic food lit me up. My personal health issues combined with my philosophical views to lead me here. "Land and love" were my tenets. Authentic passion led me, despite gaps in my skills and knowledge. Family background helped a lot. Whatever success I have got a head start from my privilege and resources. But it also took true passion, and a willingness to take risks for what felt real and important to the future.

Mission entrepreneurs need to understand the values that drive investors who are interested in their companies. Those I've worked with probably sensed my sincerity about their cause and so were willing to invite me into their business intimacy, their secret sauce, their own long-game intentions. This comes back to working with friends, or people with whom you could be friends. Do business with people you trust. Be trustworthy yourself. Having a shared purpose beyond making money can be the crucial feature that brings you an invitation into a partnership.

It vital to remember that we are on this planet for a different purpose than accumulating vast amounts of money. It's dangerous to amass too much capital without a vision for why you're doing it. Get your values and purpose figured out. Bet incrementally. Commit to lifelong learning, both practically and in your emotional life. Get your head screwed on and your heart plugged in.

Those with wealth are today's queens, kings, dukes, and duchesses—or even mini-nation-states. It's more power than most know how to handle well. Work to master that power. Refine a vision for how your power serves the future. Find good people for partners and team. Develop personal skills so you manage the ups and downs with grace.

Renewal Partners was a powerful story machine. Great stories influence the future. Carol's has. Yours can too.

Fran Seegull

is the Executive Director of the U.S. Impact Investing Alliance, which works to increase awareness of impact investing in the US, foster deployment of impact capital, and partner with stakeholders, including government, to build the impact investing ecosystem. Formerly Fran was the Chief Investment Officer at ImpactAssets, where she headed investment management for The Giving Fund—a $275 million donor-advised impact investing fund.

How did you come to do this work?

I started as a program officer at the Peter Norton Family Foundation in the early '90s. I thought we were doing some pretty interesting and creative grant-making. But over time I started wondering how the endowment was invested—if it was consistent with the mission or unknowingly at cross-purposes with it. A 5 percent grant payout is great, but it's going to be overshadowed by the 95 percent impact that the corpus, the endowment, makes.

So I went off to Harvard Business School from '96 to '98 to figure out how to use the financial capital markets for impact. That was my transition. The work that I did at HBS looked at the nature of value: financial value, but, also economic, social, and environmental value. I came out of that work with two conclusions.

One was that there was a type of venture capital that you could practice that offered both market-rate venture returns and philanthropy-style impact. This was early days, but that has been borne out over time—Renewal Funds is an example. The second was what I suspected: accumulating wealth and then starting a foundation to use 5 percent for grants—while the main corpus is invested unconsciously without regard for impact—isn't the best way to create value overall for society.

**What drove you to want to investigate
better ways of applying for-profit capital to impact?**

The world we have created—through the capital markets as they exist, industry as it exists, and philanthropy as it exists—has put us in a tough spot environmentally and socially. We face extraordinary challenges including income inequality, population growth, education, climate change, infrastructure issues, water issues, food security. All the government aid and the philanthropy in the world are not going to create the outcomes that we seek. And so I believe that we need to align our investment capital, our portfolios—both taxable and charitable—to be in alignment with our values if we want to create a world that we want to pass onto our kids and grandkids.

The driving factors I spoke about earlier create an imperative for impact, but also an opportunity for financial returns. I do this work because I've always been terrifically motivated to make change in the world, and I think that investment capital is, and needs to be, a huge leverage point.

**Do you challenge notions of getting what is traditionally
called market rate return through impact investing?**

Impact investing can deliver a range of returns. You're hearing a lot of folks now talk about market rate because that is a way to engage more mainstream wealth advisers, asset owners, and institutional fiduciaries. The problem is that it's more complicated than that. There are some impact investment types and asset classes that you can invest in and get market rate and maybe even a premium rate of return.

There are other investment vehicles that may require concessionary returns. If you're lending money to charter schools so that they can buy a facility, it's probably not going to be market-rate return. There might be certain businesses that serve the poorest of the poor, the bottom of the pyramid, people who live on one or two dollars a day. Investing to serve these groups will likely not be market rate. So it's complicated, but market rate is a good entry point to engage folks in the dialogue.

At this point in history, where we are in this
movement toward clean money? Is it early? Is it advanced?

Religious investors centuries ago pioneered socially responsible investing (SRI), which was refraining from investing in the sin stocks—firearms, alcohol, and tobacco. Since then, in the public markets, there has been a rise of interest and allocation to environmental, social, and governance (ESG) funds that take into account those factors—picking companies or funds based on ESG scores. And there's movement toward looking at different kinds of positive ESG screens versus negative SRI screens. We're looking to a paradigm of stakeholder value that goes beyond just shareholder value. Shareholders are one kind of stakeholder, but only one. Other stakeholders related to company performance include employees, vendors, clients, the communities in which companies work, the environment.

So we're making some good headway. Larry Fink is CEO of BlackRock, the largest asset management firm in the world. He recently issued a letter—that was shared in *The New York Times* and in the Twittersphere—asking his public company managers to take ESG factors into account, both in terms of risk and reward, when managing their companies. He also called for an end to short termism, where company managers must manage to quarterly returns.

Warren Buffett recently included environmental factors in his letter to investors. When investors like Larry Fink and Warren Buffett write these letters, that suggests there's a tidal shift—a mainstreaming of this idea that value is not just based on shareholder value, but that managing stakeholder value more broadly can actually drive returns.

What are the cautionary things
to consider as impact goes mainstream?

As impact investing mainstreams, we want to make sure that the impact component is front and center. When you consider a company for investment, what are the impact practices? Is impact baked into the business model? And does the company or fund measure and report impact? The goal is achieving impact investing scale through mainstreaming, but doing so with integrity.

Can we accurately assess the true impact of investments, or do we still have a ways to go in that?

We definitely have some good tools. On the public equity side there's the SASB (Sustainable Accounting Standards Board), which seeks to require companies to report on, in SEC disclosures, certain metrics that are material by industry segment. That would be a real game-changer for public companies if they had to disclose their impact in a standardized fashion. On the private equity side we have the IRIS (Impact Reporting and Investment Standards) and GIIRS (Global Impact Investing Rating System), which is more like a Morningstar for impact.

What gives you hope for the future?

Until recently, I taught a graduate class on impact investing at USC's Marshall School of Business. My students were a mix of candidates for MBA and Masters of Science in Social Entrepreneurship degrees. We studied how to raise and deploy capital to impact ventures at various stages of growth. I remain heartened by my students' level of engagement and their deep conviction that we need to move from the incumbent paradigm of shareholder value to one of stakeholder value. This more expansive view of the world is the future.

Unleashing Philanthropy

SOME LESSONS I LEARNED from philanthropic giving also carry over to the investment world. Carol Newell has been an investor on a mission for over three decades. She is respectful and wise about capital, always prioritizing doing the right thing. Her strategy is grounded in a keen sense of global trends and a very different type of money culture—good relations, honorable actions, and money as a sacred trust for higher purpose. Carol has a proven golden touch. Her instincts and people savvy keep her well ahead of the pack, in business and also in philanthropy.

Giving away money is an under-realized subset of clean money. Philanthropy is ready for a major shakeup, and Carol's innovations contain some important insights in an area with huge potential.

There is a formal foundation sector in the United States and Canada nearing $1 trillion in total assets. Generally these funds are set up so their assets will continue growing through generations. Most foundations do that by investing their assets into traditional wealth management portfolios, similar to those which dominate most wealth ownership. The majority have no ethical screen. Those that do have some screen still have major capital invested in areas contradictory to their charitable goals.

Only a small portion of the income earned from these big assets is then spent to meet minimum, legally required percentages. The asset base itself, the principal or "corpus," is never touched. These minimums change from time to time, but they are created by public policy to be under the expected average earnings for wealthy investors—and thus to enable permanent growth of the assets. (The current US legal requirement is that the equivalent of 5 percent of the endowment, taken from investment revenues on that money, be spent annually on grant making.)

Administration, operating costs, and expenses of the foundation itself absorb a significant portion of the legally required amounts they must spend each year. After this overhead, the actual money out the door to not-for-profits is typically well under 5 percent. For a $100M endowment in a given year, that gifting amount can legally be less than $4M. Meanwhile, the endowment itself can grow over that year to $102M. Thus, the asset base is designed to grow forever.

These are tax-free fortunes mainly invested in conventional large institutions and corporations, with a blind eye to their impact on people and planet. Assets are lost to the stated mission of the foundation. That must change. Contradicting a charitable mandate in this way is morally dubious and pragmatically foolish. Imagine throwing mountains of garbage out the back door of your house while paying a few pennies to trashpickers who come with hats in hand to your front door. It's outdated public policy that begs for reform.

Tax advisors encourage wealthy people to create foundations for tax reasons first. It is secondarily a way to hold family members together over generations. The common purpose is to manage the money for continued growth. Using it to actually help the world is often a minor consideration.

Larger foundations are long-term, professionally staffed institutions. Their scale dominates priorities and strategies across the charitable sector. Their power is huge. What can be said in their favor is that they at least have serious grant-making philosophies and procedures. (Closely held family foundations, on the other hand, often provide little more than handy back-pocket social status, connection-making, and barely informed hobby fun for the people involved.) The vast majority of grants from these big institutions go to the largest charities—religious institutions, wealthy universities and private schools, hospitals, disease research, or building new wings on museums. A minor, sliver percentage of all this money goes to the environment, social justice, or addressing major societal challenges.

Those foundations that do address social issues are often opaque bureaucracies. Not-for-profits must spin their work to meet the whims of these foundations and their donors, forcing the entire sector to prioritize dancing for their dinner to win grants to pay their overhead. Reporting is generally arcane, tedious, and varies for the preferences of different foundations.

My point is that there is tremendous room for creative innovation. The world needs to unleash the charitable sector in solving big problems. Foundations are monumentally important in this. They hold the keys to huge vaults of money. Foundations should be the headline makers in the world, bringing forth solutions and acting as leverage points for our greatest global challenges.

Stories of brilliant grant-making abound. There are people already doing amazing things with foundation money. Turning these sleepy asset bases into a powerhouse vanguard of a restored planet and a regenerative economy should be a top priority. Massive unlocked potential lies dormant there. Bold experimentation is possible and should be done. If you have influence on a foundation, push edges and enliven its role as the uniquely precious steward that it can be. Insist on deploying its entire resources toward savvy, tactical, and long-term change to benefit future generations.

Carol's Endswell Foundation had a mandate to explore and model how a relatively tiny foundation could embody these premises. We pushed norms, acting as a kind of R&D laboratory to demonstrate what can be done in the clean money wheelhouse with philanthropic tools. And once again, we came out with many inspiring stories.

All's Well That Endswell

From the beginning, traditional philanthropy wasn't transformative enough for Carol. "There wasn't much focus on creating systemic change," she says. "I wanted to focus on root causes. I could see that our disposable society was leading us down a road that had a dead end. One that wastes precious resources while destroying habitat, and where financial optics ignore externalities and herald consumption just to keep the ball rolling. None of it made sense to me."

Carol directed $17 million CAD of her inheritance into the birth of the Endswell Foundation. Her passion and entrepreneur's sensibility allowed us the freedom to experiment with how it was deployed. Our shared sense of urgency to meet global challenges demanded bigger action than the typical grant-making strategy, or to settle for conservative approaches to money management. Carol's overarching goal was to deploy assets today on urgent problems.

She was willing to overspend legal baseline minimums. Rather than preserve the philanthropic asset base in perpetuity and grant small percentages per year, in 2001 she authorized the spend-down of the Endswell principal. Positive financial results extended our work over 16 years. In that time Endswell made more than 1,500 grants—along with uncounted sponsorships and scholarships— amounting to $25 million CAD.

Investing the asset base in things directly aligned with our mission increased our modest dollars. These investments included SRI-screened assets, base-building loans to not-for-profits, investment in revenue-generating subsidiaries, and social-purpose real estate projects. We helped put important pieces of land into long-term protection to protect forest habitats, respecting indigenous rights and traditional uses. We made grants, loans, and investments in and with Pivot Legal Society, Canada's leading social justice legal services organization. This enabled them to purchase secure office space in Vancouver, launch a for-profit subsidiary, and invest in financially sustaining membership growth. (When Pivot chose to sell its building, Pivot and stakeholders each made money to reinvest in social change work and grant making.)

Helping not-for-profits own real estate is valuable, and can result in an endowment-like gift. Years down the road, just like other real estate investors, they will have an asset that can build capital for their work long term. Sharing the asset base for long-term ownership deals like these can have big impact.

Our grant-making practices were designed to shift the power dynamic of grant seeker and the institution. We offered general support grants as our primary model. Those are the most precious dollars an organization can get—money for basic overhead and salaries. We wanted to be a reliable, year-on-year source of funding for not-for-profits, building capacity while reducing the looming budgetary uncertainties that can cloud mission and focus. It gave more autonomy to not-for-profit leaders. It also reduced the onerous paper burden of proposal writing and reporting. Out of a $25,000 grant, why have someone spend $5,000 in staff time to write detailed reports and accounts just to keep you happy?

We knew our passion for the hot issues of the moment needed to be balanced by funding the deeper capacity and longevity of smart people—change agents who had committed to careers of service in vital issues, rather than to making wealth for themselves. We invested in the long-term resilience and strategic abilities of these individual leaders and teams by funding them to go to trainings, workshops, and conferences.

Finally, we funded the growth of two enduring institutions in the environmental and social change sector—Tides Canada Foundation and Hollyhock's leadership institute (more about those two later).

Some of my lessons from philanthropic giving that carry over to the world of finance and investment.

+ Be collaborative with the recipient organizations. They usually know more than you about their issues.
+ Resist starting new organizations because you have "a better idea how to do it." Our egos can be self-indulgent and distract precious resources from an already money-starved field.
+ Create fewer hoops, forms, reports, and administrative costs. These hamper organizations and can drain energy. Ask for thoughtful reflection and analysis of results sparingly, and without the time-sink of long, tedious forms.
+ Make longer-term, larger commitments. Smart financial investors usually plan to increase their investments over time. Not-for-profits need similar bigger funding for large initiatives, and ongoing operational funding too, just as other enterprises do.

- Use quick-decision, low-dollar grants like you might spread compost on a garden. They grow confidence and strength for changemakers. The results can be surprisingly valuable.
- Give capacity and infrastructure support in the sectors you prioritize. Those gifts keep on giving, long after you are done. Special projects are important, but we need strong, stable institutions in the change sectors for the long term.
- Get money out the door. Consider "spending down" rather than releasing slow trickles of money. Generational wealth becomes conservative and can wind up in a dusty closet of stock market investment, making social access grants and accomplishing little.
- Bring foundation assets into alignment with the values and purpose of your grant making! Exit multinational corporate stocks and bonds, particularly those in industries that create the problems you want to address with your grant dollars. Focus and be as proud of the investment side of the asset base as you are of the grants. The impact may be far larger.
- Bank locally with credit unions, community loan funds, and other regional investment options. Who and where you bank with, geographically, matters. What are they using your money for? Look for local investments if you know how, or seek out people who do. That creates ripple effects and multiple positives by circulating money in your own community.
- Take risks. The taxpayers of your nation are subsidizing you with charitable tax breaks. Go beyond what government can do. Make it count.
- Support public policy. That can change a trillion dollars of societal priorities.

Land Legacies: The Great Bear Rainforest and More

The Great Bear Rainforest (GBR) is the world's largest remaining intact coastal temperate rainforest, where, in the words of the Nature Conservancy, it is "nearly impossible to separate the land from the sea." Stretching from northern Vancouver Island to the Alaska panhandle, at about 64,000 square kilometres, the Great Bear is larger than the state of West Virginia. It is home to immense bio-diversity: the rare white Kermode "spirit" bear, over 2,500 discrete wild salmon runs, beach-feeding wolves, threatened orca and sei whales, carbon-capturing eelgrass, and all the birds that migrate up and down the northern Pacific Flyway.

It's a little known and stunning place. One huge success that came from leveraging Carol's capital was supporting two decades of work by a scrappy coalition that won legislated protection for the Great Bear Rainforest. The alliance included environmentalists, First Nations, local communities, the timber and mining industries, and provincial and federal governments. The majority of the area is now fully protected, most now managed under ecosystem-based management practices that protect traditional uses, species, and the intact major sections of its coastal temperate rainforest. The agreement ensures decision-making, job creation, and wealth capture for the local First Nations who were, prior to colonization, among the most prosperous people on the continent.

It was a vast effort. Getting there meant integrating the interests of coastal residents, First Nations, environmental groups, government, and industry (tourism, timber, and mining, among others). The long and grueling process burnt out many people. But the GBR stands as a model from which to take lessons in protecting similar, sacred, and amazing sites across the world. It is among the largest land-protection agreements ever accomplished on the planet.

We have no idea yet the importance of prioritizing such natural areas. Which essential discoveries, or essential planetary functions, may be contributed from such vast intact geographies?

Endswell supported the process through innumerable, ongoing small grants and as a lead Canadian donor for matching $60 million in public funds. We offered office facilities, conference rooms, leadership and process support, and access to Endswell's network. Tides Canada Foundation also played a seminal, multi-faceted role, as described below. Through our not-for-profit organization, the Hollyhock Leadership Institute (HLI), we provided multi-day retreats for leaders from various sectors—with a priority focus on

First Nations—for training and haggling over a cohesive and functional overall strategy.

This approach was unique in breaking out of the traditional "not-for-profit ghetto" designed for a perpetually dependent sector. HLI helped develop skills typically reserved for the for-profit business sector and those in government relations. The goal was to help nature protectors and indigenous allies be on more equal footing with other stakeholders in terms of their skill sets, and help them gain better insight into how power works on the inside.

We put a major portion of Endswell's $25 million into BC environmental groups. The list is long and diverse. It includes the Sierra Legal Defense Fund, the Pembina Institute, Forest Ethics (now Stand), Ecotrust, West Coast Environmental Law, the Dogwood Initiative, Farm Folk City Folk, West Coast Environmental Law, CPAWS, Living Oceans, Raincoast Alliance, Sierra Club, Silva Forest, the Muskwa Kechika, BC Wild, the BC Environmental Network, Wild Salmon Coalition, Northwest Institute, Taku Watershed Alliance, Skeena Watershed Alliance, Wilderness Committee, and many others.

Activating capital to mission at this scale can have incredible effects. Endswell realized short-term goals and interventions as well as significant, lasting legacies. Among other highlights of our work in the not-for-profit sector over 18 years:

- Major funder in the BC Endangered Spaces campaign, which agitated toward protection of 12 percent of critical habitat in the province. Along with helping protect 475,000 hectares in BC's Kootenay region and 500,000 hectares in the Cariboo-Chilcotin, Carol was instrumental in the creation of Tatshenshini-Alsek Park. Nicknamed "the Tat," it links three adjacent national parks to create a 97,000-square-kilometer ecological unit, now a UNESCO World Heritage Site.

- Helping create an enabling environment for supporting First Nations in their land rights issues, along with our own decolonization awareness and learning. A powerful "reconciliation" movement has begun to take hold in BC, a land mass the size of California, Washington, and Oregon combined, where only

Jody Holmes, Project Director, Rainforest Solutions Project, on Hollyhock's role in the 20-year Great Bear Rainforest campaign:

As activists who were often resistant, hypercritical, and untrusting, we came to value the exponential strategic shifts that happened only at Hollyhock. The "Hock" was the silver bullet when all else failed or when rainforest activist coalitions needed to take space to strategize, reflect, and problem-solve thorny issues that often got lost in the day-to-day bustle of the Great Bear Rainforest campaign. And when relations between environmentalists and forest industry negotiators were at breaking point, the core group (known as the Joint Solutions Project) retreated to Hollyhock with our mediator and built a durable new strategy to birth the final phase of the Great Bear Rainforest agreements.

Solution Space. Big Dream Incubator. Conflict Resolution Portal. The combination of getting away from our cell phones and computers, spending time breaking bread, walking in the forest and along the beach together, early-morning yoga, late-evening hot tubs, and the walk through lush flower gardens and intentional beauty to the sound of the food bell announcing another spectacular meal—these never failed to work their magic on insoluble problems.

The Great Bear Agreements announced on February 1, 2016 represents a sea change in consciousness. Here, we have moved from a morphogenetic field of environmental degradation, industrial greed, separation, and devaluation of First Nations history and wisdom to an emergent consciousness where First Nations co-manage their land and resources and choices are consciously made to protect the uniquely global treasure that is the Great Bear Rainforest—and to create conservation-based economies with vital and thriving local communities. Hollyhock and its visionary leadership hosted, incubated, fed, nurtured, trained, provoked, and challenged. It made unique connections, and it brought insights that were highly instrumental in developing that sea change in consciousness.

6 percent of the land is "private." Much of the province remains as disputed ancestral territory taken by force from the original inhabitants.

- ◆ Pioneering program related investments (PRIs) and mission related investments (MRIs) via loans and equity, with a small group of foundation allies in Canada. This is another way foundations can more powerfully activate their underlying assets.

- ◆ Rejuvenating Hollyhock as a lifelong leadership learning institute. Over two thousand people participate each year in social innovation, arts and culture, well-being, and leadership programs, infusing a long-term cultural and social change ethos and practical skill set for a wise, resilient future.

- ◆ Supporting Pivot Legal Society during its crucial early years to develop into Canada's preeminent social justice law firm, addressing some of the nation's toughest challenges. Pivot is a key advocate in Vancouver's Downtown Eastside, one of Canada's poorest neighborhoods, pushing for action and policy change on homelessness, sex-trade worker safety, harm reduction, and housing. Its litigations change national policies.

- ◆ Seeing over a dozen graduates of Hollyhock Leadership Institute's programs go on to be elected to public office. There is a critical need for values-inspired citizens to seek election and become decision-makers.

Tides Canada: $200 Million to Social Change So Far

Once I understood the significance, seriousness, and instinct of Carol's vision, the first person to come to mind to ask for help was Drummond Pike.

The years following my first meeting with Drummond at Linnaea Farm on Cortes saw the blossoming of an important friendship that continues today. One of the great aspects of aging is long friendships. The evolution and influence these can have on a lifetime—all the permutations, intersections, introductions, mutual advice, and love— is precious. Drummond's heart of gold, sincere service instincts, and humble wisdom offer a rare mix of insight and inspiration.

Drummond deeply knew philanthropy and its potential. He had been an investor and board member of Working Assets (now CREDO), a pioneer in using telephone services resales to move forward social issues. He knew the emerging field of values-based investment then sprouting in the Bay Area. Many of his clients were early inventors of mission-based investing. Tides itself was paid to host and manage organizations like the Threshold Foundation and SVN, as well as many of their individual members, family foundations, and larger networks of progressive donors. That he had working knowledge of the "for-profit with a mission" front edge of business was unusual and perfect. There weren't many other people with that exotic blend of expertise.

Drummond is a heroic visionary in the history of clean money. He joined us as an expert resource to support Carol and team in brainstorming and planning the evolution of the Renewal and Endswell strategies. His passion for meaningful change were essential to any success we may have had. Norine MacDonald, charitable lawyer, then Laura Campobasso, organizational development professional, and Jim Morrisey, genius tax accountant, were essential parts of our team as well.

We knew that Drummond's San Francisco-based organization, the Tides Foundation, contributed a whole other dimension to the not-for-profit social change sector in the United States, offering tools, advice, programs, and overall capacity and infrastructure. By 1996 Tides was two decades old, and already large and influential. It had been breaking new "social enterprise" ground in charity support ever since Drummond founded it "off the side of his desk."

Tides helped social change donors with problem-solving, and served them with meticulously reliable financial services. It grew from there, reaching grant transaction volumes well into the nine figures annually.

Quiet, professional, client focused, Tides handled the complex paperwork required for diverse grant making. It helped match clients with recipient organizations that were harder to find and smaller, with newer strategies. Like a national community foundation or an alternative United Way, Tides would take on the tough challenges in charity and help funders get the job done. Through great legal counsel, indefatigable patience, and smart leaders—Drummond, Ellen Friedman, Gary Schwartz, China Brotsky, Cynthia Rowland, Tom Sargeant, and many others—Tides brought a small revolution to progressive philanthropy over the years. It drove the concept of client support to a next level and proved that a social enterprise fee-for-service model could make financial sense.

A core Endswell strategy became building a Canadian version, the Tides Canada Foundation (TCF). We would license the name, review the original American model, and then design for the Canadian context. TCF launched in 2000 as a fully independent organi-

Craig Reinarman, a former University of California emeritus research professor in sociology who has focused on social justice issues for more than 25 years, spoke at a Distinguished Alumni Award ceremony for Drummond Pike at UC Santa Cruz in 2016.

In the 1970s, I did some work on prison reform and among the few philanthropists willing to fund such work was the Tides Foundation and this guy Drummond Pike. Youth unemployment in the early 1980s—again, Tides and Drummond Pike. Environmental justice? Tides and Drummond Pike. Who is this guy?! Drug policy reform? Drummond Pike again.

Economists often speak of "the multiplier effect," the idea that an increase in investment or spending stimulates other economic activity that in the end produces a greater increase in overall national income than the initial amount. Well, Drummond invented new organizational forms of philanthropy that created extraordinary synergy, making it possible for donors to achieve much more in combination than they ever could have by themselves. So it's fair to say that Drummond Pike is a walking, talking multiplier effect.

zation, with Endswell providing some back-office support until it gained stability. Drummond and I each served on that founding board for ten years, until it was well established. Already it has facilitated over $200 million in donor contributions to social and environmental causes, a large amount in the Canadian context.

TCF was the independent third-party manager and clearing-house for much of the Great Bear Rainforest funds. We gradually shifted all Endswell's grant-making over to TCF, saving significant administration costs due to the full-time capacity and team there. Carol launched Canada's first dedicated social justice fund at TCF, with $1 million to match other grants in that category. Major innovations and various First Nations initiatives were made possible or optimized through its nimble and inventive willingness to help.

Today TCF takes on large national initiatives in Canada, from Pacific Ocean marine protection to supporting the people, culture, and ecology of the North, all of which are often overlooked in the race for resource exploitation and military supremacy. Indigenous food security, urban neighborhood social services capacities, the creation of the national Freshwater Alliance, and early climate leadership are among the many important contributions of Tides Canada. In 2014 TCF established Change Capital, to give donors access to a "best of sector" impact investment portfolio for their charitable dollars.

Make Money Matter

Carol's steady, multi-year support of Tides Canada and the Holly-hock Leadership Institute have created long-term legacies, new to the existing landscape, that will have positive influence in Canada and beyond after we are long gone.

Others with significant excess money can do this work too. While this book focuses more on for-profit concerns than charitable dollars, it's important to see that when applied strategically via a larger theory of change, not-for-profit grants are a crucial component of an ecosystemic, integrated deployment of capital for social good.

So are the investment policies and creativity of the asset bases themselves! Remember that one.

We are grateful to be part of this unfolding process of regional change, rippling across a broader landscape. If you have similar opportunities, pursue them passionately, fearlessly, and with due diligence to all the legal and financial complexities.

And when the time is right, be bold and share your stories. Set aside humility and jump into the spirit of sharing. We need brave, unique stories of how people have accelerated big change. That advice goes beyond telling stories of unleashed capital. Art, culture, and community efforts all inspire others. Extraordinary accomplishments can come when deeply held values, sense of purpose, drive for meaning, and unleashed creativity combine: great documentary films, books, conferences, workshops, relationships, and regional events.

The roadmaps you leave will help others pass us on the path and take things ever further. How else will we rev up the clean money revolution?

If an inexplicable wind fills your sails, and you use that wind to create something beautiful and transformative, tell others about it.

Drummond Pike

founded Tides Foundation in 1976. Tides was the first dedicated host for donor-advised funds and collaborative-giving programs, and it currently supplies many needs in the progressive community through seven related corporate entities. Drummond now consults with several principals on philanthropic and financial matters and is a Director with Ultra Capital, a project finance impact investing firm in San Francisco focused on sustainable real assets (water, renewables, organic agriculture, and waste). His board work includes Working Assets (CREDO Mobile), the Environmental Working Group, and the Institute for New Economic Thinking.

How does philanthropy need to modernize?

Philanthropy is a tired, timid field, more focused on "metrics" than impact. To really contribute, it must become what Jim Josephs, past CEO of the Council on Foundations, once described as society's "R&D department." It should be characterized by rapid experimentation, frequent failure, and a hunger for new ideas. Too often philanthropy shuts the door on new or unfamiliar voices and avoids controversy.

A particular failing is with investments. It's often said one should maximize investment returns unfettered by values, and then do wonderful things with the proceeds. The toil of a grant-maker should focus on the uses to which money is put, not how it is being accumulated. The problem, of course, is that many ways in which people make money—foundations included—actually cause or further many of the problems we encounter today.

Why should charities and foundations prioritize the full impact of their investments?

Institutional integrity suggests a foundation's stated purposes, like environmental goals or alleviating poverty, should be honored

throughout its operations. Turning a blind eye to investment policies can undermine a foundation's mission. Oil and gas investments
support an industry that fuels climate change. Some hedge funds
move jobs offshore to pay lower costs. For foundations working on
climate change or poverty, such investments clearly conflict with
mission.

Can you name any examples of base assets being leveraged for charitable purposes?

For many years, I've argued to donors to think about investment
as well as grant making to achieve their goals. A great example
occurred with a significant Tides donor interested in increasing
voter engagement. Surveying groups working on tools in the field,
we found a start-up called Catalist that was assembling voter files,
commercial data, and a delivery system for organizers on the ground.
On a deep look, we concluded that investment in the Catalist platform would be the best use for funds. Over a period of several years,
working with this donor, Tides invested several million dollars in
developing the company's tools that are now the dominant set used
by voter registration and public interest advocacy groups all across
the country.

What can trustees of foundations do to activate their charitable assets with their vision and mission?

Any fiduciary should periodically reflect on how well the institution's current activities match its underlying purposes. They should
examine asset allocation and manager performance, and how
managers' investment policies support the foundation's vision and
mission. An easy way to achieve this is to hire an outside reviewer
familiar with ESG investing to undertake an independent look. It
wouldn't cost much and would provide the kind of perspective and
thought process that so many need and want.

What is the role of divestment in the shift to clean money?

The remarkable story of fossil fuel divestment is adding to the
tremendous shifts in the marketplace we're seeing today. The "fossil

fuel free" (FFF) approach to asset management found its legs initially in opposition to coal, the dirtiest and most problematic fuel. Early adherents avoided the losses caused by the slow demise of Big Coal, despite political protectors holding out hope for the yet-to-be-invented "clean coal" technology.

Both domestic and international agreements and legal processes are leading us away from unfettered use of fossil fuels. We'll either leave it in the ground, or accept huge rises in sea level within a relatively short period of time. This idea of "stranded assets" combined with the industry's continuing head-in-the-sand investment in exploration has caught the attention of many long-term investors, as it should.

Short-term politics aside—and that's a big aside—it seems inevitable that we will continue the rapid shift to renewable energy. If you are investing for long-term stability, going FFF is making more and more sense.

Where is this all going in the big picture for investors?

What it is all boiling down to is a different understanding of our future. Growth for growth's sake is no longer enough, nor does it speak to young people who are coming of age in an awareness of climate change. A commitment to clean money or sustainability-based investing carries us back to the imperative to preserve the commons: the land, air, and water upon which human survival depends.

There are options in every asset class you can imagine that reflect clean money values. In venture, there are emerging technologies that can move the needle toward energy efficiency and away from fossil fuel reliance. In private equity, there are plenty of opportunities to support organic agriculture, renewables, and turning wastewater into energy and productive material.

In private debt, there are myriad opportunities for project finance that support these emerging clean industries. In the public markets, it's literally getting crowded in the passive area—ETFs and mutual funds—that help investors with both negative and positive screens. And almost every major investment firm has acquired or is developing capacity for ESG and sustainability-based investing.

Goldman Sachs and Bank of America–Merrill Lynch are both great examples of this. It doesn't take a genius to conclude we are not far away from the "tipping point" where sustainability-based investing becomes the norm. It just makes sense.

Clean Money
Emergence

THE REVOLUTION IS HAPPENING. Trend lines are clear. Cleaner food, services, transportation, energy, buildings, and money are gaining traction rapidly. We are beginning the shift from what Marjorie Kelly calls "the extractive economy" to a "generative" one:

> Generative ownership designs are about generating and preserving real wealth, living wealth, rather than phantom wealth that can evaporate in the next quarter. They're about helping families enjoy secure homes. Creating jobs. Preserving a forest. Generating nourishment out of waste. Generating broad well-being.[41]

Trillions of dollars have begun shifting from the most destructive practices into more generative ones. The investment and wealth management industries, vast and entrenched, are among the hardest sectors to change. The clean money sector of the industry is still beginning, testing new financial products and language with clients. Yet the signs of change are plentiful and gaining momentum.

Entrepreneurs and investors from places like the Social Venture Network, RSF Social Finance, Toniic, and PlayBIG have been huge factors in the growth of clean money, especially in the private equity world. In the public equity sphere, socially responsible investing (SRI)—rating and screening out the worst companies based on ethics and impacts—has been a major component of the shift to a generative economy.

The Rise of SRI

In the early '90s Carol Newell's funds were managed by Genus Capital, a boutique wealth management firm in Vancouver. SRI screens were emerging in Europe and the United States, led by pioneers like Joan Bavaria, founder of Trillium Asset Management, Joyce Haboucha at Neuberger Berman and now Rockefeller, and George Gay and Steve Schueth of First Affirmative Financial Network. Other standouts include Domini, Walden, Clean Yield, US Trust, and Progressive Asset Management.

Carol was compelled by the idea of filtering the worst actors out of her stock market investments. Genus had limited capacity to evaluate the environmental and social performance of public equities. This new research burden, and its philosophical underpinnings, had not been a part of existing financial analysis. Early adopter mutual funds in North America gave a few limited, higher-cost options, the first screens mostly focusing on opting out of "sin" categories like weapons, cigarettes, alcohol, gambling, and environmental fines. In Canada the options were even slimmer: Ethical Funds, Meritas, Clean Yield, and a few others. These were mutual funds, not full service wealth management, which lagged.

Most wealth managers were still rolling their eyes at such do-gooder thinking. In fairness, they were captured by the financial product mix built by their own institutions. The idea of researching public companies and rating them based on new, additional indicators—carcinogenic products, leadership diversity, desecrating indigenous cultures for natural resources, environmental crimes, bribing foreign governments or other practices—was considered pie-in-the-sky. How could you select for "cleaner companies," reducing your total universe of large corporations, and make a similar financial return compared to a broader diverse portfolio that was intentionally "values blind" to the actual culture and practices of the company?

The job of wealth managers was to maximize financial return, the argument went, and not to be moral police. Why waste energy on this woolly-headed idea? Nice idea, client, but the world is too complex for such nuances. Just make money.

That was the orthodoxy of the day. It was not easy to break. You might call it the Friedman Effect: Milton Friedman was one of America's preeminent 20th-century economists, who in 1970 famously, or infamously, wrote a *New York Times* op-ed titled "The Social Responsibility of Business Is to Increase Its Profits." Friedman scoffed at any objectives beyond naked profit, and painted ethical approaches to commerce as part of a socialist threat to American freedom.* In that widely influential article you can see the origins of the long neoliberal hangover that SRI was helping people shake off.

As SRI questions continued to arise in their offices, they repeated the liturgical mantra: "Money is neutral. Make as much as you can, and then do good things with the proceeds." We found that philosophy depressing. Carol was not interested in exploiting people and planet just to give away a slice of the earnings. How could we choose to be blind to damage and sleep well at night?

I think about Jim Crow culture and public policy in the South when I grew up. Good people felt bad about it and saw it as unjust, but went along quietly. They had their reasons: comfort; fear of the unknown; an inability to envision, or believe in, alternatives. Rationalizing the status quo is always easier than striking up uncomfortable conversations and pushing people to see or act differently.

It's hard to point out to the emperor that he has no clothes.

When you start to question the system you find structural obstacles. In the clean economy transition, laws and regulations can

---

* "When I hear businessmen speak eloquently about the 'social responsibilities of business in a free-enterprise system,' I am reminded of the wonderful line about the Frenchman who discovered at the age of 70 that he had been speaking prose all his life. The businessmen believe that they are defending free enterprise when they declaim that business is not concerned 'merely' with profit but also with promoting desirable 'social' ends; that business has a 'social conscience' and takes seriously its responsibilities for providing employment, eliminating discrimination, avoiding pollution and whatever else may be the catchwords of the contemporary crop of reformers. In fact they are—or would be if they or anyone else took them seriously—preaching pure unadulterated socialism. Businessmen who talk this way are unwitting puppets of the intellectual forces that have been undermining the basis of a free society these past decades."[42]

block progress. Many regulations are written to serve special interests. Other times change is blocked by a lack of visibility, where the dark consequences of our economic actions are hidden in faraway places. We end-use consumers and investors understandably prefer to trust professionals around complex topics, and we often have no idea what realities are behind the products they're buying on our behalf. You could be funding oppression of indigenous peoples, toxic dumping, or slavery. Examples of these are embedded in the supply chains of many large profitable companies in the world today. Annual reports to shareholders focus on other aspects of the business, ones designed to boost their stock price. Senior executives, big financial houses, and investors focus on the allure of the highest return rate.

Residential schools for First Nations. Segregation. Debtors' prisons. These mass tragedies and many other outdated norms should remind us to not get too comfortable in our assumptions about what is done in our names. We need to understand what we are invested in or supporting with our money, and challenge practices that we know are wrong. Modern digital information makes it easier to know what our money is doing, and to search out better alternatives. We have weaker excuses now; "I didn't know" has become less convincing. We have access to vast information, as do our managers. Our job is to ask questions and give direction. Those who own large amounts of capital can afford to be informed about their money. At the very least, we can place our money with a manager with proven commitment and success that offers cleaner money as a first assumption. We have a moral responsibility to do so.

Historically a wealth manager's sole mandate has been to make more money for those who have it. We need to expand that mandate, so that money managed for personal security is also managed with an eye to the greater wealth of the world. If that sounds foolishly naïve today, it won't in twenty years. Maybe sooner. Sadly, the "make all you can, then give some away" view remains prevalent. Close friends believe it. Good people of all kinds do. Perhaps the reason is because most of us only see minimal, under-proven options.

That's why the financial sector is so ripe for innovation and building cleaner products. More successful models are needed for proofs of concept. This has been true for many years.

In Canada in the early '90s, the SRI approach was hampered by a lack of available research as much as ideology. The pioneering Social Investment Organization (SIO) led by Eugene Ellman (now the Responsible Investment Association, led by Deb Abbey), was the small Canadian gathering of SRI advisors who began the conversation.

Carol pushed back against polite brush-offs from wealth managers. Aware of the American advances in socially screened portfolios, she stubbornly insisted on a deeper look. We brought our Genus manager to New York City to meet with Joyce Haboucha, a forward-thinking early SRI advocate. Joyce later became board chair of the Social Venture Network and a leader for the Rockefeller family's shift toward values-aligned portfolio management. She provided professional credibility and thus validation to Genus that SRI was a legitimate, realistic option.

Realistic, but not easy. As noted, the central challenge was that in-depth research of each company listed on the Toronto Stock Exchange (now called TSX) didn't yet exist in a useable form for wealth managers. We began a search into the state of screening tools in Canada. We were directed to a Toronto firm led by Michael Jantzi. They were about halfway through a high-quality, professionally researched assessment of TSX listings. Their rating system weighted key screening issues for publicly traded Canadian companies. With a push from Carol, Genus became Michael's third contract. Using his data, Genus created a screened equities fund for us, keeping it quiet in the back office—testing proof of concept before risking their reputation on this new product category.

Sustainalytics: Clean Investing Pioneer

Michael's dream was cleaner money. He believed capitalism could drive societal good. As a determined values-driven entrepreneur, his gamble was a question: could a research product pay the bills *and* ultimately help shift massive money from bad actors to better companies? "I had long believed that corporations usurped any stakeholders in terms of their impact. If we were going to change their behavior, it would be through the capital markets," says Michael. That dogged determination to prove a new idea is at the core of many successful entrepreneurs. They stick with it.

Michael's "aha" moment around his life purpose had come through a CBC public radio report on SRI in the late '80s. A recent economics grad, he wanted to bring SRI to Canada, which he did by launching Jantzi Research. "A lot of people told me I was crazy," Michael recalls. "I told them to get out of my way."

Competitive and strong-willed, Michael was a pioneer. But his drive to reform investing was stymied early on by a pressing need for cash. Carol and I had knocked on his door to see if he wanted an outside investor. Michael was wary of "vulture capital"—and of losing control. He needed to trust our buy-in, patience, and shared commitment to his mission. These were fair concerns. Companies can lose their mission when driven by the growth agendas of outside partners. Michael did his due diligence on "Left Coast" Carol and Joel, and gambled on us. We invested a six-figure amount to complete the research of the entire TSX. Today he credits Renewal as crucial to the long-term survival and success of his endeavor.

Jantzi Research was central to the growth of the social screening movement in Canada. In 2007, when RBC* became the first major Canadian bank to offer investors the option of SRI funds, it was in partnership with Jantzi. When Barclays iShares—the world's most extensive family of Exchange Traded Funds (ETFs)—launched the first socially responsible ETF in Canada, it was in coordination with Jantzi. Michael expanded globally through a merger with Sustainalytics and Triodos Bank in the Netherlands. Sustainalytics, with Michael as CEO, is one of the few remaining independent research firms in the world. Most others were purchased by large conventional finance firms.

---

* RBC now manages many large SRI accounts, partly through the leadership of another old friend, Tom Van Dyck, who manages a big book at RBC out of San Francisco. Tom's clients include leading-edge charitable foundations and private clients helping push the Divest Invest movement.

This story has several happy endings. The Genus gamble on Jantzi's SRI screening gave them a pioneering approach that landed them steady new clients. They eventually announced their SRI offerings publicly and proudly. Carol and Genus have a successful relationship to this day. They are now an SRI leader in Canada, and a pioneer in other advanced products. By 2015 Genus built one of Canada's first "fossil fuel free" investment funds. These types of successes will continue driving managers globally to bet on new products that serve the growing legions of values-based investors.

Pushing Managers for Clarity and Values

SRI is now offered by the largest wealth management firms in the world. It's feeding the roots of the new economy. It's a "gateway drug" to investing with consciousness and love.

In a 2015 poll by J. P. Morgan of a thousand high-net-worth investors, 71 percent said they were interested in SRI. Statistics from the US Social Investment Forum (US SIF) show that by the start of 2016, over $8.7 trillion was invested according to SRI strategies. One in five dollars under professional management in the United States is involved.[43] These are incredible figures relative to what was going on twenty years ago. They demonstrate the tremendous scale of what is possible in the next decades. Large companies face pressures from multiple directions now. Global awareness will only push this trend further. Massive capital will flow toward SRI.

You know you're winning when marginalized ideas become mainstream. The change cycle takes time. I predict that by 2050 sin funds that exploit industries with big negative externalities (military, tobacco, fossil fuel, and others) will be the minority, chosen only by the cynical investor. Clean money will be the norm.

Carol's example shows the power of sticking to your principles. Through her insistence that her managers provide options for her values, taking risks with her investment dollars, and trusting her vision, everyone won. She made money, too.

Staying true to your values is powerful, particularly in the face of skepticism about what you know in your bones to be correct. If you believe in something that doesn't exist widely yet, and you push for it, you help make it happen. Put your own money at risk: the results may surprise you.

Those of us with "more than enough" have a rational responsibility. When we see the need for change, we have the power to influence that change. Do you know where your money is? Do you ask wealth

Leslie Christian is head of Outside Investments, a division of NorthStar Asset Management.

Increasing numbers of wealthy people, not very many but some, are waking up to the illogical assumptions of our current financial system. As more people of high net worth ask questions, and are courageous enough to buck the system that's made them wealthy, there is more opportunity for them to move to equitable and sustainable management of their money.

My challenge to the wealthy is to resist the belief that you have to have layers of so-called experts between you and your investments. I think we have too much financial engineering and not enough on-the-ground business leadership and expertise. There is an emerging opportunity for a new breed of advisor— those who have the knowledge, experience, and desire to engage at a personal, transparent, and direct level.

One way to think about this is that we need to move to a distributed economy. Distributed energy, logistics, information, manufacturing, and distributed *value*. One of the things I emphasize more and more with my clients is the beauty of investing smaller chunks of money in distributed economy projects and companies. Yes, we have to keep track, and we have to do the due diligence—but it is worth the effort and money. In addition to the direct benefit of the investment, clients are shifting fees to advisors who offer meaningful services and away from the Wall Street drive to consolidate, aggregate, securitize, and depersonalize the world.

advisors questions about the practices of companies they support with your dollars? Do you make your values clear and insist your advisors act upon them?

If you are metaphorically "patted on the head" when you talk about values, consider another manager. Condescension is not a legitimate response. Demand clarity, and speak your truth. You can help your manager by empowering them toward ethical investing. And if you see few advances in their thinking about screens and values-based investing, notice that and think about moving your money.

If you've ever felt embarrassed because you can't understand your money manager's language, make them explain things that confuse you. Demand translations of obscure language and terminology designed to wear you out and make you believe in their expertise. If your advisors can't explain in clear English what they're doing and why, you should think twice about giving them your money. In Michael Lewis's nonfiction book on the subprime meltdown, *The Big Short*, one man talks about going to investment meetings with his boss, Steve Eisman:

> "Steve's fun to take to any Wall Street meeting. Because he'll say 'Explain that to me' 30 different times. Or 'Could you ex-plain that more, in English?' Because once you do that, there's a few things you learn. For a start, you figure out if they even know what they're talking about. And a lot of times, they don't!"[44]

Clean Money Mainstreams

Big players are testing the waters. In 2015, the world's largest asset manager, BlackRock Capital, launched the BlackRock Impact US Equity Fund, a mutual fund "to invest in measurable social and environmental outcomes while seeking to generate competitive financial returns." It's a good early indicator. The Global Sustainable Investment Alliance (GSIA) estimates that "sustainable investment assets" grew 25 percent globally between 2014 and 2016. Impact investing is the fastest-growing segment, achieving a 56.8 percent compound annual growth rate in the same time frame.[45]

Other big signals:

◆ In 2017, Bain Capital launched its $390-million Double Impact Fund, with managing director Deval Patrick calling it "a small first fund."[46]

◆ Prudential has committed to building a $1-billion impact investing portfolio, up from $500 million in 2016.[47]

◆ J.P. Morgan has invested $68 million in 11 impact funds. They claim through these to have improved the livelihoods of 44 million people in "low-income and underserved communities."

◆ Goldman Sachs, which oversees more than $1.1 trillion in assets, acquired Imprint Capital in 2015. Imprint has been enormously successful as a leading, first-mover impact investing and research firm for values-aligned investors. Goldman wants to capture this new market. Their move will signal other giants that the premise is valid. These big players manage most of the wealth in the world, and we need them to want to invest in clean money.

◆ Tech entrepreneur Marc Andreessen, who in 2012 said "I would run screaming from a B Corp," now invests in B Corps through his $4-billion VC firm Andreessen Horowitz.

◆ The rise of funds such as Aavishkaar India and Elevar Equity, as Jean Case of the Case Foundation noted in a 2015 *Forbes* article, "are providing impressive rates of return by backing entrepreneurs serving the billion plus customers at the base of the pyramid."

Today, many boutique wealth managers offer versions of values-aligned venture capital funds, and new wealth managers are rapidly entering the field. Their offerings range from ultra-high net worth customized portfolios to more accessible $250,000 minimums, and offer a variety of strategies. A handful of US examples: Green Alpha Advisors, Change Finance, First Affirmative, and BSW Wealth Partners (all in Colorado); CapRock Group (Boise and Seattle); Tom Van Dyck at RBC and Sonen Capital (San Francisco);

Tiedemann Wealth Management and Veris Wealth Partners (both with offices in New York, San Francisco and beyond); and North-Star Asset Management and Fresh Pond Capital (both in Boston).

More good news is that products for lower-net-worth clients are expanding, like Calvert's exciting platform that allows investments for social good starting at twenty dollars. Crowdfunding is opening up even more new arenas.

The meme is seeded. We do not want our money to damage people, nature, or the future. We're asking questions: where is our money, and is it causing damage? We want to know it's improving things for those coming after us. We want better solutions. We want to see a major boost in clean economy careers.

Wars were historically the major catalysts of economic growth. Destroy a nation or city, and then the rebuilding creates big economic activity and wealth flows. The spoils go to the winners. We have destroyed enough through war and consumption. The opportunities now lie in regeneration. That regeneration is going to take trillions of dollars. Going through every part of our modern lives and reengineering them through a lens of respect for planetary limits and just human needs will unlock new products and industries that will help calm and heal our world.

This change will take a wave of young leaders who hear the call of this new career path—using capitalism to build a just, resilient human presence on the planet. Its economic rewards will be plentiful. To all of you considering careers in finance, or who are responding to the call to change the world: there is a boom about to happen. The clean money revolution is going to change everything. There is much to invent, money to be made, and tremendous satisfaction to be had. You can still get in early, be a leader, and make a major contribution with your life. Join with the activists and others who question authority. Find people with digital smarts who can bring the message of change to the world.

My friend Danny Kennedy is cofounder of Sungevity and now a director at the California Clean Energy Fund (CalCEF). He estimates that the $7 trillion predicted by Bloomberg New Energy

Finance to go into renewable electricity generation over the next 25 years is not nearly enough to respond to global warming. To adequately keep temperatures below 2°C (3.6°F) he believes we need to invest over $12 trillion in the next quarter century. To hit the new 1.5°C (2.7°F) target for climate, nations will require even more investment. (For more on some possible numbers for investing in a sustainable future, see Chapter 10.)

If such numbers sound impossible, they're not. As Danny wrote in a 2016 article for Greentech Media, "That's no trivial amount of money, but it's a goal that is eminently achievable. To put it in perspective, the average amount the entire world needs to invest in clean electric power annually to hit the 2-degree target is only 7 percent more than American citizens invest in car loans each year." These changes will pay off major long-term dividends. Overhauling the entire economy is labor intensive. Solar energy, as Danny points out, yields far more jobs per dollar than fossil fuel energy does.

Danny represents one of the powerful subsets of the clean money businesses. He and other former front-line activists are inventing enterprises that make money aggregating massive bases of consumers who care. They are making good profits that they can then deploy into other such businesses. They are leaders and will be a force to be reckoned with.

We can follow their example by being bold in this revolution: making what we do with money a high priority in our moral and ethical life.

Find your own alignment between your money and your values, and bear in mind the challenges of perfection. Nuances and details are important. There are no perfect people, no perfect organizations. It's easy to to be an expert armchair quarterback, quick to find fault and be outraged at the imperfections we see. Frustration is understandable, but the best way to begin—is to begin. Track what your money supports and what is hurt by it. If you're an investor, go beyond the brand name of your wealth manager. Find advisors whose values and perspectives you trust. Insist that your questions about your money are prioritized. Apply that lens to your bank or credit union, to where you shop, and what you buy.

Private Equity Gets on Board

The clean money revolution needs investors, entrepreneurs, corporations, foundations, engaged citizens, and conscious purchasers. "Impact" investing is a big tent within this massive transformation. We need everything from manufacturing clean energy infrastructure at scale to micro-financing Latin American agriculture cooperatives. Thoughtfully invested public securities are important. Directing private equity investments toward the mission-based entrepreneurs who are reinventing every part of the economy is even more exciting for me.

I love the early stage private equity world. It's full of raw smarts and heartfelt passion, a kind of rich intertidal zone of our economy where creativity, excitement, and possibility thrive. It's a learning extravaganza.

Public securities, on the other hand, are only pieces of paper traded on perceived value. The money doesn't go directly to the company. It's a conceptual transaction done at a distance. Public markets are a casino where hundreds of millions of people are betting on assumed value, based on projections and quarterly reports. When a business shows lower net earnings one quarter, analysts are disappointed and the stock price can plunge. They then start sacrificing values to cut costs and push the stock price back up. Or something happens in global commodities or national political conditions—a natural disaster, a war, a market hiccup—and a stock declines or soars.

Public securities investing creates little real value. It does create wealth for owners, including executives, if they can push stock prices higher. Once the initial capital of a stock offering has reached the company, the rest of us are just trading paper and betting on strategies usually opaque to us. This is so disembodied relative to helping a mission-based company expand its offerings within a regenerative economy. With direct investing in early-stage private companies the capital goes directly toward business effectiveness.

Investing in public markets is a valuable tool for liquidity. It can also be an interesting intellectual exercise. You can be a student of various movements of commerce and global economic developments, and then bet on your analysis. If you bet right, through luck or intellect, you can win big. While that may be fun, I think we can do much better. We need to put that kind of intellectual curiosity and pleasure to work on meaning and purpose. Imagine if all the ingenuity that went into creating the CDOs and arcane derivatives that caused the 2008 crash had instead been directed at growing the clean economy? The world might look very different to millions of people only ten years later.

Public equities investing can also backfire. Not only in the short term, and not just for emergent companies, but also on seemingly safe, long-term investments in apparently stable companies. Uncontrollable global events, market realities, and changed perceptions can wipe out value. Just ask anyone who invested in the coal industry in the past decade. As my colleague Leslie Christian reminds us, "Modern Portfolio Theory (MPT) is just that—a theory. It ignores dramatic risks, and assumes externalities will remain off the balance sheet." What is considered a norm today can be the opposite tomorrow. You can still have fun betting your money, but if you do, heed Leslie's words. There is a lot of risk being ignored in most public company reporting, accounting, and assumptions.

From a clean money standpoint, the best argument for public securities is shareholder activism. This means teaming up with others who have shares in the same company to influence corporate decisions. It also can offer a better look at some of those under-reported risks at annual shareholder meetings.

Shareholder activism is one of the great contributions that the SRI movement has brought thanks to early innovators like Joan Bavaria and Michael Jantzi, and thanks to the ongoing efforts of people like Tom Van Dyck. Tom is famous for proving financial success while adhering to strong activism and "best of class" rigor. His decades of shareholder activism have taken it to a whole next level of toughness, fearlessly going to the microphone with resolutions that challenge the policies of damaging corporate offenders. He is one of the leaders in an organized movement of shareholders across the world that has serious influence in bringing bad practices to account.

With private equity, you make a direct investment in the company, and at a much earlier stage, long before a big public offering may arise. At this stage you're dealing with the founding entrepreneurs and decision-makers, perhaps helping define and shape the DNA of a company. The entrepreneurs are not influenced by traders and institutions buying big blocks of shares. You are directly placing bets that help a company make a meaningful product or offer a service that makes the world better.

Mission Venture Capital: Investing for Change

I met Paul Richardson in 2002 through a mutual friend. At the time he was a managing partner in a Toronto law firm, and after fifteen years in that business he wanted to move to more personally satisfying career. Renewal was organizing a land transaction on Cortes Island with a large timber company. The land was important to the community and our goal was to protect it from a clear cut. Paul's integrity, values, and smarts were clear. It was obvious he would be a better negotiator than me, and I asked him to jump in, which he did.

After successive visits to complete the deal (which worked out very well, but that's a story for another book), the British Columbia coast worked its magic, enticing Paul to relocate. In 2003 he and his family moved to Vancouver. Paul helped Renewal with some legal needs and investment transactions. He has a lifelong passion for the natural world and environmental causes, and we later recruited him to a key role on the Great Bear Rainforest deal. He worked with a small team to structure and navigate the financing and protection agreement between First Nations, the BC government, the federal government, environmentalists, and local communities. Our group was committed to and extensively involved with the Great Bear initiative, and we were thrilled that Paul helped drive that historically significant negotiation.

Carol, Martha, Pam, and I were impressed by Paul's skills. Soft-spoken and easygoing, he has a keen eye for details and a commitment to exacting background research. He has a quality that is hard to name—an intuitive sense for seeing how complex circumstances can reach harmony and move forward. It's a rare and valuable skill. In 2007 we began discussing a new Renewal fund to attract outside investors to put capital into mission-based companies. The fund, seeded with money from Carol—and some smaller dollars from Paul and others of us—would have majority outside capital. We three, plus team members Mike Cormack, Nicole Bradbury, and Pamela Chaloult, made up the management company partners. Paul became CEO and president and I became the chair. We described our work as "social venture capital," later changed to "mission venture capital"—attempting to make clear our differentiator. The premise was still very new. Our tag line was "Investing for Change."

The Renewal Funds team would scout, assess, and do the diligence on companies in which to invest. Our focus was on US and Canadian businesses, as that's a big enough geography to travel. The premise was that organic food and environmental innovations were seeding new industries where good money could be made—and that these new-economy companies, and the greening direction of mainstream culture generally, were still being overlooked by capital. We hoped the idea would be attractive to investors. It was a giant, "low hanging fruit" opportunity. We believed that pulling off this new kind of fund would help catalyze an emergent wave of new financial thinking that still needed proof of concept. We wanted to be a seed pod for the clean money revolution.

"We saw all these young companies and not many people putting money into them," recalls Paul. "The terms that people are all using now really didn't exist. Impact investing wasn't being talked about. Mission investing was being discussed a little but it was much more theoretical."

Our goal in Renewal Funds was to transform the norms of investing and prove investments could focus on doing good while making money. "We are living in a very unsustainable way on this planet and we've got to change things dramatically," says Paul. "There are many different ways one can make a contribution to that change and you've just got to figure out what your best possible contribution is. Mine is working with purposeful companies in trying to determine whether they're good investments, and then work hard to make sure that things work out."

We hit the road for two and a half years, doing seemingly endless private meetings, panels, events, conferences, and all the communications that go with it: newsletters, press releases, emails, social media. Sweating and fretting, we built upon early commitments by truly brave spirits. By closing time we'd assembled $35 million. The investors were roughly half from Canada and half from the United States, with a few from Europe and beyond. We also gained commitments from a few edge-pushing charitable foundations, as another of our agendas was to break open that foundation asset base and prove the compounding value for the mission and purpose of foundations. We even got some toes in the water from several wealth managers for individual clients. Thanks to a very friendly loan from Carol to supplement the management company expenses, we closed the gap on costs. (Friendly loans can have very large leverage.)

Our timing of 2007 for raising that money added to our challenges. We were just in time for the big Wall Street crash that circled the globe. As first-time managers of other people's money, it was daunting to set sail in the midst of a financial crisis. We were told regularly, "If you can't raise $100 million, then don't even bother. You can't make the numbers work."

We began assembling a portfolio of companies that solved ecological challenges, or put healthier, cleaner food into grocery carts, or both.

We placed our first-round $35 million into companies you can peruse on our website. In 2014, we brought in $63 million for our next fund, Renewal3. More are likely in the future. The investor mix is of individuals, families, and charitable foundations, with a few front-edge wealth managers who have brought us their clients.

Mainstream venture capitalists are often maligned as "vulture capital." The culture of the industry is seen to be all about fast, ruthless money. Of course, there are exceptions, but the label is widespread and legendary. Maxims like "two fly, eight die" and "kill early and often" guide a harsh, live-or-die type of analysis. We have a different approach to creating lasting value. We want to see more companies succeed, even if simply as solid performers rather than headline successes. Our preference is for a collaborative partner culture, rather than the "money is all that matters" ethic of traditional venture capital.

"If you assume that eight out of ten investments will fail, as is common in venture investing, you really have to expect spectacular returns out of all of your successful investments," says Paul. "The two that make it have to carry you through. We'd rather do more diligence up front, have a longer conversation and interaction with entrepreneurs and find people that we want to partner with for the road ahead. It's only by spending time with people that you can discover whether they have special something within them that makes you believe that they can build an important, purposeful company. We are willing to be a little patient and are comfortable with good long-term growth. We'd rather avoid having to mourn deaths."

Our patient partnership approach to investing has been borne out in our portfolios. Only one of the companies we've partnered with has been a write-off. As of mid-2018, we have investments in almost twenty companies, with six exits. These companies account for hundreds of millions in sales and many quality jobs. The majority are now B Corp certified. We encourage them to go through that measuring process, as we have with Renewal Funds itself. We have an excellent team of younger smart people, who seem delighted to have careers in a financial company they feel good about. Of course, we have hard days and disappointments. There are so many obstacles and detours on the road to growing a successful company.

Are people investing with us based on our mission and charm? Or is it our ability to prove we can put together robustly growing companies doing meaningful work, while showing a strong financial upside? I think it's more weighted to the latter. You have to innovate at the pragmatic edge and plan for a long lead time when you want to change capitalism. My hope is that early tough slogs beget the next round of easier advances. Then the momentum builds and eventually rapid change can kick into gear.

For young people who saw the Facebook movie *The Social Network* and believe they should make billions before they reach the age of thirty: be wary. It does happen, but very rarely. Most business-building is grinding hard work. Financial change, an under-attended dimension of social change, will take a generation of such work.

Paul leads our team, and is a gifted investor and captain. Each year more than four hundred companies come to Renewal Funds looking for capital. We choose only the top 1 percent—three or four per year. Paul's commitment "is to give the investors who have faith in us a good experience. We want to prove out the model of mission investing to people who have more capital and capacity than we had at Renewal. We know if we continue to do that, the implications are huge."

Here are a few stories of the companies with which Renewal Funds has partnered.

Alter Eco

Alter Eco Europe is a fair-trade organic distribution specialist. Inspired by its success in Europe, two Parisians, Mathieu Senard and Edouard Rollet, moved to San Francisco and bought North American (and later Australian) distribution rights from the parent company for a line of foods: fair trade and organic quinoa, rice, sugar, and chocolate. Alter Eco was founded with strong values and passion. Their premise is that "food is fundamental to life—and whole, healthy, delicious food can make life better for people all over the world." Direct relationships with small farming cooperatives around the world, from India to Thailand to Bolivia, help empower fair trade and organic practices, preserve heirloom grains, and enrich local ecology. They are a GHG Protocol 3 Carbon Zero business, offsetting more carbon than they emit. Mathieu and Edouard have helped lead a consortium of food producers to create a compostable, biodegradable packaging replacement (packaging in organic foods remains a big problem that needs solving).

Paul and I met Alter Eco at SVN in in 2009 and loved the story, mission, people, and inherent cascade of positives. After big growth in sales, Alter Eco sold to a family office that intends to hold the company long term while committing to enhance the mission further.

Cascadia Windows

A group of engineers based in the Vancouver area, deeply committed to the green building movement, are manufacturing the most energy-efficient windows in the industry. They are a perfect fit for Vancouver, which is pushing forward energy-efficient building codes as part of its "Greenest City in the World" commitment. Cascadia makes fiberglass window and door frames for custom homes, and for large buildings with LEED Gold and Platinum requirements. Fiberglass is the leading energy-efficient material for heat retention in windows and doors, increasingly in demand as regulations mandate less energy waste and consumption. Demand for Cascadia's products is strong and getting stronger. The market will grow dramatically as large commercial buildings move to fiberglass. Cascadia is profitable and growing quickly, with a new expanded plant coming soon.

Sweet Earth

Kelly and Brian Swette are successful former executives in a midlife new marriage. In 2012 they set out to build a meat alternative company based around a plant-based protein alternative. Called seitan, it tastes good, and is versatile and ready to eat. Brian was an executive of PepsiCo, a COO at eBay, and board chairman of Burger King. Kelly was head of marketing at Calvin Klein, and is now an expert food designer creating new meat-alternative, ready-to-eat foods for the world. Based in Pacific Grove, California, their tasty "Benevolent Bacon" and "Harmless Ham" and a wide array of burritos and meals-in-a-bowl are now moving into big chain stores across the United States. People love the products. Food giant Nestlé is shifting away from many of its candy products, making a new, long-term commitment to "plant-based foods." In 2018, Sweet Earth was sold to Nestlé at a significantly higher price.

Aquatics Informatics

Ed Quilty's career began while working for the British Columbia provincial government as a water quality specialist, and later as an aquatic ecologist for the BC Conservation Foundation. After years standing in streams manually collecting data, he took his expertise in automated aquatic monitoring and data management and started Aquatics Informatics. With Dave Ferguson and their team of over fifty software developers in Vancouver, Ed has helped lead significant change in water testing analytics, now branching into the crucial and fast-growing global water protection sector. Their big break was winning the US Geological Service lead water software contract. Advanced comprehensive software systems and "software as a service" is their growth and distribution model. Wherever their systems are used, they help protect precious water resources. After sustained growth, Aquatics Informatics was acquired in 2017 by a consolidation of clean water–related companies in a deal backed by XPV Water Partners.

Farmhouse Culture

A classically trained chef, Kathryn Lukas is a lifelong "food alchemist." She first fell in love with sauerkraut and fermentation while cooking in a restaurant she owned in Stuttgart, Germany. She founded Farmhouse Culture in 2008. Kathryn's life is dedicated to making natural health available to everyone. Farmhouse Culture's products focus on organic, non-GMO, plant-based, and gluten-free. Looking back to long-evolved food traditions, Kathryn is interested in kraut and related products for their extremely high probiotics content. The culinary possibilities of kraut—like their kraut juice beverage called "Gut Shot," and forays into other probiotic rich foods like kimchi, with many others to come—are providing a large runway for this company. Farmhouse is attracting extraordinary senior leadership along with the capital to succeed, as people become aware of how nutritious and delicious probiotic foods are. Renewal Funds invested in 2015 and growth is robust.

Prana

Marie-Josee Richer, Alon Farber, and Haim Shoham founded Prana in Montreal in 2005. They sell fair-trade and organic nuts, seeds, and snacks. Their passionate enthusiasm combines with the rare qualities of calm nerves and good humor while rolling through tough issues. They offer inspiring education in a fun way to their loyal customers, who see them as a beloved lifestyle brand. Successful in Canada, they are now launching in the United States. Prana is expanding strongly in Canada and is now gaining a foothold in the United States. The organic snack and ingredient market continues to enjoy accelerating growth.

Let's Be Impatient for Patient Capital

The global ideas, debates, and creativity around mission-based investing are far beyond what I can fully track anymore. That's excellent news. People are thinking beyond the baseline of how to shift money-making from "values-blind to values-aligned." They want deeper change, sooner. I consider the whole spectrum of values alignment, whether modest or major, to be part of a crucial transition—the visionary advancement work that Deborah Frieze and Meg Wheatley remind us of in their book *Walk Out Walk On* (see boxed excerpt in Chapter 2).

Slow Money Principles, from Woody Tasch's organization Slow Money:

1. We must bring money back down to earth.

2. There is such a thing as money that is too fast, companies that are too big, finance that is too complex. Therefore, we must slow our money down—not all of it, of course, but enough to matter.

3. The 20th century was the era of Buy Low/Sell High and Wealth Now/Philanthropy Later—what one venture capitalist called "the largest legal accumulation of wealth in history." The 21st Century will be the era of nurture capital, built around principles of carrying capacity, care of the commons, sense of place, diversity, and nonviolence.

4. We must learn to invest as if food, farms, and fertility mattered. We must connect investors to the places where they live, creating healthy relationships and new sources of capital for small food enterprises.

5. Let us celebrate the new generation of entrepreneurs, consumers, and investors who are showing the way from Making A Killing to Making a Living.

6. Paul Newman said, "I just happen to think that in life we need to be a little like the farmer who puts back into the soil what he takes out." Recognizing the wisdom of these words, let us begin rebuilding our economy from the ground up, asking:

   - What would the world be like if we invested 50 percent of our assets within 50 miles of where we live?
   - What if there were a new generation of companies that gave away 50 percent of their profits?
   - What if there were 50 percent more organic matter in our soil 50 years from now?

Myriad forces are rising to the clean money revolution challenge. It will take billions more individual steps, and much hard work remains, but this movement is now unstoppable.

The elephant in the room of global finance has to do with speed, liquidity, and an industrial-era ethos of faster and faster turnaround of capital. We need a serious rethink of the idea of infinite growth. Carol points out that we have forgotten that all this money came from Earth and people, and we never "let it rest." We expect, even demand, that it is making us more money around the clock, while we pursue our careers and hobbies, raise our families, entertain ourselves, exercise, worship, go surfing (waves or the Internet), make art, or shop.

Woody Tasch is a lead thinker in this arena. Woody was another early investor in Stonyfield, through his role as treasurer at the Jessie Smith Noyes Foundation. He later led Investors Circle, the original pioneering network of angel impact investors. Woody eventually tired of the hamster-wheel syndrome of placing money for the quick upside—getting in and out, then placing the cash for the next quick gains. He is now founder and chairman of the Slow Money Institute, whose mission is to "bring money back to earth" by catalyzing the flow of capital to local food systems.

As Woody notes in his book *Inquiries into the Nature of Slow Money: Investing as if Food, Farms, and Fertility Mattered*: "Products produced cheaply create ugly work lives and ugly households and ugly communities. Profits produced quickly cannot purchase patience and care. Patience is beautiful. Restraint and care are beautiful."[48]

Why aren't we supporting companies for decades, rather than joining the team forcing them to grow fast, sell fast, and make a jackpot—so the founders and their backers can just go out and do it again? That's the game for most investors.

How much is enough? Why? What then?

Woody directs us back to nature and how soil is built. We must invest like soil builders, like the workhorse earthworms who build the soil slowly—creating the compost, fuel, and matrix for other living things. Soil takes time and particular conditions to build well. Modern agriculture, and the high-paced system of financial exploitation behind it, hammer the soil and living things with artificial fertilizers, pesticides, herbicides, fungicides, growth hormones. Through repeated tilling and turning for more efficient short-term production we erode and deplete the Earth, and release massive carbon into the atmosphere, accelerating climate change. If you review the facts on the carbon capture possible with proper grazing on perennial grasslands, it will shock you.

Can we instead invest like earthworms, making long-term contributions to life cycles? As Woody puts it: "Every investment we make is a statement of intention, a statement of purpose, a speculation about the future of man and his role in the scheme of things, not merely a financial speculation." We need to rethink and reimagine our system of rapid computer trading of currencies and exotic financial instruments that most can't understand—as well as the building, flipping, and consolidation of companies into megacorporations who set wage levels, influence public policy, bake in planned obsolescence, and determine what's in our households and our minds.

Woody draws from the deep roots of Wendell Berry, Wes Jackson of the Land Institute, ecologist Allan Savory, and permaculture, bringing poetry and history to his ideas. That depth has helped "patient capital" regain traction and esteem, especially among wealth holders with an eye for the long term. Woody's work is broadening through Slow Money investment clubs (eleven in North America at last count, along with 17 local networks) where smaller dollars are pooled and group decisions made on local food system loans and investments. In Vancouver, Rory Holland helped launch "Knives and Forks," a co-op model slow-money club funding small food businesses.

Patient capital will grow along with the clean money movement. It just makes sense. I like being part of a business for decades, watching it evolve, and building steady asset value and distributions. Dave Whorton's work through Tugboat Capital promotes investing for long-term, dividend-making, stable companies.

The "pump and dump" frenzy that followed the emergence of wild west, small-company stock exchanges has mainstreamed into a Wall Street norm. It may as well be casino gambling, devoid of anything other than the momentary thrill of winning.

"Fast money does violence to the web of relations on which the health of communities and bioregions depends," writes Woody. "It is not enough to steer money in new directions. We must slow money down."

Woody's thought leadership has an important place in the ecosystem of a clean money revolution. He has challenged all of us to take more seriously our responsibility for what money is doing. Not all money will make that choice, but each credible alternative broadens our exposure to innovations, opens minds, generates options. It takes natural-system thinking to build the soil for clean money and change the world.

One Step, Then Another

Most of us care deeply what happens seven generations into the future. It is in our DNA. I hope that five hundred years from now, people will be highly advanced, living in a better world where poverty, disparity, lifestyle diseases, slavery, climate chaos, and refugees are stories from history. One where our infrastructural systems—food, housing, buildings, travel, goods and services—work intelligently within natural limits and thriving ecosystems for an appropriately sized human population.

Sound like a pipe dream? Cynicism is understandable. But we need a long-term vision. Getting there requires suspending our overly critical minds to consider the tremendous questions before us.

Intellectually, I'm highly pessimistic. Logic tells me we are in a heap of trouble. But I have no clue what the future will bring. I'm simply not smart enough for that. I've planted my flag in the camp of hope, faith, love. I must believe in a brilliant, resilient future.

We need to be grounded in positive outcomes. It helps to remember the many victories of the ages that brought the world this far. I think again of the civil rights and environmental movements.

Look back over the past fifty years and soak in just how much has changed. What might change over the next fifty? Our minds and intentions do make a difference. We thrive best with a grounded and hopeful future vision.

Being familiar with today's pioneers, who are working this minute building solutions, is fuel for my spirit. We need millions of stories of a better future. We need legends. We need mythology, poetry, art, song, and stories. I believe those alive in the next fifty-year period will make a mighty effort, and that widespread collective energies will cohere, moving trillions of dollars from highly damaging uses into fully regenerative ones. We can rebuild the global economy.

What could you accomplish in your fifty years? How might your work contribute to the world? Let's infuse patience and long-term thinking into rapid innovation. Let's use money as a sacred substance, as if the future matters. Support political leaders who understand that. Find advisors to move your money to better uses. Remember ancestral responsibility. Everything we do now creates the future. Let's keep imagining the future that we wish for ourselves, our children, our nations, and all species. Then let's take one step after another toward the outcome we dearly hope for.

We can do this.

Rha Goddess

is founder and CEO of Move the Crowd, an entrepreneurial soul coach who works with change-makers, cultural visionaries, and social entrepreneurs. Her focus is on a "whole self" approach to entrepreneurship as the key to a more just and sustainable economy and culture. She has presented to Bioneers, SVN, Women Donors Network, Emerging Women, and many other organizations.

Describe your work as a "soul coach" for entrepreneurs, and what your organization Move the Crowd is all about.

My work is supporting people in making their highest contribution. I engage people in strategies to help them make their vision—the change they want to bring to the world—really viable. I see that as a soul journey. Move the Crowd is an entrepreneurial training company that works with purpose-driven entrepreneurs who are willing to take that full journey.

In society we talk a lot about the entrepreneurial spirit, which is that get-up-and-go, maverick energy. At Move the Crowd we're very much interested, however, in the entrepreneurial *soul*, which for me is much more about dharma, purpose, and lifelong impact. It's about finding true north in terms of the path and really tapping into the purest essence of who we are.

Your soul is that essence. It only aspires to be what it is, and to be expressed in the world. From that essence emerges the contribution that you're here to make. I help people find and stay on that path, and develop a viable expression from it.

That maverick, driving spirit can really lead to incredible achievements. It can also lead down a path of exhaustion, overwork, even toxicity. Is that what you help people guard against?

That's exactly right. There is a narrative about what entrepreneurship looks like, and many of us have bought into it. It's that Lone Ranger, "balls to the wall" thing, where you're going to put your stake in the ground and build your empire. You'll conquer a marketplace or industry and it's going to be all about you and your genius and your brilliance. In that mainstream narrative people can burn up and burn out. And if we are not careful in this socially responsible, triple-bottom-line movement, it will be more of the same with better branding.

Being an entrepreneurial soul coach is about providing the space where I get to ask people: "What does your soul say about what you're here to do? What does it say about what you're here to build and contribute?" I help people understand that, give voice and life to that — and help them build a vehicle for it, a strategy.

How did you begin doing this work? Why you do it?

I was born into the intersection of the civil rights and hip hop movements. My parents were born in the 1920s, and they traversed decades of Jim Crow segregation. They were very much on the front lines of the struggle for basic dignity, respect and access to opportunity. That's in my bones. I have three older siblings, so in my family I heard those stories of struggle firsthand, where in this systemic way people were being disenfranchised from opportunity.

I felt a lot of anger and frustration as a young person. To figure how to navigate racism successfully is a full-time job and then some. But I grew up in the hip hop community and in a lot of ways that culture saved me. It gave me a creative outlet for the rage, frustration, and alienation, and tapped me into a whole other level of community. I had the opportunity to help carve out the forefront of what is now known as hip-hop activism.

I got very clear about my passion and purpose, and really began to engage in a deep way at the national and international level. I was doing great work. But I couldn't pay my rent. I had the personal development piece, I had the arts and transformation piece, I had the social impact piece, but I didn't have the money piece. That took me on a journey to get an unorthodox business education, one that transformed my own financial reality in a very short period of time.

After that I knew I needed to be teaching what I'd learned to people who needed it—artists, changemakers, entrepreneurs. That was the impetus for Move the Crowd.

How can the financial system be more inclusive?

As humans we tend to stay where we're comfortable. We stay where it's convenient, where we've always known. That can mean staying within the boundaries of culture, class, gender, or geography, and many other things too. That happens across the board. So inclusion begins with a willingness to be in relationships outside of your comfort zone, to cross those thresholds of identity and engage "the other."

We all have an opportunity to cultivate—and this is the key word—*authentic* relationships outside of the bounds of what is comfortable and familiar. *Authentic* means crossing those thresholds in an authentic way. Too often we have an agenda in a relationship that doesn't necessarily include the well-being of the other person. They've got something we want and we're trying to get it. We have to tell the truth about our agendas and be willing to do our work around them, so we can see others as they are and be willing to relate to them in a real way. This is an absolutely critical skill for everyone, and especially for those with wealth.

For those with wealth or excess income, what skills do you recommend in order to be courageous with money?

The first skill I would name is the ability to listen. Listening begins with the ability to listen *internally* to where and how you are being called to be good stewards of what you've either earned or inherited. In philanthropy there's a long history of casual giving. "I wrote a check to the Red Cross because it was the right thing to do," or, "My buddy bought a table at this charity event so I joined him and brought all my friends, but couldn't really care less about what was going on on the dais."

So additionally we need to cultivate the ability to listen deeply to the world, the world beyond our own cul-de-sac. What speaks to you in the world? What is really going on out there that needs your particular passion? We know that casual giving is very, very different from impassioned giving, aligned giving, purposeful giving. People with resources have the opportunity to discover and ask themselves: What does passionate, purposeful giving look like for me?

Any other advice for those who want to do good with their wealth?
Having money can cause you to insulate yourself out of fear of los-ing it—or out of fear of being inundated and pressured by requests to give in ways that aren't right for you. So that's back to listening deeply, and developing the skill to honor your "yes" and your "no." Creating good boundaries.

Listen to your soul voice and engage from that place. Then you're bringing your whole self to the party. You're not just bringing your checkbook—you're bringing your creativity, your wisdom, your perspective, *and* you're bringing your checkbook, if that's right to do. And that's awesome.

At the same time don't assume that money makes you smarter than anyone else. Sometimes we think that money comes with knowing it all. That's not the truth. Wisdom and knowledge move in lots of different ways. Take the time to become smart about how you're sharing your wealth. Money doesn't make you any more special, but it also doesn't make you any less special. Be willing to cultivate all of yourself so that your money becomes the icing on the cake. And your giving becomes a natural extension of your commit-ment to the kind of world you want to see.

Evolutionary Leadership

"What's the single most important thing young entrepreneurs can do for future success?" That's a question I often get asked when I'm promoting clean money at business schools or incubators.

My answer is always: "Learn inner skills."

Cultivating insight and mastery of yourself is the secret of a successful life. You can know all the mechanics and necessities of business, but if you skip learning how to handle conflict, how to understand your own feelings, and how to be in relationship, you will likely wreak havoc. You might succeed financially, but you may die unhappy and leave a tainted legacy. Financial success and power can have big value, but there is much more to life than that. We must be successful as human beings.

As children we absorb habits, behaviors, and assumptions from our parents and siblings. We endure later struggles and even traumas—everything from broken relationships and hurt feelings to personal failures and violent assaults. As has been well articulated by addictions specialist Dr. Gabor Mate, these ingrained patterns leave scars that affect how we respond to the world. Our negative experiences can leave us wounded and perpetually recreating what was familiar. That can mean abusing and wounding others in the process.

Our careers can also work against us. Menial labor and poor industrial work conditions can damage the body and undermine creative potential and self-determination. In the white-collar world we can suffer stress and damage to our family life and emotional well-being. Self-employment and entrepreneurship can bring yet larger pressures—the anxiety of scrambling for the next client, seeing others as means rather than ends, and breeding a winner-take-all aggressiveness that ultimately damages us. We can win the race for money, and find ourselves unhappy, lonely, and alienated.

More enlightened states—compassion, joy, honesty, self-esteem—are at risk. Even the most fortunate of us face realities that can confuse and distort. Vexing challenges greet us throughout life. Strong as our Western culture is on intellect and ambition, it is proportionally weak in delivering good skills for thriving relationships, balanced power dynamics, crisis management, emotional health, and peace. We lose what Martin Prechtel has called "the honey in our hearts." Addictions to food, alcohol, sex, and work are pervasive.

It's impossible to keep personal issues and damage from showing up in our careers and relationships. Our psychological and emotional selves tag along in our business, financial, and political lives. We then learn leadership on top of a base of accumulated, unresolved personal experiences—navigating mostly alone, or through random good luck with a wise mentor or friend along the way. Mass media is a dubious teacher.

Money is the sly foil, the crass seducer. It can lure us further from the sacred into the profane—and lead us into making it a deity or a religion. An obsession with growing and clinging to money can damage us and those we love. We need self-awareness and spiritual grounding for safe, healthy engagement with this kryptonite-like substance.

Money is embodied energy. It's a tool. Making it into a god is tragic. Using it with a divine intention to help others is wonderful.

Without some inner guidance to steer by, lust for wealth can become the meaning and purpose of life. The clean money revolution is about causing less harm and doing more good. It is also about cleaning up our relationship with money. That means learning how to notice, acknowledge, and address our own inner damage. Maintaining a mental block about the mischief our money is doing—to whom and what, right now, on our behalf—is a corrupt morality.

What will our descendants think of our choices? What will we tell our children when they ask: "Didn't you know that you made your money investing in climate change and injustice?" They may suffer knowing you had choices you ignored. Do they need money and power, or do they need our inspiration as role models who show us good pathways to fulfilling opportunity? They may want both, but without the latter, they may be spiritually empty and aimless.

A friend shared a story. Her family was visiting a Buddhist monastery in Burma. Her teenage son asked the teacher why he was a monk. His reply, paraphrased: "I wanted a life where I never had to think about or engage with money."

Why would someone go so far into spiritual practice simply to have a life free of thinking about money? Where do we learn to navigate the clever seductions of wealth while keeping our integrity and balance—and to heal and restore from inner life damage? Where are the roots that grow our self-esteem confusion into "money lust disorder"? How do we unwind the knot of pain that ambition and greed medicates for us?

There are many wise people we can turn to as resources in finding our center. I've been blessed with exposure to so many teachers and spiritual guides who demonstrate that inner skills can be learned and enhanced with intention: David Abram, Stephen Aung, Ysaye Barnwell, Joan Borysenko, Caroline Casey, Charles Eisenstein, Kim Eng, Robert Gass, Casey Gerald, Margie Gillis, Lori Hanau, Roshi Joan Halifax, Roshi Reta Lawler, Joanna Macy, Atum O'Kane, Jill Purce, Gibran Rivera, Gordy Ryan, Tami Simon, Sobonfu Some, Dr. Michael Stone.

As we challenge our preconceptions, shine light on blind spots, and stretch our emotional comfort zones, we will activate our spirits toward honorable, satisfying mastery. We can leave legacies we'll be proud of.

A Hidden Network

After the '60s, organized protest against war and for civil rights fed into the back-to-the-land movement and rising demands for clean food, clean air, clean water. That heady time was later overcome by the Reagan era of the '80s, which unleashed a tidal wave of greed and selfishness.

Yet beneath these dominant cultural trends, a progressive moral and spiritual impulse in North America has been quietly tended by enduring leadership and consciousness centers—place-based organizations cultivating personal depth as the essential ground for social and cultural change. I think of venerable institutions like the Highlander Research and Education Center in Tennessee (founded in 1932), Green Gulch Zen Center in Marin County (1962), Esalen in Big Sur (1962), Findhorn in Scotland (also 1962!), Omega Institute in Upstate New York (1972), and Hollyhock in British Columbia (1982). An important, more recent addition that brings inner and outer together is the Rockwood Institute in Oakland, founded in 2000. Burning Man, other intentional festival communities, modern-day "mystery schools," and many other emerging practices are creating a vibrant global mix.

Centers like these, where leadership meets personal development, have formed a network of progressive values and inquiry—oases of reflection in a desert of self-interest. They offer a widening contribution to the inner lives of business leaders, change agents, creatives, people in the helping professions, and citizens across the socioeconomic spectrum. As consumerism and commercialization become ever more ubiquitous, they are essential to a sane future.

I was born to an entrepreneurial, ambitious, first-generation American father whose parents had emigrated from Russia. My mother, creative and career-centric, was the descendant of German Jews. I wanted to be strong and tough, like the male role models the world celebrated. Growing up in the Bible Belt under Jim Crow, and as an adolescent in the rebellious '60s—watching the "summer of love" and anti-establishment protests for civil rights and against the Vietnam War—I had many reasons to question authority and the status quo around me. But through my twenties I was afraid to question myself. I was suspicious of therapy and self-examination. In retrospect, I had much inner conflict and confusion to explore: moderate depression, repressed anger, self-doubt, flailing for direction, endless vociferous opinions, and a sense of humor that was often at the expense of others.

My dad's model of toughing it out through all circumstances ultimately left him with a bereft emotional life. He had few close relationships or personal interests outside of business, and there were few people at his side when his kidneys failed. In lieu of inner work and community, he found his purpose in earning money, like many men of his generation. I'm very grateful that he left me a solid financial base. I wish I had learned more from him about being a good, whole man. I'm so grateful to my mother, whose inner struggles were more open. She sought help from therapy and feminist-inspired self-examination, and she seeded that possibility in me. When I faced big questions of purpose in the silence of nature at OrcaLab, I had few tools for facing vulnerabilities and unhappiness, but I did have some models if I was willing to look at them. Voracious reading and silence helped crack my shell. The symphony of the natural world and reading wise teachers and brilliantly insightful novelists reoriented my thinking and pushed me to deep self-reflection.

Over the next three decades, exposure to perennial wisdom, personal development, and the warrior-ship of an inner journey path was my greatest blessing. Hollyhock gave me that miracle.

Hollyhock Magic

My experiences with communities at Farallones, Linnaea, OrcaLab, Threshold, and Social Venture Network all nourished my spirit and growth. Hollyhock became my soul home, where inner skills were the necessary root for true success and integrity. That understanding was my steady base from which to navigate worldly pursuits. Hollyhock's founders—including Rex Weyler, Shivon and Lee Robinsong, Rick Ingrasci, Peggy Taylor, Charles Steinberg, and Torkin Wakefield—were the visionary mentors I learned from. I liked their eclectic "no guru, no Bible, no path" approach that drew respectfully from diverse traditions and holistic perspectives.

The themes of Hollyhock work are *healing* to advance inner skills; *activism* to stand for what is important; and *generational responsibility* to balance business and purpose, respect ancestors and elders, and do our best for true security for the future. True security is about peace, fairness, and a soft landing.

Hollyhock's origin history is as fascinating as the people who go there today. What we can deduce—from shell middens, culturally modified trees, reading, and many conversations—is that the land itself was used as an active summer gathering camp for First Nations bands from around the region, including the Klahoose, also based on Cortes Island. It is easy to imagine that the stunning location was a preferred destination for trading, winter food preparation, meetings, celebrations, sharing knowledge, and storytelling.

Hollyhock land was first "homesteaded" early in the 1900s by a man who had moved from the Finnish community of Sointula ("place of harmony") on Malcolm Island—an initially utopian cooperative made up immigrant Finnish miners. When the ferry and electricity linked Cortes Island to modern times in the mid 1970s, Richard Weaver bought the property and converted the old farm into a personal growth center called the Cold Mountain Institute. Weaver had trained at Esalen in Big Sur and was a brother-in-law of one of its founders. He wanted a remote and special spot to offer the work he felt was essential to the world.

When Richard died, his widow Jean Weaver put the land up for sale. Shivon Robinsong—with her husband Lee and their daughter Erin Skye—were helping caretake the property. Rex Weyler and Shivon had worked together at Greenpeace, and after a stint as an editor for *New Age Journal* in Boston, Rex came to visit Shivon on Cortes Island. She wanted to find a way to purchase the now-dilapidated facility—whose farmstead and "retreat center" buildings were being overgrown by blackberries and rainforest mold. The BC coast likes to eat buildings, cars, and infrastructure.

Rex has a great story of what happened next for him:

In the summer of 1981, I attended the Vancouver Folk Festival, as I had every year since it started. At midday, on one of the small stages, a group of seven women from Hungary performed astounding vocal harmonies. The oldest woman appeared about 70 and the youngest girl about 12. The other women ranged in height and age. This, I thought, is culture. The old woman was once the little girl. The little girl will one day lead this group as an elder. This is how real human culture works.

As the women sang rounds and chants and complex harmonies, the older woman, the leader, held out a brass pot before the crowd. "Cast your rings into the pot," she declared. "Learn your fortune." She walked from the stage, followed by the other women and girls, all singing, and wandered through the crowd, down to the edge of the pond. "Cast your rings into the pot. Cast your rings into the pot. Learn your fortune." Stepping in among the bulrushes, the old Hungarian woman dipped the pot into the pond, took up some water, and led the procession back up toward the stage. People reached forward and placed their rings into the pot. Inspired by the performance, I caught up to the grandmother and cast my ring into the pot.

Back at the stage, the women still singing, the old woman pulled rings from the pot, one-by-one, handed them to the owners, and whispered a fortune to each person. When she drew out my ring, I stepped forward. She handed me the ring and whispered in my ear: "Red hollyhocks growing above the hedge. Look for them. They will be very important to you."

Red hollyhocks? That's my fortune? I mused over this for several weeks. At the end of that summer, I went to Cortes Island for the first time, with my friend Kim Bothen, to visit Lee and Shivon Robinsong, who had recently moved there.

We stayed at their home, walked in the woods, and I told them about my cryptic hollyhock fortune. The next morning, we took a long walk, south along the beach toward Sutil Point.

We passed an upland farm and came upon some abandoned buildings, a farmhouse and a cottage on the beach. "What's this?" I asked. Shivon explained that the newer buildings were built by the former Cold Mountain Institute, a gestalt therapy center from the 1970s. The Institute had grown slightly famous in BC history as the site of early, cutting edge "encounter groups," and humanistic psychology seminars. Now, a lone caretaker, Xanon by name, lived in the beach cottage.

I wanted to investigate, so we wandered up the hill into the main farmhouse and lodge. I had been working in Boston, still had a flat in Vancouver, but had considered leaving urban life for the bush. Only a few months earlier, on the Pine Ridge Reservation in South Dakota, I had been working with the Lakota people, who had lost most of their land to colonizers, then lost most of their treaty land to swindlers. They lost children to residential schools, and were still fighting for basic human rights. At a gathering in the Black Hills, the traditional chief, Fools Crow, had thanked me for helping, but told me: "The best way to help the indigenous people, is to be one. Sooner or later, you must find a place, where you can stay, and you must protect that place." After this I had decided to return to the West Coast of Canada. I found myself falling in love with this magical spot on the beach. Was this the place that I should stay and protect? The fact that the buildings appeared neglected, stirred my interest. Someone should look after this place, I thought.

My friends moved through the lodge and out another door. I sat alone in an oceanside room before a stone fireplace. Overgrown brambles poked through broken windows.

Spiders had set up neatly in the corners of the windows. I have nothing against spiders, but I felt an overwhelming sensation that this place needed someone to love it and bring it back to life. I felt as if the apple trees and buildings were asking to be cared for. A strange sense of responsibility invaded me. I am a fairly practical person, not generally inclined to mystical epiphanies, so I can't explain any of these feelings. It just happened that way.

At that moment, Shivon and our friend Kate returned from their wanderings, quite excited. "Rex, come here. You have to see this." I followed them out onto a deck, facing a magnificent forest of cedar, hemlock, and fir trees. Between the forest and the lodge, an enormous garden appeared, completely overgrown with brambles and grass. Except, there before me, above a hedge, stood bright red hollyhocks, just as the Hungarian woman had described.

Now, my head spun and my knees felt weak. My practical, rational brain could not put all this together. Listening to whispering trees and fortune-tellers was not my usual way of making life decisions, but I felt helpless. Destiny appeared to have her way with me.

Shivon, Rex, and their partner founders (including me, two years later) pulled together the dollars to purchase and invest in the property. More years passed. At a major transitional point for the organization, Carol Newell invested significant capital in this leadership learning experiment. Her generosity and foresight helped transition Hollyhock from a struggling visionary dream—one with a good foothold—into a widely renowned organization, attracting teachers, leaders, and guests from around the world.

The Examined Life

Today Hollyhock offers a rich mix of teachers and immersive learning, including courses in meditation, yoga, and mindfulness as well as facilitation, leadership, and conscious entrepreneurship. I met most of those teachers I mentioned earlier at Hollyhock. It is a place where you can find courses that merge inner and outer development. Hollyhock, of course, is special to me.

Mike Rowlands is President and CEO of Junxion Strategy. Based in London and Vancouver, Junxion supports mission-minded founders, pioneers of corporate social responsibility, non-profit executives, and philanthropists with strategy and branding.

I no longer believe it's possible to separate personal development from professional and organizational capacity. This notion that businesses are like machines, and that each of us has a role to play as if we were cogs in a mechanism is flawed and dangerous.

Instead, businesses are better conceived as communities— networks of people who work together, cooperating for the greater good of the group. In this concept, better people make for better organizations. And better organizations make for better societies. That's a key part of Hollyhock's perspective, and of mine.

I've been visiting Hollyhock since 2009, when I first attended Social Venture Institute, an annual conference that brings together over 140 social entrepreneurs with advisors, financiers, and other supporters of socially responsible business. It quite literally saved my business. I was in dire straits after the 2008 meltdown, and SVI taught me the skills and gave me the network of connections I needed to weather the storm. It helped me to keep focusing on building a business that delivered social, environmental, and financial returns.

Whenever I return, I learn a little something valuable about myself. And the camaraderie of shared time with such a remarkable group of "thoughtful and committed citizens" is a vital energizer. Hollyhock has made me a better leader, a better entrepreneur, and a better human being.

There are high-value reasons to seek out such places. In the age of the screen, we risk being too physically passive and sedentary. We must continually outsmart the devices we depend on to avoid the modern afflictions of isolation, loss of contact with nature, and "sitting as the new smoking." We are increasingly aware of the need to be active, experience nature, and eat healthy, avoiding processed, chemical-laden foods. This is good. Rates of diabetes, obesity, cancer, heart disease, liver toxicity—often lifestyle-induced afflictions—are steadily growing. They are killers.

It is also all too common to be *emotionally* sedentary and *spiritually* passive. We know that our physical health is inextricably linked to our psychological health. Spiritual maturity gives us a sense of place and purpose, and makes us far more resilient. It's wise to commit time to learn the inner realms. Today's competence demands that we navigate our emotions, conflicts, and relationships, and that we have resources to fall back on when we face disorientation. We can develop better access to intuition and insight. Managing anger, self-doubt, and confusion follows from knowing your own heart and mind.

Raj Sisodia is the author of *Firms of Endearment: How World Class Companies Profit from Passion and Purpose*. In a 2015 interview in the Indian economics and management quarterly *Thinkers*, he was asked about the behavior of exploitive organizations. Sisodia responded that businesses generally operate "with a narrow perspective and a lot of it has to do with the wholesale importing of the old American-style capitalism.... we have to raise the consciousness to get people to see that this is not about sacrificing performance for the sake of these other things, but it's about aligning all the forces together so that you actually create a lot more value for everybody."[49]

People in business may feel forced to be cutthroat by external imperatives, like boosting shareholder value. (We as shareholders can forget our role in creating negative consequences by our demands for ever-higher return rates.) Negative, dominating behaviors can result from unresolved confusion about our own true value. Damage can compound exponentially.

We know the better business leader understands their own insecurities, fears, reactions, and ego. Organizations that motivate people, build self-esteem, and support self care and conflict resolution do more good for everyone. Without those practices we become narrower. As the inner world of leadership contracts into fear and negativity, our businesses, organizations, and institutions suffer. Our families suffer, too. We grow callous. We teach our children and others we influence to perpetuate our poor or reactive examples.

The examined person thinks creatively and more independently. They trust an inner knowing, the mix of intuition and practicality. They get things done with flow and ease. They express clear boundaries. Nurture themselves. Speak truth to power.

Such people live adult wisdom. They inspire. They are model ancestors. They are peace warriors for the future. They are all in. They show the way.

The wise advice of entrepreneurial coach Rha Goddess reminds us to look critically at the narratives we're living in our careers and how we're relating to the people in our lives. Otherwise, "if we are not careful in this socially responsible, triple-bottom-line movement, it will be more of the same with better branding."

Good business leaders must retain employees and customers, create useful products and handle mounting demands. Inner skills are gold in this context. Fortunately, there is a vast world of wisdom available. Wise guides redirect us to our deep knowing. Counseling and therapy give us space to reflect and hone our emotional intelligence. Learning retreats help us feel silence and deeper awareness. Nature-based settings usually enhance the experience, adding the most accessible wisdom teacher of all. We learn to face fears and gain tools for successful relationship, with others or, most importantly, ourselves.

Catherine R. Bell is the founder of BluEra, an executive search company in Alberta. Her 2015 book *The Awakened Company* highlights leading from the quality she calls "presence":

Presence is an energy, transmitted almost like light—unseen, and yet capable of revealing everything it touches. Consequently, when we are around a person with great presence, we experience a palpable feeling of our interconnectedness.... effective leadership is a dance between, on the one side, inspiration, motivation, intellectual challenge, and the ability influence others, and on the other side the everyday execution of multiple roles and responsibilities. Because this dance flows from presence, it's both graceful and serene. For these reasons, leading from presence is devoid of the desperate role-juggling we encounter among egos in so much of the business world.[50]

How to increase presence and flow in our lives?

Bell points to aligning your life with your values, and to practices like yoga and meditation. A 2010 study of managers at four European companies showed surprising results from meditation for businesspeople. Summarizing in the magazine *Corporate Knights*, Adria Vasil wrote that "approaches that involved mental silence meditation and relaxation techniques led to significant improvements in social consciousness and socially responsible behaviour, even when CSR principles weren't actually mentioned. The meditating managers were more apt to prioritize social welfare over economic profit and even more likely to prioritize protection of the natural environment over productivity. Plus, they had a greater overall sense of responsibility and inner harmony."[51]

Raj Sisodia, commenting on the same study, noted that corporations that offer relaxation and meditation to their employees in the hopes of reducing stress or absenteeism may find their employees' values and motivations changing. "The consciousness part of conscious capitalism requires that we be more mindful and more awake and see the whole reality, all the interconnections and interdependencies," said Sisodia. "[Meditation] is one of the best ways that we know how to accomplish that."[52]

Corporate professionals, entrepreneurs, artists, homemakers, parents, hourly workers, students, retirees—we all need more awareness of and facility with our inner lives.

Knowing how to love, how to be a good person, how to reduce fear or the suffering of stress—understanding our mind-body relationship and how to enhance it—these are skills of the examined life. There are well-worn but unique and individualized versions of these skills for each person. As we navigate the seductions and distractions of daily life, we should take these concepts seriously. As you master emotional skills, you will feel good. "Feeling good" is more elusive, and potent, than meets the eye. It's contagious. It increases trustable leadership and right action.

Consciousness practices grow clean money revolutionaries!

The Keys to the Ferrari

Leadership is the underlying theme of Hollyhock's mission, pedagogy, and long-term offering to people and planet. Lifelong leadership work starts at Hollyhock by addressing what has made us who we are. Then it offers the teachers, tools, peer support, and empowerment needed to increase skills. The programs there are multifaceted and holistic, adapted to our roles as leaders in all walks of life.

What is leadership? Leaders are perceptive contributors and collaborative directors—strong stewards of what matters most. Family, community, organizations, businesses, and public service all benefit from wise guidance and effective direction. Leadership underpins all the roles in which we seek to create a world that is fair, fulfilling, and resilient.

There are so many qualities of good leadership: the ability to guide, motivate, and inspire; willingness to empower and share opportunity; authentic devotion to best outcomes for others; empathy; and modeling emotional and spiritual maturity.

Without inner work, leadership is impaired and can become toxic. Poor leadership is self-centered, reactive, and short-sighted.

It can cause lasting damage to people, organizations, and entire cultures.

Learning inner skills should be compulsory for investors, entrepreneurs, managers of public budgets—and, most of all, for those who own massive wealth. In the clean money revolution, we need honest self-assessment of our skills and abilities. We must continually improve and seek help where we need it. Those who handle large sums of money are stewards with monumental responsibilities. As dollars change hands, transactions hurtle them around the planet. Too often blood is spilled with, around, and for the power to hold that money. Pull out a piece of currency and you might not be able to see the blood stains on it—but behind it, can you feel the exhaustion, the fear for one's children, the drudgery of long days of hard labor?

For high-net-worth individuals wanting to invest in change, I offer a note of caution. Owning money does not confer effectiveness at investing, managing, or leading. Wealth increases options but is no guarantee of financial or other specific skills. Those have to be learned separately. Inheriting wealth can be like being handed the keys to a space rocket when you've only ever learned to ride a bicycle. Imagine giving a twelve-year-old the keys to a Ferrari. What's going to happen? Disaster. And the harm won't just be to the inexperienced driver. Many innocent bystanders may suffer.

Assess your abilities carefully. Be humble. There is a lot to learn. As the child of an entrepreneur I had received some limited business experience, but I had many skill and experience deficits. The privilege of inherited money got me better access, and education opened some doors. My status as a white male increased my assumed power in a fundamentally unequal culture. Many connections came easily. But any skills I have—inner, outer, financial, and otherwise—came through hard work, steady practice, and diverse experiences.

When I went "back in" to the business world after my time at OrcaLab I was able to move into organic food investing gently, thanks to years of prior organic gardening involvement. I learned slowly along the way with many blunders. I advanced with small tests, watching dozens of others and blessed with many guides, stories, and opportunities for hands-on practice. I had many things to learn and many mistakes to make.

The entitlement that comes with owning big money is a devilish trickster. It can fool us into ignoring or hiding our gaps. We may have no training or real experience in the practical and emotional skills involved in money transactions. Compassionate self-honesty about one's true skills, vulnerabilities, and ambitions is crucial. Invest first in your own knowledge, talents, experience, and maturity. For clean money investors going into the for-profit "impact investing" space, some basic questions to ask yourself:

- Why do you want to make money?
- How much is enough?
- What will you do with the money?
- What legacy do you want to leave?

Even if our vision and values are perfect, we need to assess our skills.

- Am I ready to take money away from financial advisors who invest my wealth in companies that do unacceptable damage to people and the planet?
- What is my capacity for evaluating investments?
- Who can best help me?
- Am I willing to lose money?
- Am I ready to own the power of my money and align it with who I believe I am?
- What is my lifelong leadership program for my own growth and wisdom?

Be wise with money or it will screw you up, along with others you mean to help. People can use the power of money to get all kinds of things to compensate for emptiness or pain in their lives: sex, fame, power. You probably know just what I mean. Be humble and learn to handle money with grace and smarts. All of us who aspire to a role in the clean money revolution should continue self-inquiry and self-assessment. Get help! Seek those with expertise.

Carol Newell knew she wanted help. She built a strong, empowered team. Big outcomes followed. Others who have tried to do it all by themselves, determined to prove their brilliance without putting in the work to earn it, have caused many messes. Sincere intentions don't insulate you or others from consequences.

What are our strengths? What are our gaps? What type of team do we need? Which key advisors? What is our pathway of practice needed to master crucial skills? Are we better being our own entrepreneur—or would be do less harm and more good by finding and hiring other intermediaries with integrity and talent to help shift our capital from destructive and exploitative uses to generative ones?

Experiment and learn with smaller parts of your resources. Wisdom and instinct will develop over time.

Back to the Bonfire

I moved back to Tennessee when my father died in 1984, but every year since, the allure of Hollyhock has brought me across the continent for one transformational experience after another. I joined the board in the early '90s. In 1998 I met my wife, Dana Bass, on the floatplane dock near the Vancouver airport, as we both waited to head to Hollyhock. My Nashville pal Mark Deutschmann was there too, his own love of the place still pulling him back there from such a distance after all those years.

After getting to know Dana's background and sensibility, I asked her after just three days, "Would you like to run this place some day?" She was speechless.

Why did I do that? Instinct, perhaps. But she was the first hospitality and wellness management professional we'd seen who was familiar with unique, eccentric facilities. She understood the depth and complexity of what we were up to on this remote little island. She was moved by the potential. Unbeknownst to me, she had already been feeling a calling inside herself, seeking a life change. Our personal development workshops were growing, the working team was past the all-volunteer era, and it was time to accept that the work underway needed professional management and better structures—along with new eyes, ears, and some magic.

Two years later, we recruited Dana to move with her daughter Noelle and son Dusty, full time, from the Joshua Tree area. Her elder sons Garrett and Trever stayed in school in the States. She became Operations Director, then soon later CEO, of Hollyhock's then-private company. A new era had begun.

Dana and I are now happily married business and life partners. Hollyhock has been a huge part of the meaning and value in our lives. A consistent thread of involvement has been my volunteer role in producing and hosting crafted gatherings in the incredible natural setting—delivering transformational experiences to hundreds of social entrepreneurs and social change activists.

Hollyhock changes lives. It influences its region's culture and mindset with its eclectic mission. Thousands have been directly and indirectly inspired by its ongoing harvest of personal stories and profound outcomes. Nestled in a breathtaking natural setting on the continent's edge, it is a modern mystery school. Such places are important for breaking the bonds of conventional money thinking and creating new approaches. These are eclectic learning gatherings offering delicious organic food, beach fires, ocean swimming, and hot tubs. They build trust and connections. You can imagine the unique value for investors and entrepreneurs able to meet in this way, rather than making a pitch across an office desk!

Hollyhock events attract funders and veterans with big successes from many sectors, as well as starter-level entrepreneurs, creatives, and those who dedicate their lives to positive change. At gatherings like the Social Venture Institute, the Social Change Institute, Summer Gathering, Story Money Impact, Web of Change, Activate, Reel Youth, Indigeneyez, and more, we deliver "life-changing" as if it were a repeatable educational pedagogy. I think it is. We believe this work is about long-term culture change, drawing from the inspiration of natural systems with the strength of diversity—and continual regeneration. We aim for 50 to 70 percent new people at each event in order to welcome fresh voices and perspectives into the mix.

It adds up to a less-understood yet essential big-picture cultural change strategy. A clean money thread weaves through it all. The massive contemporary brewing of local, organic, craft, renewable, and high-tech solutions needs to be supported with the gatherings, leadership development, and cross-pollination that happen at places like Hollyhock.

Gibran Rivera, master facilitator and the creator of the Evolutionary Leadership workshop:

I work on my own growth and transformation and I encourage others to do the same. But I really see little point in personal growth absent a commitment to social transformation. So my focus in life is supporting the development of leadership networks and organizations that are committed to our next evolutionary leap.

Hollyhock's emphasis on collective possibility, on providing a space that yields community among change agents, entrepreneurs, and activists is the most important thing it could be doing. It provides a space that nurtures greater authenticity in relationship. It nurtures trust. These qualities are integral to the change we want to see in the world.

My first time I went to Hollyhock was as facilitator of Web of Change in 2009, and it wasn't just the beauty of the land that got me hooked—it was the magic I found there. Something was happening among participants that was unlike anything that happened anywhere else I had facilitated.

This magic is what keeps me coming back. Our ancestors knew that some places were more conducive than others; they honored and sought places conducive to ritual and connectivity, and I seek to do the same. This is why when I created the Evolutionary Leadership workshop I chose to launch it at Hollyhock. I want to see change agents thrive as they learn to hold and support each other along this arduous marathon to justice.

The revolution needs people with increasing self-mastery. Moving trillions from damaging investments to regenerative ones requires a sense of calling. That calling is our birthright. To engage it we need the skills of personal resilience. We must know ourselves. Then we can serve others better.

Do you have meaningful places where you can connect and share vulnerability? Do you have trusted networks where you get honest feedback? Are your friends able to talk about and take responsibility for their feelings, and understand how to channel strong emotions like anger? Is your work environment generative and inspiring? Are you happy?

There are real tools available to all of us, if only through books or online. We can't all regularly attend places like Hollyhock, but we can find coaches, therapists, support groups, or good friends, who can be wizards with and for us. Their support helps us own our unresolved emotional wounds that can blind us to opportunities, or that can sabotage those opportunities when we get triggered by them. Once we see ourselves and learn new tools, it's GAME TIME!

If you need some Hollyhock medicine, find us just across the water from the end of the gravel road, at the end of the highway, on the left coast of the continent. Amidst the West Coast rainforest, one of the last great green places on Earth, you will find change agents, activist warriors, timeless wisdom, amazing teachers, new-wave companies, and old-school hospitality.

You may just discover, or rediscover, the meaning and purpose of your life.

Danny Kennedy

is a clean energy pioneer. In 2007, Danny co-founded Sungevity, Inc., the country's largest privately held solar company. He is now managing director of the California Clean Energy Fund and president of CalCharge, a membership consortium that drives breakthroughs in energy storage technology. He is the author of the clean energy manifesto *Rooftop Revolution: How Solar Power Can Save Our Economy—and the Planet—from Dirty Energy.*

How did you come to do what you do?

My early career was as a global activist, in energy and climate broadly, along with other issues thrown in—all of which, strangely, turned out to be good grist for the mill of starting a business. I had a long campaign career in Greenpeace and other related organizations, mostly climate and energy issues. I worked in Australia, Papua New Guinea, and Fiji, and I helped set up Greenpeace China. When my business partner was trying to talk me into starting Sungevity, I said, "I know how to hurt a company, I don't know how to start one." And he said to me: "It's the same, it's the same." And he was right. The human skills of being an activist and an entrepreneur are very similar. Start something with nothing. Inspire people and make things happen.

Around 2006 I burned out on the activist side and needed to push a different path. I felt like we'd convinced people we had a climate change problem; we needed to have a solution. I started Sungevity to scale solutions and demonstrate them, partnering with two people who made it possible.

Of which Sungevity achievements are you most proud?

We demonstrated that solar could be sold through the Internet. That was really the kind of key intellectual property that we developed—the idea of "sunshine online," using web commerce as a way to scale deployment rapidly. We created a great customer experience, which is really the key to any business succeeding. Our goal was to get solar out of the cottage industry zone and into a high-tech customer service business. Now we're now the largest privately held solar company in America. We're also working across Europe, in Germany, the U.K., and the Netherlands. So this company I started with two mates is now worth more than Peabody Coal and serves tens of thousands of customers, with more every month. Spreading sunshine online—I can't complain! It's a great thing to do.

The fall of coal has been a real wake-up call to a lot of people.
We talk about energy disruption and we don't yet really understand what that word means. It means really dramatic change, and the coal industry's fate is an example of that. I think it's going to befall other fossil fuels.

**How much capital can the clean energy
sector absorb in the next couple of decades?**
The renewable sector is currently absorbing about $250 billion to $300 billion per annum. That's just on electricity, not transportation. This means rewiring parts of the world that already have electricity infrastructure, like the United States, Europe, Australia, and Japan. That's a big enough effort, but the heavy lift is bringing electricity to places that don't yet have that infrastructure—huge areas of India, Indonesia, the Philippines, and Africa. Global population is expected to be over eleven billion by the end of the century, and Africa's population will likely double by 2050. That's one billion more people in Africa alone.

There are more humans on Earth today that don't have electricity than there were when Edison was around. They're all going to get electricity in the next couple decades, and they're all going to get it from clean energy. And so the numbers will soon grow to the range of $500 billion annually, more than double what we're currently doing, up to around $1 trillion annually by 2030. Even under a business-as-usual scenario, Bloomberg New Energy Finance

(BNEF) is forecasting something like $7 trillion to be spent in clean energy build-outs over the next 25 years. That's crystal-ball gazing, but it's a pretty reasonable forecast. BNEF makes the point often that for the last few years the alternative energy has actually been coal, oil, nuclear, and gas. There's been less money on that side than there has been on wind, solar, water, and clean energy for three years now.

That is good news long term but at the same time the urgency is there. In the lag phase of this ongoing disruption, for many people and species the climate changes are unbearable. They're dying because of them. When you take into account the Paris climate talks and the commitments made to stay below 2 degrees Celsius, and hopefully "1.5 to stay alive"—you're going to need to increase that businesses as usual number by about 75 percent. So you'd be close to seeing an investment in renewables of $12 trillion over 25 years.

That might sound like a ton, but relative to global capital it's not that big a number. Americans spend about $500 billion every year on their car loans alone. It's a drop in the ocean.

What is the California Clean Energy Fund? What's your role there?
I moved on to the California Clean Energy Fund (CalCEF) in late 2015. It's 12 years old, an organization here in the Californian firmament that connects money to ideas, investors, and investments. We're also managing a $25-million grant program for very early stage entrepreneurs in sustainable energy in California. We have also a 501(c)(3) which educates financiers, policy makers, and regulators around ways to do climate-solution finance. We've started some companies out of that, based on where we've identified needs and gaps. We also have a 501(c)(6) that is basically a trade association. The main program on that side of the house is CalCharge, which is a public-private partnership working to accelerate the tech on battery and energy storage.

That's some of what we do. Now we're growing globally and trying to bring some of our experience, lessons, and models—and capital—into Asia and Africa, where global energy capacity is going to be built out in the next couple decades. My role is to help bring some international focus to it, because it's been a very California-oriented model.

What does bringing an international focus to a California-based clean energy fund mean?

California would be the eighth-largest country on Earth if it were a country, and there's this amazing reality that it has gone from coal dependency twenty or thirty years ago to almost no coal in the mix now. It will be 50 percent renewable by 2030 by law, and it'll probably get to 100 percent renewable way before anyone else. California has all the political will in the world and it's been good for the state. We've built jobs. There's Google and Apple in the mix of course, but also Tesla and SolarCity and Sungevity have created more jobs and wealth than any other industry in the state. That's a good news story we want to share with the world. The learning, lessons, policies, and pieces that make that happen need to be rapidly replicated if we're ever going to deal with climate change.

One of the things that we always underestimate with clean energy is that it's job-dense. It's labor-rich, whereas fossil fuel is capital-intensive and labor-light. You create something like 24 million jobs in a doubling of clean energy. And if we were to do what Paris requires, it's way more than doubling by 2030.

If an investor wants to get into clean energy, there's a broad swath of what might be labeled that way. But it's not always clear: the U.N. for example does not consider big hydro projects to be clean energy. What should investors be looking for under the clean energy umbrella?

There's a portfolio of products. They may not be as 100-percent pure as the driven snow, but they are clean. I agree with the analysis that big hydroelectric is not clean, but run-of-river hydro might be, along with canal-based solutions. But I think they're going to be less important. Wind and solar are the dominant generating resources. And then there's a whole lot of smart energy improvements that'll be made to existing grids—and will be implemented in the new grids that these leapfrogging nations adopt.

These new grids won't follow the old centralized model. They'll be more like a fractalized web of micro-grids. The key technologies there are actually storage and micro-processing power to manage a just-in-time supply of electricity to meet demand. So there's a range of things. I'm personally quite convinced that a hundred years from now, photovoltaic solar will be the dominant source. There'll be a transitional period where we'll use whatever we can, while we accelerate the adoption of clean energy for dirty energy as we realize what we've done to the weather.

But we as a civilization will end up being largely solar powered, because semi-conductors become cheaper the more you make them. We've just hit the threshold in the last year or two and now we're pretty much cheaper than anything. And so we're going to start scaling production and that's going to drive down cost. And before you know it, electricity will be this thing that comes out of flat-plate semi-conductors called PV at almost no marginal cost wherever you put it. And that will just mean a massive adoption of this product over decades. By the end of the century we'll be largely a solar-powered society.

Does clean energy have a social justice aspect?
Can the rise of clean energy actually help with
wealth disparity and income inequality?
I bring a strong equity lens to this work. "One hundred percent clean energy for a hundred percent of the people." That's our vision. To have the right social impact as you rewire the world and take over the commanding heights of the economy, you should be intentional about who you seek to serve and how. We need that equity focus. To date that equity piece has been I think a bit sidelined by the clean energy industry, just because we've had our heads down and been focused on execution.

I want to make sure that as the clean economy rises—which it inevitably will now—that it happens in a better way, lifting all boats on its tide. By that I mean that it involves a more diverse community. It shouldn't just make more rich the people that are already rich care of last century's energy system. I often say that clean energy has much more than an environmental benefit. The moniker I use is 3D energy: not just *distributed*, but *decentralized* in terms of ownership and *democratized* in terms of control.

The three Ds are basically a distributed architecture, versus running the big central coal power station way out of sight and out of mind. Your power source is closer to home, if not right on top of your head. That means decentralized ownership. Those assets in society that power our lives, lifestyles, industries, and economy could be owned by local capital. You see that in Germany, which has adopted 35 gigawatts of wind and 40 gigawatts of solar or something in that ballpark on an 86-gigawatt base capacity. Most of that solar and wind is locally owned. Farmers, cooperatives, and things like that.

So the community can have control of the heights of the economy that used to be centralized in the hands of the few, because fossil fuels were weirdly concentrated in place—and required intense capital to extract and transport and refine and deliver. At a high level it gives me great optimism because sunshine is spread pretty evenly. If it's even more abundant anywhere it's amongst the poorest of the world population. I'd hope to see these people taking this opportunity to leapfrog some nasty power structures that would otherwise control their destiny. With a battery and a bit of PV you can better control your destiny. And that is technologically possible today.

The $100 Trillion Question

HUMANITY IS ON the edge of a precipice.

We know the headlines. Ecological emergencies. Mass refugee flights from failing states. The distortions of late-stage capitalism eroding basic trust, tolerance, and hope. Common decency and respect is starting to seem anachronistic. Worship of money and celebrity rules the media, while our ties to land, loyalties, and love are severed.

Yes, it's also "the best of times." Many diseases have been eradicated or are manageable. Modern science and industry have brought sanitation, clean water, and industrial food to billions worldwide. Smart phones and the Internet give us access to unfathomable volumes of information.

There are competing trends. Decay and chaos on one hand, integration and regeneration on the other. As $100 trillion changes hands in the next twenty years, the question is, which future wins? Will this generational wealth transfer help us rebuild, or will it throw gasoline on the fires of rampant greed?

There are so many ways we can turn that money to transforming the world. We can rethink taxation to make it more fair. We can price carbon. We can create schools and hospitals for all. Feed the world sustainably. Make pollution and other externalities illegal and guard smart use of resources. What else could the clean money revolution accomplish with $100 trillion?

Thanks to the passion and wisdom of so many great leaders over the past fifty years, our basic ethical premises about self-interest, ecology, and life itself are starting to shift. We have further to go as a global culture that will only become more intertwined. Despite what some segments of our society would prefer, there's no going back. What if we agreed that the meaning and purpose of life was not only to enjoy it, but to use our energies to ensure a liveable future for dozens of generations into the future? What if our Golden Rule and central religious belief was that we be responsible for leaving the Earth better than we found it, restoring it rather than degrading it?

$100 Trillion Vision

Here are some foundational elements for a resilient future civilization.

+ Fair taxation
+ Gender, race, class, or sexual preference equality
+ Global carbon pricing
+ Elimination of fossil fuel subsidies
+ Legal ownership of pollution and externalities
+ Life cycle manufacturing responsibility
+ Money out of politics
+ Proportional representation voting
+ Degrowth prosperity
+ Slowing population growth
+ Minimum guaranteed income
+ Just social safety net
+ Housing as a human right
+ Prison and drug law reform
+ Gun control and demilitarization
+ Quality public health care and education

Clean Money Transition Costs (2017–2050)

Reparations for colonialism and slavery	$10T
Transition to renewable energy	$20T

Sustainable transportation	$10T
Green and living buildings	$10T
Soil restoration and carbon capture	$10T
Guaranteed income, health care, education	$10T
Zero waste	$10T
War and weapons industry reduction	$10T
Steady state economy transition	$10T
Total	**$100T**

These numbers are symbolic. Please tear them apart. Do your PhD on more precise ones. Debate, skewer, and improve them. Map out more accurate visions with research. At this early stage the exact numbers are less important than recognizing the need for a massive shift of capital from destructive uses to regeneration.

That is our chance for a soft landing and a resilient future civilization.

There are precedents and estimates to get us started. The World Bank noted in 2010 that moving global economies to a net-zero emissions trajectory will take $700 billion to $1 trillion per year of investment. The sustainable business advocacy group Ceres has called for $36 trillion to be invested in clean energy between 2014 and 2050 in order to have an 80 percent chance of capping global warming at 2°C.

At Davos in 2014, World Bank president Kim Jim called for removing the $1.9 trillion in global subsidies to the fossil fuel industry—a number that includes externalities the industry itself causes—then turning that money toward clean energy investment.[53] Many statistics exist to inform a $100 trillion shift.

The point is, are these numbers wrong? How would we know? We need to study, discuss, map, design, and empower solutions strategies that show the way.

We now see how much money we will lose and how much human suffering we face from global warming and other ecological and social catastrophes. One scenario shows that up to $31.5 trillion of pension assets are overvalued with respect to climate risk.*

There are no doubt efforts already underway to determine the costs of achieving needed changes. They are probably rapidly emerging for scientists, academics, economists, insurance companies, governments, and military. We should fund those doing the modeling, and popularize a map for shifting to a positive future history. We may still avert massive disaster, and empower a steady-state society of enlightened self-interest.

We need a financial plan for achieving a safe world in the next thirty years. This period will be crucial as social and ecological externalities come home to roost. We need a rapid reinvention of capitalism, finance, and wealth management. We need to rethink power and purpose. Otherwise this revolutionary moment where "the 20 percent could consciously shift trillions of dollars" will be replaced with "global meltdown, all bets are off, retreat to your bunkers, hope the military can protect you."

Let's remember our responsibility for the long game. To a "seventh-generation" vision, quarterly and annual results are only minor blips on a chart. We need MBAs and academics and investors and citizens to consider the world in five hundred years. Then we can map out the first fifty-year stage. Part of that is identifying a viable human population total that Earth can sustain, and planning for that. That's evidence of a wise society.

I hope smarter people than me will help us clarify this roadmap to the future. Those of us with resources and influence can complement the visioning process by pushing intelligent conversations and policy change, and shifting our own investment decisions.

---

* Economist John Hewson, a former leader of the Australian Liberal Party, is a fellow in economics at the Australian National University and chair of the Asset Owners Disclosure Project (AODP). The AODP tracks how corporations manage climate risk. "In our work, only 7 percent of the top 500 asset owners of the world of our last year's survey could actually measure the climate risks that they were running. And only about 1.5 percent actually had a strategy for managing those risks. In my view, financial markets consistently underprice risk. They don't particularly understand it and they underprice it."[54]

Find your purpose. Connect your actions to it. Step up and run for office. Lobby for fair taxes. If you own a business, shift toward a generative rather than a zero-sum extractive model.

We all have a role. We are ancestors. We are responsible for future generations.

Eriel Tchekwie Deranger is a member of the Athabasca Chipewyan First Nation (ACFN) in Alberta, Canada. A founder of Indigenous Climate Action, Eriel has worked with the Indigenous Environmental Network, Sierra Club, Rainforest Action Network, and the UN Indigenous Peoples' Forum on Climate Change.

What's your role in the sustainability transition?
Much of the Alberta tar sands is in Athabasca Chipewyan territory. I'm helping the ACFN be more engaged in the governance of our lands and territories. Historically we haven't had any real say in that. The underpinning of my work here is that indigenous people hold unexplored ideologies about governance and economics. They know how to develop their lands and resources in a way that's not just respectful to their cultures and identities, but to regional ecology and global sustainability. These can help move the world's energy systems and economies in a way that is critical right now as we face global climate change.

How does the world of finance and investment relate to your work?
There's a money aspect to all this. If you follow the root cause, we've disconnected our monetary systems from the impacts they have on the ground. The systems that are currently running everything—the New York Stock Exchange, the London Stock Exchange, the Toronto Stock Exchange—are still run on antiquated policies and antiquated risk analysis and antiquated ways of forecasting profits and losses. When these systems were created, it

was okay to have slaves. And indigenous people were considered backward people of the forest.

I don't understand how we can adopt progressive policies at the highest levels internationally and still have our economic systems run on these policies, simply because a few powerful people are afraid it's going to affect their bottom line.

Do you feel momentum for a clean money revolution or that we're still going uphill?

I think we're winning. There has been a huge shift in the consciousness of society as a whole and there's a huge desire for systemic change. It's those that are maintaining the systems as they are, and profiting from them, that are holding on for dear life. They've got their death grip on these archaic structures of capitalism. Meanwhile we have an entire society and a new generation that's saying, "No. These systems are based on colonial, patriarchal methods and ideologies that just don't work for us anymore."

It's time for the business world to think outside of the box. This is a new era. In my work I've met people that are really pushing the boundaries of what a capitalist business model can and can't do.

How would you deploy $100 million for the greater good?

If somebody gave me that money, it wouldn't be about investing in wind or solar or this or that technology. It would be investing in people. I'd want to bring jobs and opportunities to marginalized communities. Along with that I'd bankroll bringing economists and others to these communities to learn from them. Because I do think that their voices, knowledge, and economic systems are vital to a real global solution. Don't be fooled just because people are poor: they have advanced economic structures of bartering and trading and assessing value and living sustainably. I'd use that money to see their voices and concerns merged into new systems of wealth distribution and just economic development.

Inspiration Everywhere

All the voices in this book have made the case for an awakening of consciousness. We should listen, and admit that how we make money cannot be separated from our morals and ethics. As Danny Kennedy pointed out in the Q&A at the end of Chapter 9, we need new ways of closing the gaps and creating wealth for the global poor that "leapfrog" old power structures and distribute capital and jobs more fairly.

There are charitable foundation boardrooms managing billions in financial assets, with directors who are focused on growing those assets but ignoring what they do to the world. Meanwhile their grants put bandages on the damaging side effects their investments create. Major universities have invested endowments so large that they are often referred to as "hedge funds with universities attached." They concentrate more and more wealth while doing more and more damage. It's the same with pension funds, insurance companies, sovereign wealth funds, banks, charities, and family offices. Each have enormous power to change how money is used. It's time for these entities to include the well-being of the commons in their definition of "fiduciary responsibility."

Fiduciary responsibility has traditionally meant making the highest return rate for owners, exclusive of the damage such investments cause. That mindset must be reinvented. It must change to include the long-term health of the whole planet. Anything else is a form of blindness, And insanity. It is not just imprudent to make extra money by poisoning water, people, or future generations. It's immoral, and should be illegal. These pools of capital must begin moving 50, 75 or 100 percent of their endowments and assets into the emerging clean economy.

Pension funds can't continue investing in ways such that retirement becomes more dangerous. Foundations need to direct assets to restoration and fairness, not degradation. Universities should invest in their local communities and a safer future world for their graduates, along with the economic stability of their workers' families.

As Peter and Jennifer Buffett of Novo Foundation say: "The most radical way to advance meaningful change is to shift economic, social, and cultural power to those who don't have it."

This is a crucial part of the needed equation. My allocation of $10T for "reparations for colonialism and slavery" refers to this point made by the Buffets.

With a stroke or two of a pen, those of us in the 20 percent can shift our money away from terrible mischief. Examine whether "highest return rate" is the true test for your wealth. If you need high return rates, narrow the field to drivers of the clean money transition. Decide how much is enough, and do that first. We can no longer morally justify "as much as I can get" as a reasonable or ethical answer.

Do you have a well-developed intention for how you intend to use the "more than enough" part of your money for the good of others? Will you risk passing excessive wealth to your family assuming it will make them better, happier, more realized people? Might the ownership gift you are giving instead cause suffering to them, and to those affected by how they use the money? Be sure they understand how money is created, down to the source of who and where is impacted.

I invite you to make your own journey of discovery. If you have wealth, use what you need for your own evolution, personal and financial. Look at the origins and supply chains you profit from. You are smart and have smart people who can help. Do a study of your financial transactions, your investments, your stock portfolio. Look into who worked for what wages, under which conditions, for the low-cost materials needed to earn your profits.

As Gandhi pointed out, history will judge us for how justly we act toward those who are most vulnerable. It's the unborn who are most vulnerable of all. "Intergenerational justice," like "rights of nature" or reparations for colonialism and slavery, remains obscure. These concepts are moving toward the center, as other once-ignored and now obvious truths have done.

The change is happening. We are now past the vision, invention, and seeding of these ideas. We are in the early growth stage. Social entrepreneurship, enlightened investors, the questioning of conventional wealth management assumptions, and the emergence of a new generation of values-aligned leaders are combining into a powerful formula.

Matthew Palevsky is the son of Max Palevksy, a computer pioneer and founding director of Intel. Matthew has organized civic engagement on climate change, political corruption, drug policy reform, and workers' rights. Currently chairman of Ethical Electric, he has spent the past two years practicing Zen Buddhism at Upaya Zen Center in New Mexico. He was recently ordained as a novice Soto Zen priest and is an Master of Divinity candidate at Harvard University.

What are the biggest challenges and opportunities today?
In the United States, pervasive distrust has spawned many of our national injustices. We are suffering from political divisions not seen statistically since the Civil War. This distrust undermines the effectiveness of local and federal governments as well as civic organizations and business. Donald Trump's ascendancy is a useful illustration of just how grotesque this has become, and it's difficult to see a way out. But the core cause that we have to address is inequality, in terms of both wealth and access—to things like education, a decent job, healthy food, and safe housing.

Globally, however, climate change is our greatest challenge. In the long run, it holds the potential to bring us together as a global community, but in the meantime it may inflict human suffering on an unprecedented scale—mass refugee migrations, direct suffering from extreme climate events, wars sparked by scarcity.

Regarding solutions, here in the United State we need to consider our roles as members of a capitalist democracy. We have certain responsibilities as citizens that dovetail with our roles as consumers—and, for a lucky few, as investors. We need not only to educate ourselves, vote, and be civically engaged, but also to question and improve the system itself. As consumers, this means questioning how we shop, what we buy, and what we expect from the market. If we're a job creator, consider what kind of jobs we're creating and how we treat people who work for us. If we're an investor, ask if our capital improves access to healthy food, education, and other basics, or perpetuates existing inequalities.

Why does clean money matter?

Socially responsible investment and consumer activism address these issues by taking money out of public markets and putting it into companies and NGOs that work to solve them. I'm the Chairperson of Ethical Electric, where we help people purchase local renewable energy instead of energy produced by fossil fuels. We have tens of thousands of customers choosing their own energy provider. And the people on our team largely have organizing backgrounds—we've taken the lessons of mass mobilization, and some of the incredible tools built for movements like Obama's '08 campaign, and applied them to consumer movements in scalable companies that can have a mass impact.

Tom Matzzie, CEO of Ethical Electric, was formerly at the AFL/CIO and a leader at MoveOn. He has applied his experience as a political activist to the economic impact an innovative business can have. Another example is Billy Parish, who started Mosaic, a solar company I'm involved with. Before Mosaic he was behind the Energy Action Coalition, a large global alliance of climate change activists founded over a decade ago. Then he said, "There's a large role for businesses to play. I'm going to start a crowdfunding platform where people can invest in putting solar panels on the roof of their local YMCA."

After a lot of hard work, Mosaic is now a leading platform for financing rooftop projects, a crucial component of the fledgling residential solar business. Tom and Billy were activists first, and we share similar perspectives about how change occurs. I enjoy working with entrepreneurs like the two of them—people inspired by their social change background.

Are Millennial and Boomer responsibilities different in the clean money revolution?

My emphatic response would be that we all have the same responsibilities! Every generation has a valuable perspective. Our problems require cross-generational communities because we're all bringing something different to the table.

Your advice on aligning ethics with investment?

Investing is a political act. All the ways we steward wealth are political acts. We need to invest with the same consideration we give to how we treat people in our lives. The first step is to ask yourself what you really care about, and if your investments reflect that. Ask that sincerely, and try to ask it as if you've never considered it before. That can release a lot of the heaviness that comes from thinking about money.

Other than that, I've continuously benefited from seeking advice from people I trust and respect. It's an intimate question and best dealt with in an intimate conversation. No website, manifesto, or formula has the authentic answers for you. Money is sticky, really sticky. As Joel Solomon says, it's a mix of the sacred and the profane. Money is love, it's sex, it's laziness, it's greed, it's our ego, it's our family, it's our entire society. Money is an imaginary receptacle for all of that, and, of course, is none of it. The clearer we can get about our relationship to money and the hidden values we imbue it with, the less stuck we might be when dealing with it.

Inspiration Everywhere

The clean money revolution is gaining credibility, proof of concept, and momentum toward mainstream acceptance. Wealth managers feel the trend via pressure from clients. They're struggling to provide comprehensive, satisfactory solutions. Firms now highlight their efforts in these directions. New products are being launched. Wealth management firms that understand this demand, its value to the world, and how to relate to clients that want it, will grow robustly.

I return to the incredible example of organic food. Decades of early adopters persevered with businesses that grew, processed, manufactured, distributed, and retailed organic foods. They worked in virtual obscurity. Only a small committed consumer helped this early stage. Organics then began to show up on mainstream grocery-store shelves in the 21st century. Growth has seen double-digits, outpacing conventional food. In the United States, what was a $3.6 billion market in 1997 was valued at over $39 billion in 2014.

Organic food remains well under 10 percent of North American food sales, but it will grow ever larger. The common sense of healthy food, people, and ecosystems is too compelling. As Campbell's Soup executive Denise Morrison admitted in Chapter 3, Big Food is on the defensive, trying to overcome "mounting distrust." An entire agricultural and manufacturing system that jeopardizes health, worker safety, rivers, topsoil, and other areas is now facing the threat to reform or die.

The same cycle is steadily evident in renewable energy, efficient transportation, green buildings, carbon pricing, regulations to protect the commons, worker's rights, taxation reform, and many other areas.

People are making exciting moves in every arena. The Gates Foundation pledged at least $2 billion to renewable energy investments. Warren Buffett is investing big money into wind energy. Jeff Skoll has built a compelling media company called Participant, which is behind Pivot Television Network, TakePart digital advocacy group, and 70 feature films and documentaries including

An Inconvenient Truth, Spotlight, and *Food, Inc.* Al Gore is helping deploy a large venture capital pool to better, cleaner products with Generation Investment. Kat Taylor leads Beneficial State Bank, owned by a charity, driving access to capital in underserved communities. Vancity Community Credit Union is leading a global values banking movement. Diverse impact investors are being connected by Dana Lanza via Confluence, Charly and Lisa Kleissner with Toniic and 100% Impact, Michael Whelchel and his partners at Big Path, and Rodney Foxworth of BALLE.

Young entrepreneurs are eager to build businesses that make a better world. Incubators, accelerators, investment funds, professional advisors, and universities are waking to the crisis and eager to help move those businesses faster. Forward-thinking entrepreneurial mayors are recalibrating cities like Vancouver, Paris, Stockholm, and Portland. They are thinking longer term, taking sober looks at coming challenges, and acting boldly now to prepare for soft landings.

Spiritual leaders like Pope Francis, the Reverend Lennox Yearwood, and Joan Halifax are speaking truth about the pickle we have created, making a call to action to put our intellect and resources into a global movement for a safer future.

Every sector of the economy needs overhaul. Yes, clean energy will be massive. But so will clean transportation, clean buildings, clean water, clean air, clean food, clean mining, clean logging, clean clothes.

Do any of us deserve to make gigantic profits because we own distribution systems? Because we are clever at selling things people don't need? Because we can take advantage of regulations, corporate welfare, tax loopholes, or the exploitation of impoverished people who have no choices about their own labor?

For this transformation to root permanently, we need awakened spirits, healed emotional bodies, examined lives. We need clarity of meaning and purpose. We need *we*: all of us. Those with wealth and power are lucky we still get the choice to step into this movement. We've been fitting into norms we have been taught are correct. We need to step up as visionaries, leaders, honorable citizens, and world-changers.

Let's do it while we still have the chance.

Astrid Kann-Rasmussen is the granddaughter of Villum Kann Rasmussen, founder of a Danish window company now known as the VELUX Group. She is the chair of the V. Kann Rasmussen Foundation in New York City, and vice-chair of the international KR Foundation. Both focus on funding effective responses to climate change through a systems approach.

What is your role in the clean money revolution?
I've been working in the foundation world for 16 years. My big passion is climate. It's the most significant problem we face as civilization. The consequences of climate change affect every one of us in an unprecedented way. If we do not get this right, every other problem will be magnified or forgotten entirely.

I've realized that a big barrier to real change is the money system we have created in Western civilization—banking, insurance, investment, and finance. I used to believe in some kind of evil force, in a group of influential decision makers that obstructed real change. The reality is that the money systems we use have their own inertia and were not invented to protect our planet or recognize its limitations. Most people are just trying to survive or do the best for their families. It's our collective use of the money system in its current form that is the problem.

What is the first step in creating real change?
In the philanthropic world, we have to change our approach to investment. It's not just how we make grants, but where we are invested. We need to use common sense and vigorously engage with our financial advisors to help them make the right choices.

I remember sitting at a board meeting years ago where they were trying to find ways to fund climate change solutions. I saw the investments of the foundation, in petro-companies like Exxon and others, were counter to everything we were trying to do about climate. I raised it with the board and it wasn't taken seriously. The prevailing attitude was, "Of course we need to make money to give it away." I think in my generation, and in the next generation that's now emerging, it's becoming very clear that investing in the same problems that you're trying to stop does not make sense.

We need to ask ourselves hard questions. Where do we put our money and where do we invest it? What kind of world is that creating? We need to look at every company and every fund, and ask ourselves if it reflects our values and the change we are looking for. There is no easy way, but the world of investment is luckily maturing to meet this challenge. It will be easier with time.

What is your advice for young people for the new economy?
Find like-minded people. Find your tribe. The sooner the better. Find networks where it is not just about meeting "the right people" but where there is a sincere wish to change things, and a chance for honest, confidential dialogue. It's very important to talk to like-minded people regardless of what background you come from.

That said, I have so much confidence in the promise of coming generations. I am meeting incredible young people all the time who understand this on a completely new level. I learn more from them than they do from me.

Billionaires of Love

I've shared all the stories I could reasonably fit in this book. I've communicated my own doubts and inadequacies. This book is written in the hope that people like you will help push the clean money revolution forward—joyously, successfully, and pleasurably as you can. There is grave seriousness aplenty. I hope you find your own way into the positive revolution around the meaning and purpose of money, in all its dimensions. Be driven by love whenever possible, and by tough love when needed.

The wealthy can model what is needed by moving assets, personal or financial, toward the grand planetary effort needed today. We have a job to do. We must fulfill our generational responsibility to the future. Accumulating infinite wealth, with no higher purpose, is naked greed at worst, self-imposed banality at best. It's simply not right.

It is imperative that all of us, at our own scale, with or without money, use our power and passion to bust open the truth about what money is doing right now, and to change that story. The time is now. We can now move money further and faster, toward a safe, resilient, soft landing for the future of civilization.

True security is a strong peace, where a fair, regenerative economy thrives. True love is love of the future, of the whole.

Let's be billionaires of good deeds, billionaires of love, billionaires of meaning and purpose.

The return on that investment will be a great blessing. Dying with the most money is pointless. It's about what we do to help those who will follow us.

Remember the land.

Remember the future.

Remember love.

Acknowledgments

My first acknowledgment is to those ancestors whose dreams and hard work led me to a land where I could live in such privilege and opportunity. I extend equal gratitude and sense of debt to the indigenous people upon whose land I live. May your patience, insight, and knowledge help this world to transform, and may your communities thrive for centuries to come.

My partners and our extraordinary team at Renewal Funds kindly supported my focus on this book. Tyee Bridge, my co-author, has been a perfect partner. Your constant patience, insight, and savvy about the craft of writing has made it all possible. Many thanks to Rob West, our editor at New Society Publishers, for understanding what we were hoping to do with this project, and his help in framing and greatly improving it.

New Society Publishers, our partner in producing this book, has taught me for over twenty years that small book publishing makes a big influence on the world. A paragon of good jobs in a small community, your ability to innovate in a topsy-turvy era of publishing is inspirational. Renewal Partners' investment role with NSP has been one of our proudest relationships. I was thrilled when cofounder Judith Plant and our editor Rob West agreed to bet on this book. Judith's late husband Chris "Kip" Plant is dearly missed, and was a far-sighted thinker of the highest integrity. I'm honored to be in the NSP author family.

My father Joel "Jay" Solomon gave me business sense and love of people. My mother Rosalind Solomon opened my eyes to the world, emotional complexity, and the drive for meaning. My sister Linda Solomon Wood is my lifelong friend and guide as well as a warrior for authentic journalism.

My wife, Dana Bass Solomon is my true love, best friend, and life partner. Dana brought me her four capable, savvy children, Trever, Garrett, Dusty, and Noelle, who have added infinite joy to my life. Johanna Robertson and Sofia Robledo are my two adult godchildren who teach me constantly. Shivon Robinsong saved my life with her singing kidney, an unfathomable gift. With Rex Weyler, they gave me Hollyhock as a profound guidepost in my life. Along with Paul Spong, they were my first three mentors in activism and breakout understandings.

Andrew Weil steadied me in health philosophy over decades. Carol Newell gave me the opportunity of a lifetime, opening the experience that makes this book possible, and proving that money can indeed be magic. Martha Burton bet on me early and has remained a steadfast business partner for over thirty years. Jim Morrissey, tax and structure genius, made so much possible. Paul Richardson has been my brilliant partner in our mission venture capital business and a deeply trusted ally. Mark Deutschmann is an enduring compadre, and the strength of that bond only grows over the years.

The list of mentors and friends to whom I owe gratitude is long. Among the powerful people who keep me on track while we scheme the future, I'd like to thank Ibrahim al-Husseini, Jeanette Armstrong, Menie Bell, David Berge, Tzeporah Berman, Chuck Blitz, David Boyd, Adrienne Marie Brown, Nadia Chaney, Rebecca Cuttler, Stephen Deberry, Chris Desser, Pamela Chaloult, Sandi Chamberlain, Elizabeth Crook, Jesse Finkelstein, Robert Gass, Lori Hanau, Amy Hartzler, Ken Hays, Dave Henson, Gary Hirshberg, Ryan Taylor-Hood, Thomas Huffman, Kristin Hull, Rick Ingrasci, Kevin Jones, Debra Joy, David Karr, Jon Kinsey, Theodora Lamb, Reta Lawler, Patrick Lee, Jocelyn MacDougall, Ross McMillan, Dawn Magee, Mike Magee, Karen Mahon, Josh Mailman, Konda Mason, Jason Mogus, Marian Moore, Clayton Thomas Mueller, Charlie Murphy, Babatunde Olatunji, Katie Ormiston, Matt Palevsky, Esther Park, Bob Penner, Richard Perl, Cara Pike, Drummond Pike, Peter Poole, Julia Pope, Ajay Puri, Astrid Rasmussen, Vanessa Richards, Andrea Reimer, Gregor Robertson, Christopher Roy, Holton Rower, Mike

Rowlands, Richard Russell, Gordy and Zoe Ryan, Tom Sargeant, Eduardo Schwartz, Don Shaffer, Niki Sharma, Rupinder Sidhu, Nina Simons, Sherry Stewart, Mary Stranahan, Kat Taylor, Peggy Taylor, Annemarie Templeman-Kluit, Kelly Terbasket, Jessy Tolkan, Ziya Tong, Mark Torrance, Francesca Vietor, Mark Vonesch, Torkin Wakefield, Victoria Watson, and James Weinberg. Thank you Arthur Colman for your guidance.

Michael Stusser, you taught me French intensive biodynamic gardening, setting me on the path. Then you delivered Dana, my foundation.

President Jimmy Carter, you modeled impossible success and public service. Al Gore Sr., you awakened me to politics, and Al Gore Jr., seeing my Tennessee homey bring climate to the fore makes me so proud.

Eli and Lev Krag Solomon, my nephews, all these forces of nature mentioned are your guides when needed.

Curating this list has been bittersweet. So many other profound influences—you know who you are. I am a mosaic of your gifts and belief in me. Forgive me for my omissions.

This book is in honor of the ancestors and the future of our dreams.

Endnotes

1. Wright, Gavin. *Sharing the Prize*, p. 4. Belknap Press of Harvard University Press, 2013.
2. "Modern Slavery Estimated to Trap 45 Million People Worldwide," *New York Times*, May 31, 2016. Stats based on data from the 2016 Global Slavery Index. nytimes.com/2016/06/01/world/asia/global-slavery-index.html
3. "Wealth: Having it All and Wanting More," p. 3. Oxfam Issue Briefing, January 2015. oxfam.org/sites/www.oxfam.org/files/file_attachments/ib-wealth-having-all-wanting-more-190115-en.pdf
4. Ibid, p. 3.
5. Reward Work, Not Wealth, p. 10. Oxfam Briefing Paper, January 2018. oxfam.org/en/research/reward-work-not-wealth
6. Laurie, Julie. "If You Own a Pitchfork, You Will Grab It When You See This Chart." *Mother Jones*, March 16, 2015.
7. "Wealth: Having it All and Wanting More," p. 2.
8. *Report on US Sustainable, Responsible and Impact Investing Trends.* ussif.org/sribasics
9. "Coal and Gas to Stay Cheap, But Renewables Win Race on Costs." Bloomberg New Energy Finance, June 13, 2016: Seb Henbest, head of Europe, Middle East and Africa for BNEF, and lead author of NEO 2016, commented: "Some $7.8 trillion will be invested globally in renewables between 2016 and 2040, two-thirds of the investment in all power-generating capacity, but it would require trillions more to bring world emissions onto a track compatible with the United Nations 2°C climate target." about.bnef.com/press-releases/coal-and-gas-to-stay-cheap-but-renewables-still-win-race-on-costs/
10. *2006 Cone Millennial Cause Study.* "This civic-minded generation, 78 million strong, not only believes it is their responsibility to make the world a better place, they (78%) believe companies have a responsibility to join them in this effort." conecomm.com/research-blog/2006-millennial-cause-study
11. *The 2016 Deloitte Millennial Survey*, p. 11. deloitte.com/content/dam/Deloitte/global/Documents/About-Deloitte/gx-millenial-survey-2016-exec-summary.pdf

12. "Is the Future Our Choice or Our Fate?" Posthumous excerpt from Donella Meadows manuscript. See: donellameadows.org/archives /is-the-future-our-choice-or-our-fate/ and alternet.org/story/10707 /donella_meadows_celebrates_earth_day_from_beyond_the_grave

13. "The Powell Memo (also known as the Powell Manifesto)," Reclaim Democracy webpage. reclaimdemocracy.org/powell_memo_lewis/. See also pp. 188–90, *Justice Lewis F. Powell, Jr: A Biography* by John C. Jeffries, Jr: Fordham Univ. Press, 2001.

14. Harvey, David. *The Condition of Postmodernity: An Enquiry into the Origins of Cultural Change*, p.43. Basil Blackwell, 1992.

15. Vogel, David. *Fluctuating Fortunes: the Political Power of Business in America*, p. 198. Beard Books, 2003. Judis, John. *The Paradox of American Democracy: Elites, Special Interests, and the Betrayal of Public Trust*, p. 121. Pantheon, 2000.

16. Reuss, Alejandro. "That 70s Crisis." Dollars & Sense, dollarsandsense .org/archives/2009/1109reuss.html

17. Vogel, David. *Fluctuating Fortunes*, p. 198.

18. "The Powell Memo (also known as the Powell Manifesto)," Reclaim Democracy webpage.

19. Graves, Lisa. "A CMD Special Report on ALEC's Funding and Spending," PR Watch, July 13, 2011. prwatch.org/news/2011/07/10887 /cmd-special-report-alecs-funding-and-spending

20. Vanden Heuvel, Katrina. "Building a Progressive Alternative to ALEC." *The Washington Post*, July 29, 2014. washingtonpost.com/opin ions/katrina-vanden-heuvel-building-a-progressive-alternative-to -alec/2014/07/28/36ee41a6-1697-11e4-9e3b-7f2f110c6265_story.html

21. Rizzo, Salvador. "At Arizona Gathering, ALEC Teaches Lawmakers How to Turn Conservative Ideas into Law." *The Star-Ledger*, April 1, 2012. nj.com/news/index.ssf/2012/04/at_arizona_gathering_alec _teac.html

22. Mukunda, Gautam. "The Price of Wall Street's Power," *Harvard Business Review*, June 2014. hbr.org/2014/06/the-price-of-wall-streets -power

23. Korb, Lawrence, et al. "A Historical Perspective on Defense Budgets." Center for American Progress, July 16, 2011. americanprogress.org /issues/budget/news/2011/07/06/10041/a-historical-perspective-on -defense-budgets/

24. Dickinson, Tim. "How the GOP Became the Party of the Rich." *Rolling Stone*, November 9, 2011. rollingstone.com/politics/news/how-the -gop-became-the-party-of-the-rich-20111109

25. Libin, Kevin. "A Charity with Plenty of Very Long Tentacles." *National Post*, November 20, 2010.

26. Braun, Adam. *The Promise of a Pencil*, p. 65. Scribner, 2014.

27. Chattanooga/Hamilton County Air Pollution Control Bureau. apcb .org/index.php/about-us/history

28. Jones, Van and Keith Ellison. "Pollution Isn't Color-Blind." *The Guardian*, July 23, 2015. theguardian.com/commentisfree/2015/jul/23 /black-lives-matter-air-pollution

29. Carrington, Damian, and Emma Howard. "Institutions Worth $2.6 Trillion Have Now Pulled Investments out of Fossil Fuels." *The Guardian*, September 22, 2015.

30. Safina, Carl. *Beyond Words: What Animals Think and Feel*, p. 398. Picador, 2015.

31. Henderson, Hazel. *Ethical Markets: Growing the Green Economy*, p. 2. Chelsea Green Publishing, 2007.

32. Gunther, Mark. "Stonyfield Stirs up the Yogurt Market." *Fortune*, January 3, 2008. archive.fortune.com/2008/01/03/news/companies /gunther_yogurt.fortune/index.htm

33. Wahba, Phil. "Campbell Soup CEO Says Distrust of 'Big Food' a Growing Problem." *Fortune*, February 18, 2015. fortune.com/2015/02 /18/campbell-soup/

34. "Walking towards a Happy City: An Interview with Charles Montgomery." Walk21 Vienna. walk21vienna.com/2015/07/24/walking -towards-a-happy-city-an-interview-with-charles-montgomery/

35. Quoted in Jagpal, Niki, and Kevin Laskowski. "Philanthropy Is Commendable but Is It Dangerously Altruistic? Reflections for Martin Luther King, Jr. Day." National Committee for Responsive Philanthropy website: blog.ncrp.org/2011/01/philanthropy -is-commendable-but-is-it.html

36. Katayama, Lisa. "Doughnuts to Dollars: How a Business Scion's Son Went from Burning Man to Angel Investing." *Fast Company*, December 3, 2010. renewalpartners.com/blog/pamela-chaloult/how -a-business-scions-son-went-from-burning-man-angel-investing

37. "The Story of Our Founding," Social Venture Network website, svn .org/who-we-are/about-svn

38. 2014 video interview of Wayne Silby by Valerie Mosley of Valmo Ventures, youtube.com/watch?v=wSvzOCO4ozs

39. Ibid.

40. *Organic Foods and Beverages Market Analysis by Product*. grandview-research.com/industry-analysis/organic-foods-beverages-market

41. Kelly, Marjorie, and David C. Korten. *Owning Our Future: The Emerging Ownership Revolution*, p. 11. Berrett-Koehler, 2012.

42. Friedman, Milton. "The Social Responsibility of Business Is to Increase Its Profits." *New York Times Magazine*, 1970.

43. ussif.org/sribasics

44. Lewis, Michael. *The Big Short*, p. 23. W. W. Norton & Company, 2010.

45. *2016 Global Sustainable Investment Review*. gsi-alliance.org/wp-content/uploads/2017/03/GSIR_Review2016.F.pdf

46. Bank, David. "What We Know about Bain Capital's $390 Million Double Impact Fund." *Impact Alpha*, July 18, 2017. impactalpha.com/what-we-know-about-bain-capitals-390-million-double-impact-fund-8dd4e0c90571/

47. Sathe, Ommeed. "Impact Investing." prudential.com/personal-insights/impact-investing. See also Devin Thorpe, "Prudential Working to Double Impact Investing Portfolio Focuses on Newark." forbes.com/sites/devinthorpe/2016/12/13/prudential-working-to-double-impact-investing-portfolio-focuses-on-newark/#684e56892dc5

48. Tasch, Woody. *Inquiries into the Nature of Slow Money: Investing as if Food, Farms, and Fertility Mattered*, p. 98. Chelsea Green Publishing, 2010.

49. Kapoor, Amit. "The Raj Sidodia Interview." *Thinkers*, February 12, 2015. thinkers.in/the-raj-sisodia-interview/

50. Bell, Catherine. *The Awakened Company*, p. 126. Namaste Publishing, 2015.

51. Vasil, Adria. "The Mindful Corporation." *Corporate Knights*, Spring 2014. corporateknights.com/channels/workplace/the-mindful-corporation-13971444/

52. Ibid.

53. "World Bank Group President Jim Yong Kim Remarks at Davos Press Conference." The World Bank, January 23, 2014. worldbank.org/en/news/speech/2014/01/23/world-bank-group-president-jim-yong-kim-remarks-at-davos-press-conference

54. Phillips, Sarah. "'World Headed to Recession if Climate Change Ignored,' John Hewson warns." *ABC News* (Australia), April 4, 2016.

Index

About the Authors

JOEL SOLOMON is Chairman of Renewal Funds, a $98-million mission venture capital firm. He has invested in over 100 early-growth stage companies in North America, delivering above-market returns while catalyzing positive social and environmental change. Solomon spent ten years building businesses in Nashville's deteriorating urban core, where he cofounded Village Real Estate, Core development, and the Bongo Java chain of coffee houses. Solomon is a founding member of the Social Venture Network, Business for Social Responsibility, Tides Canada, and is Board Chair of Hollyhock. He a Senior Advisor to RSF Social Finance in San Francisco.

CREDIT: ZACK EMBREE

TYEE BRIDGE is a Vancouver-based writer whose work focuses on progressive change-makers, ecological issues, and the power of story. His writing has received many honors, including four National Magazine Awards and seven Western Magazine Awards. He is the founder of Nonvella, which specializes in short works of literary nonfiction, and of Arclight, a custom publishing firm.

ABOUT NEW SOCIETY PUBLISHERS

New Society Publishers is an activist, solutions-oriented publisher focused on publishing books for a world of change. Our books offer tips, tools, and insights from leading experts in sustainable building, homesteading, climate change, environment, conscientious commerce, renewable energy, and more—positive solutions for troubled times.

We're proud to hold to the highest environmental and social standards of any publisher in North America. This is why some of our books might cost a little more. We think it's worth it!

DON'T
EAT
THIS
BOOK
(but you could)

- We print all our books in North America, never overseas

- All our books are printed on **100% post-consumer recycled paper**, processed chlorine-free, with low-VOC vegetable-based inks (since 2002)

- Our corporate structure is an innovative employee shareholder agreement, so we're one-third employee-owned (since 2015)

- We're carbon-neutral (since 2006)

- We're certified as a B Corporation (since 2016)

At New Society Publishers, we care deeply about *what* we publish—but also about *how* we do business.

Download our catalog at https://newsociety.com/Our-Catalog or for a printed copy please email info@newsocietypub.com or call 1-800-567-6772 ext 111.

New Society Publishers
ENVIRONMENTAL BENEFITS STATEMENT

For every 5,000 books printed, New Society saves the following resources:[1]

30	Trees
2,695	Pounds of Solid Waste
2,965	Gallons of Water
3,867	Kilowatt Hours of Electricity
4,899	Pounds of Greenhouse Gases
21	Pounds of HAPs, VOCs, and AOX Combined
7	Cubic Yards of Landfill Space

[1]Environmental benefits are calculated based on research done by the Environmental Defense Fund and other members of the Paper Task Force who study the environmental impacts of the paper industry.

Certified

Ⓑ

Corporation

FSC
www.fsc.org

MIX
Paper from
responsible sources
FSC® C016245

new society
PUBLISHERS
www.newsociety.com